FOOD LOVE

# Food Lovers
# Guide to
# Maine

## First Edition

*Best Local Specialties,*
*Markets, Recipes, Restaurants*
*& Events*

*Margaret Hathaway*

gpp

Guilford, Connecticut

Editor: Amy Lyons
Project Editor: Lynn Zelem
Layout Artist: Mary Ballachino
Text Design: Sheryl Kober
Illustrations © Jill Butler with additional art by Carleen Moira Powell
Maps: Design Maps Inc. © Morris Book Publishing, LLC

ISBN 978-0-7627-7016-8

Distributed by
National Book Network

Printed in the United States of America

All the information in this guidebook is subject to change. We recommend that you call ahead to obtain current information before traveling.

# Contents

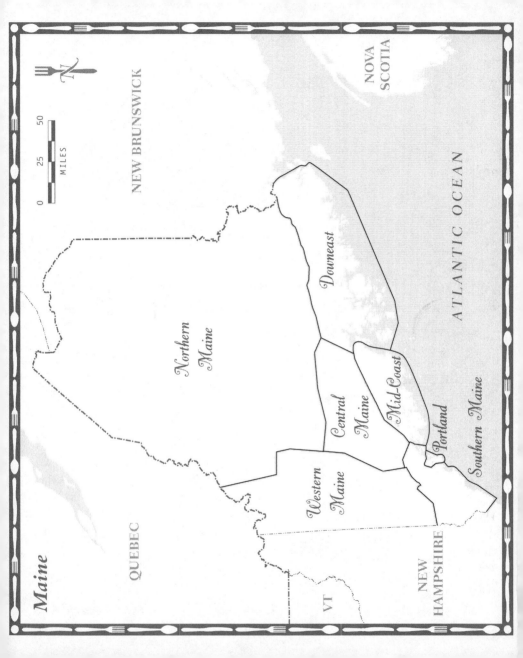

Maine

QUEBEC

NEW BRUNSWICK

NOVA SCOTIA

Downeast

Northern Maine

Mid-Coast

Central Maine

Portland

Western Maine

Southern Maine

ATLANTIC OCEAN

NEW HAMPSHIRE

VT

MILES

0    25    50

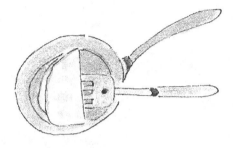

## Central Maine, 251

For Karl, my favorite dining companion

# About the Author

Margaret Hathaway is the author of *Living with Goats* and *The Year of the Goat*. She lives with her husband, Karl Schatz, and their two children on a homestead in southern Maine, where they raise dairy goats and poultry, tend a large garden and small orchard, and make cheese. Visit them at www.tenapplefarm.com.

# Acknowledgments

Though I'm the author, in truth this book has been a collaboration, combining years of my own foodie wanderings with the advice and recommendations of others. Whether it's my dental hygienist telling me about a great place for strawberry shortcake (thanks, Jennifer!) or the food guides that I scan whenever I'm looking for a new spot for supper, I'm never eating alone.

Thanks go to the wonderful food writers of Maine who've steered me to many a great meal: Nancy English, Kathleen Fleury, Anestes Fotiades, Meredith Goad, Nancy Harmon Jenkins, Jonathan Leavitt, Hilary Nangle, Joe Ricchio, Michael Sanders, Cynthia Finnemore Simonds, and Lindsay Sterling.

For everything from restaurant recommendations to recipes to distracting my children so I could work, thanks go to Stacy Brenner, Flora and John Bliss, and Emma Cooper; Caroline and John Bliss; Allison, Connor, and Ian Duffy; Jody Fein and Robb and Luisa Hetzler; Erin, Raymond, and Owen Dulac (and Ray, thanks for the roof!); Don and Samantha Hoyt Lindgren; Leslie Oster; and Elise Richer and Harry, Archie, and Mark Rubin.

Specifically for recipes, thanks go to Dean Bingham, Nicole Chaison, Craig Lapine and the folks at Cultivating Community, Krista Kern Desjarlais, and Colin Woodard.

For their support and enthusiasm (and patience), thanks to my agent, Jill Grinberg; to my editor Amy Lyons; and to project editor Lynn Zelem and the whole team at Globe Pequot.

Thanks to my mom, Jeanine Hathaway, for spending her holidays entertaining my children while I finished up the manuscript; to my dad, Steve Hathaway, for accompanying me to countless diners, lobster shacks, and ice-cream stands; and special thanks to Bruce and Nancy Schatz for sharing their extensive knowledge of the state and its food. Finally, thanks to Karl, Charlotte, and Beatrice for embracing this project and the pleasures of the table with such gusto.

# Introduction

To the uninitiated, the words "Maine food" conjure a single, simple image: a lobster dinner, the plate piled with steamed clams, corn on the cob, and a cup of drawn butter, followed by a slice of blueberry pie. It's a lovely vision, and an even lovelier meal, but it represents only a tiny taste of what Maine has to offer. Though its history is that archetypal Yankee tale of sturdy pilgrims, heroic sea captains, and stoic farmers, over the course of centuries, the Pine Tree State has become a place of diverse preferences and palates.

Myriad influences have shaped Maine's dynamic food culture, but the greatest is a convergence of communities unique to the state. From inhabitants of college towns to close-knit islands, from Portland's urbanites to the organic farmers of the Saint John River Valley, Maine's people are a fascinating lot. The state is home to farmers and fishermen, mill workers and vacationing millionaires, back-to-the-landers and Bowdoin professors, and immigrants from every corner of the planet. Maine's terrain is equally diverse, including fertile fields, primeval forests, blueberry barrens, salt marshes, mountain ranges, sandy beaches, and gently sloping pasture—all of which contribute to the wonderful flavors available to cooks.

Among Maine's foodies, tastes are discriminating but democratic, and the same people who flock to upscale farm-to-table restaurants may begin their days at the neighborhood doughnut shop (yes, I'm speaking of myself). Today, you'll find classic diners just steps away from Vietnamese takeout, and hand-rolled pasta on the same block as spaghetti with red sauce. Lebanese kibbe may be on the menu with boiled dinner, while Korean tacos pile kim-

## Lobsters in the Mail

If you're missing the flavors of Maine, never fear! The state's thriving mail-order lobster industry ships live lobsters—tucked in a bed of seaweed and packed with such necessaries as butter, corn, and a pint of chowder—to your door. Most lobster pounds do overnight shipping, but in case you're stumped, here are a few options that specialize in long-distance orders:

**Hancock Gourmet Lobster,** 104 Taylor Rd., Cundys Harbor, (866) 266-1700; www.hancockgourmetlobster.com.

**Maine Lobster Direct,** 48 Union Wharf, Portland; (800) 556-2783; www.mainelobsterdirect.com.

**Port Clyde Lobster,** Port Clyde; (207) 372-8686; www.portclydelobster.com.

chee and beef short ribs on a corn tortilla. And then there's seafood: Whether you're slurping oysters with a pint at a wharf-side bar or savoring a dish of pan-seared scallops, you know your meal is fresh, brought in that morning by local fishermen.

Given the culinary climate, Maine's chefs feel the freedom to borrow from many traditions, creating, at their best, meals that are distinctly Maine: reviving heirloom fruits and vegetables, experimenting with unusual fish and cuts of meat, and spiking local ingredients with spices "from away." The beauty of Maine's food scene is its inclusivity—we've all contributed to the meal, and we're all welcome at the table. Enjoy!

## How to Use This Book

For the purposes of this guide, the state has been divided into seven geographical regions, starting in the south and gradually working north. Each region has its own chapter, discussing the area's distinctive flavors and food traditions. I've tried to group areas by culinary specialties, but in some cases, the borders between regions are a bit arbitrary, drawn by roads and county lines rather than kitchens. Particularly if you're traveling up the coast, have a look at offerings in the bordering chapters—something fabulous may be a short trip away. I've given the city of Portland its own chapter, which includes the bordering towns of South Portland and Cape Elizabeth. Maine's largest city and cultural heart, Portland's food life is dynamic and could probably fill an entire guide on its own.

## Price Code

Restaurants and Landmark Eateries follow a pricing guide so you have some idea of what to expect.

$      inexpensive, mostly quick bites with entrees under $10

$$      moderately priced, most entrees in the $10 to $20 range

$$$      expensive, most entrees over $20

$$$$   special treat, expect a prix-fixe menu of $65 or more and plan not to skimp on recommended wine pairings

Within each chapter, you'll find the following categories:

### Bakeries

Bakeries come in many guises, from French patisseries to sweet shops specializing in whoopie pies and filled hermit cookies. This section visits the full spectrum, but the shops are unified by one thing: Their main attractions come from their ovens. In many cases, these bakeries also offer soups and sandwiches on their own breads, so they're good stops for light lunch or picnic supplies. (Note: Several shops listed as bakeries also make homemade doughnuts, but many doughnut shops are listed as Landmark Eateries. If you're looking for a hot doughnut, fresh from the fryer, check Appendix B for a listing of the state's best doughnut shops.)

### Brewpubs & Microbreweries

A brewing renaissance began in Maine in the mid-1980s, and the movement toward small-batch and craft brews has only strengthened over the decades. The Maine Brewers' Guild (www.mainebrewersguild.org) has an active membership of more than two dozen microbreweries, and many of the country's most celebrated brewpubs are dotted throughout the state. This section includes breweries that offer tours and tastings, brewpubs that serve up pints crafted on-site, and beer bars that offer a wide range of local and imported brews on tap and by the bottle.

### Farm Stands

Farm stands sit by the side of most rural roads in Maine, from card tables offering a surplus of cucumbers and zucchinis and an honor-system cash box, to more elaborate shops selling honey and maple syrup, pies, and seedlings. This section is a listing of some of the state's best, though it's not by any means comprehensive; if you're driving by and the produce looks good, close the book and just stop!

### Farmers' Markets

The farmers' market in Portland is the oldest continually operating market in the country, and with that example to follow, the state is home to dozens of small markets, selling seasonal produce, eggs, cheese, meats, and baked goods. This section offers listings of some of Maine's larger farmers' markets, but keep in mind that hours, days, contact people, and locations can change each season. If you're in Maine on a summer weekend, chances are good that you're within a short distance from a weekly market—call ahead or ask around to confirm.

### Lobster Shacks & Fishmongers

No visit to Maine is complete without a little lobster. Whether it's mounds of succulent, lightly dressed tail and claw meat on a buttered roll or a shore dinner complete with steamed clams and corn on the cob, Maine lobster is an unforgettable treat. This section guides you to some of the state's most iconic lobster shacks (mostly seasonal, where you can get a full meal), lobster pounds (often open year-round, where you can buy live lobsters and sometimes have them boiled on-site), and fishmongers (where you can buy all kinds of fresh seafood in addition to lobster, which are usually live in tanks).

### Food Happenings

Mainers take great pride in their culinary traditions, and this section is a guide to some of the state's foodiest

## TOURS & TRAILS

**The Maine Beer Trail (www.mainebrewersguild.org):** Take a self-guided tour of the state's best beers with the Maine Brewers' Guild map of brewpubs and microbreweries. Download from their website, or find a printed copy at information centers throughout the state.

**Maine Foodie Tours (www.mainefoodietours.com):** Local food enthusiasts lead guided walking tours of Portland, exploring the culinary history of the city with stops for a bite here or there. Tours include the Culinary Walking Tour, the Port City Beer Tour, and the Culinary Delights Trolley Tour.

**The Maine Wine Trail (www.mainewinetrail.com):** Like their brewing cousins, the Maine Winery Guild has compiled a map of the state's producers of wines and spirits. Download the map from their website to take the self-guided tour.

festivals, organized by month. Look here for celebrations of everything from potatoes to *ployes*, chocolate to chili, and barbecue to blueberries. Note that statewide events are found in Appendix C: Food Happenings.

### The Maine Ice Cream Trail

California has a wine trail, Vermont has a cheese trail, and in Maine, we have ice cream. Rich, sweet, hand-churned ice cream is a summer tradition in the Pine Tree State, and seasonal stands are tucked down rural roads in every county. This section provides a listing of some of the best. Because they're open seasonally, it's best to call ahead if you're making a special trip, as hours can vary.

### Landmark Eateries

Ranging from candy stores open since the 19th century to floating restaurants docked in the harbor, landmark eateries have been chosen because of their distinctive personalities, as well as a certain amount of longevity. Many restaurants in this section are throwbacks to another time—drive-ins that still have carhops, diners in train cars, old-fashioned seafood spots with homemade rolls and pies. Some, though they've been around for half a century, have adapted with the times and are notable for their continuing place in the community. Most are not fine-dining establishments but are a good bet for a fun, memorable meal.

### Learn to Cook

With its high concentration of chefs and easy access to local ingredients, Maine is a great place to hone your kitchen skills. From organized classes in teaching kitchens to casual workshops and participatory meals at home, culinary experts are eager to share their skills. This is a listing of some of the state's most interesting offerings, teaching participants to make everything from simple stocks to aged cheeses.

### Made or Grown Here

From small-batch vodkas to organic apple butters, the artisans and producers of Maine are crafting amazing things from local ingredients. This section offers a list of some of the best bets for everything from chocolate truffles to foraged mushrooms. This is also the section that includes coffee shops that roast their own beans and *gelaterias,* whose frozen treats are distinct from classic ice cream.

### Restaurants

Maine has an abundance of wonderful restaurants, from elegant dining rooms to casual bistros. Young chefs are drawn to the region by its great produce, fresh seafood, and pasture-raised meats, and the foodie community embraces all they have to offer. While this section doesn't include every wonderful restaurant in the region—that would be too encyclopedic!—I've tried to identify a range of good eats, hitting all price points and satisfying many palates. Descriptions here are not reviews, but if I've included it, chances are it will be worth a stop.

### Specialty Stores & Markets

From high-end gourmet markets to crunchy natural foods co-ops to custom butchers, this section lists shops that have a specific focus. Many do one thing very well—handmade sausage, for instance, or supplies for brewing beer—but some are generalists, offering a range of treats. Wine and cheese shops are listed here, as are a variety of

# Up-to-the-Minute Food News

Food scenes are fluid, and restaurants emerge and disappear more quickly than books can be written. If you're planning a visit to somewhere off the beaten path, make sure to call ahead so you're not disappointed. For the most up-to-date listings, check out the following online sources:

**www.downeast.com:** *DownEast* magazine's website includes a food section with all the state's dish—from kitchen gossip to restaurant guides.

**www.eatmainefoods.org:** The *Eat Local Foods Coalition of Maine* has developed an online map to find farmers' markets, farm stands, restaurants serving local foods, and more.

**www.portlandfoodmap.com:** A comprehensive map of local eateries, with links to reviews and foodie news.

**www.themainemag.com:** In print and online, *Maine* magazine focuses on culture, people, destinations, art, and food in the state. Their "eat" section visits a specific region each month and reports back with the best bets. For candid opinions about the Maine food scene, visit their Facebook page. With more than 10,000 fans contributing to the conversation, you're sure to find a recommendation: **www.facebook.com /EatMaine.**

markets that offer catering. Note: A number of these shops serve sandwiches, light meals, and prepared entrees, so they're a good stop for lunch or a quick supper.

### Pick Your Own

Farms listed in this section are open to the public for fruit and vegetable picking. Many also have farm stands and seasonal cafes offering hot or cold beverages and homemade snacks—several apple orchards are known for their doughnuts. Because every season is different, make sure to call ahead to check picking conditions and availability.

## Recipes, Etc.

A scattering of recipes can be found throughout the book, as well as notes on ingredients, brief guides to local delicacies, and explanations of the specialties of each geographical region. I've included these to give you a fuller sense of Maine's tremendous food culture. Recipes showcase local flavors and cooking techniques, while notes aim to give you a head start before you dive into the food scene. I'm grateful to the chefs and producers who helped me pull these together—they're named in each recipe. Please know that any mistakes or omissions are entirely my own.

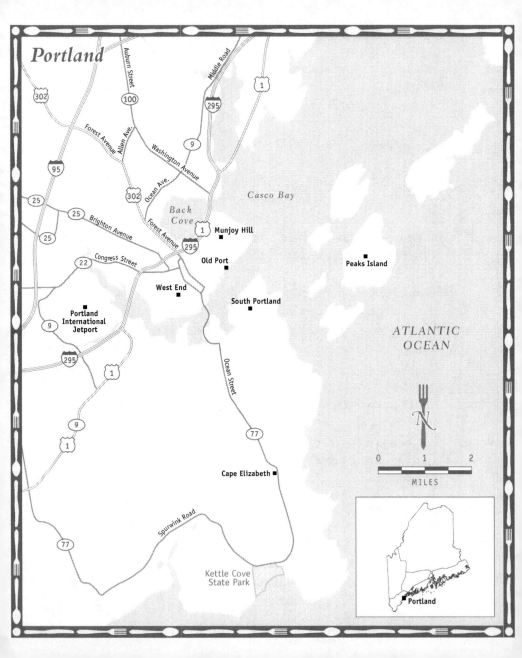

# Portland

Maine's cultural and culinary heart, the city of Portland is a cosmopolitan place, buzzing with thriving independent businesses, a lively arts and music scene, and an energetic food community. The town's history is deep: At the mouth of the Fore River in Casco Bay, the peninsula on which Portland sits was originally settled in 1633, and the town was incorporated in 1786. A seaport and railway hub through the early 19th century, much of the city was destroyed in the Great Fire of 1866, though one institution has remained constant—the Portland Farmers' Market, founded in 1768, is the country's oldest continually operating market of its kind.

As in many cities, the 20th century marked a gradual migration out of Portland's downtown, but an urban revitalization movement began in the 1990s, which has energized the city and turned the Old Port into a tourist destination. The historic neighborhoods of Munjoy Hill and the West End are alive with restaurants and small markets. In between them, the Arts District on Congress Street, named for the Maine College of Art at its center, is home to galleries and storefront art spaces, as well as coffee shops, ethnic markets, and funky restaurants. The Portland Museum of Art, also on Congress, was designed by I. M. Pei and houses an extraordinary collection, including the works of many Maine artists.

Portland is widely considered to have one of the country's most vibrant food scenes, and in 2009 it was named "America's Foodiest Small Town" by *Bon Appetit* magazine. Restaurants range from chef Sam Hayward's pioneering farm-to-table mecca, Fore Street, to divey holes-in-the-wall, and include everything in between. Wander the streets for just a few blocks and you'll find an Eritrean cafe, a beer garden with more than 300 brews, a Japanese noodle bar, a restored club-car diner, and a *gelateria* run by a family from Milan. An active Slow Food convivium (chapter) holds potlucks, lectures, and events, including the annual Writer's Night, in which food writers read from their works, and a winter CSA fair, at which participants can sign up for a summer farm share.

It's impossible to sample all of Portland's kaleidoscopic culinary offerings in just one visit, but with enthusiasm and an adventurous palate, you'll have fun trying.

## Bakeries

**Borealis Breads,** 182 Ocean Ave., Portland; (207) 541-9600; www.borealisbreads.com. A leader in the commercial revival of Maine-grown grains, Jim Amaral, owner of this European-style bread bakery, uses more than 80,000 pounds of Maine-grown

# THE BREADBASKET OF NEW ENGLAND

Before the advent of cross-country railroads and the 1825 opening of the Erie Canal made it possible to move grain across the continent by the train car, Aroostook County was the source of much of the wheat consumed in the East. For a time, it was considered the breadbasket of New England, though eventually potatoes edged out grains for commercial growth. Over the past decade, however, there's been a resurgence of interest in Maine-grown wheat. **Jim Amaral of Borealis Breads** (see p. 14) has been a leader in that movement, buying much of his bakery's flour from farmer and miller **Matt Williams at Aurora Mills** (http://auroramillsandfarm.net) in Linnaeus. Young bakers are also joining the movement, and further south, **Michael Scholz of Albion Bread Company** (available at farmers' markets) mills his own wheat, and is converting the old County Jail in Skowhegan into the Somerset Grist Mill. As The County's floury history comes back to life, more fields are being sown with hardy heritage grains, a trend encouraged by the scholarship of the **Northern New England Local Bread Wheat Project,** a community collaboration organized jointly by the Universities of Vermont and Maine, and by the enthusiasm of bakers at the annual **Maine Kneading Conference** in Skowhegan (www.kneadingconference.com).

organic wheat per year. The resulting loaves showcase local flavors: favorites include fresh rosemary, Aroostook wheat, Maine potato, and Maine Coast Focaccia, which includes a sprinkle of seaweed. Available at retail locations throughout the state, the company's flagship store is its Portland bakery and bistro, where beverages, light meals, and pizza are also available.

**Cranberry Island Kitchen,** 52 Danforth St., Portland; (207) 774-7110; www.cranberryislandkitchen.com. Begun in a small cottage on Little Cranberry Island more than 20 years ago, this sweet dessert bakery has expanded and moved south but has retained its simple, homey flavors. Owners Carol Ford and Karen Haase have recently received national attention for their desserts, which use locally produced ingredients in whimsically shell-shaped whoopie pies and cookies and in subtly spiced Island Buttermilk Cake. In addition to the retail shop, baked goods are available to order, both for parties and in charming Maine-inspired gift tins.

**Cream & Sugar Bakery,** Portland; (207) 775-6701; www.creamandsugar bakery.com. Cream & Sugar's rich, buttery desserts are available at coffee shops around Portland, but the bakery is distinguished by one trait: home delivery. Owner Elise Richer delivers warm baked goods, both sweet and savory, from Scandinavian-style cardamom pound cake to chocolate-raspberry layer cake to honey-walnut bars by the dozen. Made with locally sourced ingredients, these treats are perfect for a gathering, and make a great gift from afar. See Cream & Sugar Bakery's recipe for **Chard & Egg Pie** on p. 18.

**JulChris Cookies,** 382 Cottage Rd., South Portland; (207) 899-2825; www.julchriscookies.com. In a bright, cheerful storefront, this cookie bakery offers sweet, chewy treats packed with chocolate, toffee, nuts, and fruit. The bakery was named for owner Deborah Integlia's children, Julia and Christopher, and the cookies have similarly familial tags: The bakery's most popular item is My Husband's Favorite, a chocolate-chip cookie with chopped walnuts and sweetened coconut. Other popular cookies include Patenglenns, a butter cookie with white chocolate and cranberries; Julskis, a peanut butter cookie with chocolate filling; and Butterbrickle Tims, a toffee cookie dipped in dark chocolate. Self-serve coffee and seats by the window make it easy to linger here.

**Scratch Baking Company,** 416 Preble St., South Portland; (207) 799-0668; www.scratchbakingco.com. Known for its perfect hand-cut, hand-shaped bagels and homemade English muffins, this bustling bakery also makes divine desserts and has a rotating selection of scones, coffee cakes, cookies, and brownies. A small market offers breakfast staples (local eggs and bacon, milk, and tubs of cream cheese), as well as "things that go with bread," like a nicely curated selection of cheeses and wines.

**Standard Baking Co.,** 75 Commecial St., Portland; (207) 773-2112. Open the heavy wooden double doors of this European-style

# Chard & Egg Pie

*This savory pastry makes a great brunch dish and can be made as individual pies or in one large crust. Cold-loving chard grows abundantly in Maine, and when Elise Richer makes these for patrons, as often as not she will have cut the greens from her own garden. The recipe, based on a traditional Italian Easter tart, is one of Cream & Sugar's most popular items.*

1 large bunch Swiss or rainbow
    chard
1½ tablespoons olive oil or
    butter for sautéing
Salt and pepper
2 ounces cream cheese (use
    more or less to taste)

Bread crumbs
Parmesan cheese
Dough for a double-crust
    9-inch pie
6 eggs

*Sauté chard in oil or butter until wilted, seasoning to taste. Remove from heat and gently stir in cream cheese, until melted and well mixed. Let cool. Pour off any excess liquid. Season again to taste, and add enough bread crumbs to*

bakery and the smells of butter and yeast billow out. Considered by many to be home of the best baguette in Maine, this bread and pastry bakery rounds its menu with a wide variety of staples and sweets. Special favorites include savory olive bread, sweet fig bread studded with walnuts, and, of course, classic French baguettes.

*absorb extra liquid. Add Parmesan to taste. (The chard filling should be fairly strongly seasoned as the egg is unseasoned.)*

*Divide dough into 2 parts, one slightly larger than the other. Roll each piece into a circle, the larger piece for the bottom crust, the top piece for the top crust. Place bottom crust into pan.*

*Spoon enough chard filling into the pie pan to cover the bottom crust. Gently crack each egg directly on top of the chard (try to keep the yolk intact), spacing them evenly around the pie. Spoon additional chard on top of each egg, then place top crust over and crimp. Use a small sharp knife to cut a vent in the top crust, without piercing the egg inside. Chill filled pie until ready to bake.*

*Place a rimmed sheet pan in oven and heat to 425 degrees. Place pie on heated sheet pan and return to oven. Bake for 30 minutes. If pie needs more time, reduce heat to 350 degrees and bake until golden brown. Let set a few minutes before eating. Also good at room temperature.*

*Serves 6. (When slicing, try to give each person an egg.)*

Recipe courtesy of Cream & Sugar Bakery (p. 16).

Croissants are crisp and buttery, hazelnut brioche is light, and desserts are rich but not too sweet.

**Two Fat Cats Bakery,** 47 India St., Portland; (207) 347-5144; www .twofatcatsbakery.com. Located down a few steps in an unassuming building on the edge of the Old Port, this cozy American-style dessert bakery prides itself on homey sweets baked from scratch. The vintage decor complements such classic cakes as coconut, lemon, red velvet with creamy vanilla frosting, and carrot with cream cheese frosting. A large selection of pies ranges from single fruits such as local blueberry, pumpkin, and apple, to inventive combinations like mixed berry, blueberry rhubarb, and raspberry peach. Cupcakes, cookies, and whoopie pies are perfect for an afternoon pick-me-up.

# Brewpubs & Microbreweries

**Allagash Brewing Company,** 50 Industrial Way, Portland; (800) 330-5385; www.allagash.com. Retail store, beer tastings, and brewery tours available daily, except Sat (in winter) and Sun (year-round). Call ahead, hours vary by season.

**Brian Boru Public House,** 57 Center St., Portland; (207) 780-1506; www.brianboruportland.com. A fixture in the Old Port, this Irish pub offers Guinness on tap, live Irish music, and hearty pub fare. Look for the Guinness toucan mural—a bright spot in the cityscape.

**D. L. Geary Brewing Company,** 38 Evergreen Dr., Portland; (207) 878-2337; www.gearybrewing.com. New England's first microbrewery, Geary's has been brewing and bottling its ales in Portland since 1986. Founder David Geary trained with brewers in Scotland and England before creating his own recipe for pale ale, which is available bottled and on tap throughout the state. Call ahead for tours.

**The Great Lost Bear,** 540 Forest Ave., Portland; (207) 772-0300; www.greatlostbear.com. Since 1979, this Woodford-area landmark has served beers, burgers, "hearty, spicy junk food" (their words), and a surprisingly large selection of vegetarian entrees. Pints flow from 69 taps serving more than 50 craft beers from the Northeast in a fun, boisterous atmosphere. This local institution has a following beyond the state, and is considered by many—from *All About Beer Magazine* to *Gourmet*—to be among the great beer bars in the country.

**Gritty McDuff's Brewing Company,** 396 Fore St., Portland; (207) 772-2739; www.grittys.com. For more than two decades, this English-style pub has been brewing award-winning ales on the premises of its Old Port location. The workings of the brewery are visible to patrons, and Gritty's growing array of beers is available bottled as well as on tap. **Now with two additional locations:** 68 Main St., Auburn; (207) 376-2739; and Lower Main Street, Freeport; (207) 865-4321.

**The Inn on Peaks Island,** 33 Island Ave., Peaks Island; (207) 766-5100; www.innonpeaks.com. With a view of the water and Portland's skyline, the inn's restaurant features classic pub fare and cask-conditioned Shipyard ales on tap. Make sure to check the ferry schedule for your return trip—though if you miss the last boat, they may have a room.

**Maine Beer Co.,** 1 Industrial Way, #3, Portland; (207) 221-5711; www.mainebeercompany.com. This very small microbrewery is committed to being green: The company's electricity is 100 percent wind powered; used grain, yeast, and grain bags are donated to local farmers; and 1 percent of all sales go to environmental nonprofits. Call ahead for tours.

**Novare Res Bier Cafe,** 4 Canal Plaza, Portland; (207) 761-2437; www.novareresbiercafe.com. With 25 rotating taps, 2 hand pumps for traditional cask beer, and more than 300 types of bottled beer, this beer bar is a serious celebration of artisan-crafted brews. The food menu complements the beer, with hearty sandwiches and a meat-and-cheese bar. A small but well-chosen list of wines and spirits is also available.

**Shipyard Brewing Co.,** 86 Newbury St., Portland; (800) BREW ALE; www.shipyard.com. This growing brewery—with ales now available in 38 states—hosts full guided tours by reservation every Tuesday night from April through December. Make sure to try their new, nonalcoholic Capt'n Eli's Soda, made with natural cane sugar and available, like their beers, in bottles and kegs.

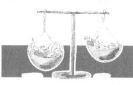

## Farm Stands

**Alewive's Brook Farm,** 83 Old Ocean House Rd., Cape Elizabeth; (207) 799-7743; www.alewivesbrookfarm.com. Named for the tiny fish that spawn in the farm's brook, this stand sells fresh lobsters, clams, crabs, and snails; seasonal produce from their fields; and turkey raised on the farm. Open 9 a.m. to sundown year-round, every day except Christmas.

**Jordan's Farm,** 21 Wells Rd., Cape Elizabeth; (207) 767-3488; www.jordansfarm.com. One of only six working farms remaining in Cape Elizabeth, this local landmark helps to preserve the rural feel of the town. Offering their own seasonal produce—from early lettuce to late squash—grown on the 60-odd acres the family cultivates annually, and a variety of products from across Maine. The farmers work year-round, but the stand is open from June through Nov.

## Farmers' Market

**Portland Farmers' Market,** Apr through Nov, Sat at Deering Oaks Park from 7 a.m. to noon, Mon and Wed at Monument Square from 7 a.m. to 2 p.m.; www.portlandmainefarmersmarket.com. One of the oldest continually operating farmers' market in the country,

Portland's thrice-weekly seasonal market has been serving the community since 1768. Several dozen area producers participate in the market, offering everything from fresh seasonal vegetables to honey to meats and cheeses.

## Lobster Shacks & Fishmongers

**Benny's Famous Fried Clams,** 199 West Commercial St., Portland; (207) 774-2084. This seasonal clam shack, near the highway on an empty stretch of outer Commercial Street, is beloved by locals for its ample baskets of fried clams, scallops, and Maine shrimp; unadorned lobster rolls; and hand-cut fries. Drinks are self-serve from the cooler, and seating is at outdoor picnic tables by the busy road, but the reasonable prices for fresh seafood more than make up for the stripped-down atmosphere. Open Memorial Day through Columbus Day weekend.

**Browne Trading Company,** Merrill's Wharf, Portland; (207) 775-7560 or (800) 944-7848; www.brownetrading.com. Known to chefs throughout the country for wholesale fresh and smoked seafood and fine caviars, Browne Trading Company's retail market adds an extensive selection of wines and lunch service to its exquisite seafood offerings. Seafood is processed on-site, and shellfish and salmon (among other fish) are cured in a boutique smokehouse adjacent to the market.

**Free Range Fish & Lobster,** 450 Commercial St., Portland; (207) 774-8469; www.freerangefish.com. The briny smell promises good things will come from this no-frills fish shop, steps from the docks of Portland's waterfront. Friendly, knowledgeable fishmongers crack jokes with patrons while helping navigate mountains of mollusks and whole and filleted fish. Large tanks hold lobsters of all sizes, and the staff is happy to give instructions on preparation. A small wine section and baskets of lemons and choice condiments help to ready the feast. Look for the enormous mounted lobster, and you'll know you're there.

**Harbor Seafood,** 9 Custom House Wharf, Portland; (207) 775-0251 or (800) 370-1790; www.harborfish.com. Since 1969, the Alfiero family—father Ben Sr. and sons Nick, Ben Jr., and Mike—have sold live lobster, fish, and shellfish from this waterfront fishmonger, located above the pilings on one of the Old Port's wharves. Fresh seafood glistens in the long glass cases that line the shop (more than 50 linear feet of display), and the charming historic storefront has been used as the backdrop for myriad advertisements. Customer service is a priority, and staff operates by the motto: "If it's not fresh enough for us to take home and prepare, then we're not going to sell it. Period." Closed Sun and major holidays.

**The Lobster Shack at Two Lights,** 225 Two Lights Rd., Cape Elizabeth; (207) 799-1677; www.lobstershacktwolights.com. The sweeping view from this iconic lobster shack perched above the sea is renowned throughout the state. A landmark since the 1920s, the quaint dining room and outdoor seating overlook two lighthouses and Portland Harbor. Boiled lobster dinners, lobster rolls, and fried local seafood are on the menu, as well as clam chowder and lobster stew. Open late March through late October.

**Portland Lobster Co.,** 180 Commercial St., Portland; (207) 775-2112; www.portlandlobstercompany.com. Serving tasty lobster rolls, boiled lobster dinners, and fried fish, this seasonal waterfront restaurant is a great stop on a day of sightseeing in the Old Port. The atmosphere is a little kitschy—a plastic lobster vibrates when your order's up—and can be boisterous when there's live music (daily during the summer; bands are listed on the website). A tented bar with local beers on tap is convenient to plentiful outdoor seating on the pier. Open May through Oct.

## Food Happenings

### March

**International Food Festival,** SMCC, South Portland; (207) 741-5662; www.smccme.edu. Southern Maine Community College hosts this annual festival and silent auction, featuring global cuisine, student stories, music, and film. Proceeds benefit scholarship funds for international and multicultural students. Held each March on the college campus.

**Slow Food Writer's Night,** www.slowfoodportland.org. This evening of literary and culinary delights pairs food writers with local chefs each winter for an event that celebrates local foods and engaging writing. Authors from near and far read from their works, and the menu highlights ingredients discussed by the speakers. Readers are available to sign copies of their books, which are for sale, after the program.

## June

**Annual Greek Food Festival,** Holy Trinity Greek Orthodox Church, 133 Pleasant St., Portland; www.holytrinityportland.org. More than 10,000 visitors are drawn each June to this three-day celebration of Greek food and culture. On the grounds of the West End's historic Holy Trinity Church, volunteers prepare homemade souvlaki, dolmas, moussaka, spanakopita, baklava, and more. In addition to the great food, a traditional Greek band provides music and folk-dancing lessons; Greek art, clothing, jewelry, and gifts are for sale; and tours of the church and its icons are offered.

**Cultivating Community's 20 Mile Meal at Turkey Hill Farm,** Cape Elizabeth; (207) 761-GROW; www.cultivatingcommunity .org. Incorporating vegetables raised and harvested by Cultivating Community's youth growers, this annual fall fund-raiser features tastings of "hyper-local" dishes, both sweet and savory, created by the area's best chefs. With live music, farm tours, and family activities, the afternoon is a festive conclusion to the growing season. Throughout the summer, Turkey Hill Farm also hosts regular Twilight Suppers, smaller fund-raising dinners that showcase single chefs, who volunteer their time to create meals with ingredients from the farm. See Cultivating Community's recipe for **Squash of Hope** on p. 29.

**Harvest on the Harbor,** (207) 772-4994 (Greater Portland Convention & Visitors Bureau); www.harvestontheharbor.com. This annual celebration of the flavors of Maine features three days of food and wine tastings, cooking demonstrations, culinary-themed tours, and more. Held on a waterfront pier in the Oceanside Pavilion tent, the festivities include the Maine Lobster Chef of the Year Competition, a meal crafted by local James Beard Award–winning chefs (working together as a team), and a daily marketplace featuring more than 140 Maine-made products. Tickets available in advance; must be 21.

# Squash of Hope

Portland-based nonprofit Cultivating Community's motto is "Feeding our hungry—empowering our families—healing our planet," and their mission is to strengthen communities by growing food, preparing youth leaders and new farmers, and promoting social and environmental justice. The organization works primarily with immigrants, and in community gardens they teach students to grow vegetables, which are distributed through their CSA and sold at farmers' markets.

    This recipe comes from a member of the high school Community Culinary Crew: "I learned how to cook mashed squash from my mother when I was nine years old in South Sudan, two months after surviving a serious ambush by the Sudan Liberation Movement. Our homes were all blown up and there was no food relief. The only food that was available at the time—squash."

**Fresh winter squash**
**Butter or olive oil**
**Salt**
**Garlic, chopped**

**Any herbs that you like to get the flavor and texture you want**

Peel the squash. You want to cook it the old-fashioned way in a pot, steaming it until soft. Add olive oil or butter and salt, as well as garlic and any herbs to taste and then . . . mash them all together.

Serves 4.

Recipe courtesy of Cultivating Community (see p. 28).

## November

**Maine Brewers Festival,** Portland Expo, 239 Park Ave., Portland; www.learnyourbeer.com. For almost 20 years, this two-day November festival has celebrated Maine's craft brews. Live music and tasty foods—pretzel necklace, anyone?—make the event a party. With admission, attendees receive tickets for twelve 4-ounce pours of great local beers. Sign up as a designated driver and cost of admission is converted into food tickets. Must be 21.

## The Maine Ice Cream Trail

**Kettle Cove Creamery and Cafe,** 2 Bowery Beach Rd., Cape Elizabeth; (207) 799-3533; www.kettlecoveicecream.com. Old-time hard-serve in 32 flavors, including the Maine favorite: Grapenut. Cafe offers coffee drinks, smoothies, and a selection of sandwiches. Open seasonally, Mothers' Day to Labor Day.

**Lib's Dairy Treats,** 32 Auburn St., Portland; (207) 797-4133. Homemade soft-serve, known for homey touches like zest in the orange ice cream and extra coating on dipped cones. Open seasonally.

**Red's Dairy Freeze,** 167 Cottage Rd., South Portland; (207) 799-7506; www.redsdairyfreeze.com. Opened in 1952, this beloved soft-

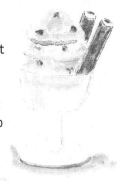

serve landmark was gutted by fire in May 2010, but it reopened for the 2011 season.

**Willard Scoops,** 427 Prebble St., South Portland; (207) 232-3618. This seasonal ice-cream shop is open on Thurs nights in the off-season, serving hand-packed quarts and hot fudge to go. Otherwise open from Apr through Oct.

## Landmark Eateries

**Amato's,** 71 India St. (and locations throughout Maine); (207) 773-1682; www.amatos.com; $. Founded in 1902 by immigrant Giovanni Amato, this landmark sandwich shop began as a cart on the waterfront, selling lunch to dockworkers. More than 100 years later, the so-called "real Italian sandwich" is still going strong (see sidebar, p. 32), and Amato's has locations throughout New England. Sandwiches are served on rolls made at Amato's Bakery and are heaped with meat, cheese, veggies, and oil. Pizza, pasta, and salad are also available.

**Becky's Diner,** 390 Commercial St., Portland; (207) 773-7070; www.beckysdiner.com; $. On cars throughout New England, the number of bumper stickers reading "Becky's Diner, Nothin' Finah" are rivaled only by Red Sox emblems. This wharf-side diner, still

## PORTLAND: THE HOME OF THE REAL ITALIAN SANDWICH

Known by many names—sub, grinder, po'boy, hoagie, hero—a long sandwich on a soft white roll, split on one side and filled with meat, cheese, vegetables, and a splash of oil is called, in Maine, an "Italian sandwich." 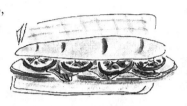 Its mythology in the state begins with Giovanni Amato, an Italian immigrant to Portland who sold sandwiches out of a cart to his countrymen who worked the docks, and went on to found Amato's Sandwich Shop, now more than a century old. Over the years, more Italians have gotten into the sandwich game, and in Portland alone there are myriad Italians to choose from. The best in town can be found at **Colucci's** on Munjoy Hill (135 Congress St., 207-774-2279), **DiPietro's** on Cumberland Avenue (171 Cumberland Ave., 207-772-4084), and, of course, **Amato's** (see p. 31).

run by the eponymous Becky, opens at 4 a.m. to serve coffee and a filling, homemade meal to lobstermen, students, workers getting off the swing shift, and anyone else who happens to be up and hungry. Cheerful staff offers attentive service with a smile. Open for breakfast, lunch, and dinner 362½ days a year.

**DiMillo's Floating Restaurant,** 25 Long Wharf, Portland; (207) 772-2216; www.dimillos.com; $$. With seating for more than 600, this former ferry turned restaurant offers a menu of classic New England and Italian-style seafood dishes from its dockside dining room. Family owned and operated for decades, it's the only floating restaurant on the upper East Coast and offers beautiful views of the harbor, generous portions, and a full bar. Lunch and dinner service year-round.

**J's Oysters,** 5 Portland Pier, Portland; (207) 772-4828; www.jsoysters.com; $$. Opened in 1977 by Janice "J" Noyes, this unpretentious waterfront raw bar was the first of its kind in Maine. Raw oysters are served by the baker's dozen from beds of ice and seaweed in the center of the bar. Raw scallops, steamed mussels, and shrimp and lobster-claw cocktails can be washed down with the local beers on tap, while baked oysters, oyster stew, chowders, and seafood entrees make a hearty meal. Seasonal outdoor seating has a view of the docks, and the indoor bar is peppered with regulars slurping oysters and spinning yarns.

**Miss Portland Diner,** 138 Marginal Way, Portland; (207) 210-6673; www.missportlanddiner.com; $$. Housed in a dining car built in 1949 by the famed Worcester Lunch Car Company, this classic diner has moved several times in its 60-odd years, most recently in 2007 after a total restoration. Now reopened, the diner offers breakfast all day, and lunch and dinner after 11 a.m. The menu is homemade comfort food with a few twists—crab Benedict and eggplant fries liven things up—and the warm atmosphere is kid friendly.

**Tony's Donut Shop,** 9 Bolton St., Portland; (207) 772-2727; $. Founder and namesake, Tony Fournier, lived by the motto inscribed on his doughnut-shaped tombstone: "As you wander on through life, no matter be your goal, keep your eye on the donut and not on the hole." His son and daughter continue the family tradition, turning out hundreds of hand-cut, hand-fried, and hand-glazed doughnuts each day. Locals gather at tables in the front to talk politics and high school sports over morning coffee, and the cases and racks fill with classic doughnuts, bismarcks, and turnovers (try the mince!). Get there early for warm, old-fashioned molasses doughnuts, a cakey spiced ring with a crispy "blossom" and a devoted following.

**Top of the East Lounge,** Eastland Park Hotel, 157 High St., Portland; (207) 775-5411; www.eastlandparkhotel.com; $$. With panoramic views of Casco Bay and the city skyline, this sophisticated rooftop lounge is a Portland institution. Deep leather couches and wing chairs add a pleasantly clubby feel. Service includes a full bar and appetizers in the evening, with lunch served daily.

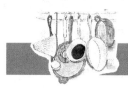

**Five Seasons Cooking School,** 87 St. Lawrence St., Portland; (207) 780-0738; www.fiveseasonscookingschool.net. With a focus on whole grains and macrobiotic cooking, classes offer instruction on dishes that are both healthy and delicious. Wellness coach Lisa Silverman also offers personal chef services, catering, and consultation.

**Patty Howells Cooking,** Portland; (207) 752-0126; www.patty howellscooking.com. In her kitchen or yours, classically trained chef Patty Howells teaches informal classes in culinary techniques that range from fundamental soups, stocks, and seasonal braises to pastries and hors d'oeuvres. Chef Howells is happy to work with groups to design classes of special interest, and participants leave with a sheaf of recipes. Also available for catering.

**Quimby Colony,** 769 Congress St., Portland; www.quimbycolony .org. In a historic building that once held an Italian restaurant, this nonprofit teaching space and artist's colony was begun by Roxanne Quimby, founder of Burt's Bees products, as a forum to nurture creativity in the culinary, textile, and fashion arts. In addition to a residential program, the space offers lectures, classes, and guided tastings in the commercial kitchen and dining room. Events are listed on their website.

**Arabica Coffee House,** 2 Free St., Portland; (207) 899-1833. Known for well-brewed coffee, a clean, quiet atmosphere, and Portland's best toast, this cozy coffeehouse is a great spot to read the paper or meet a friend. Fresh baked goods, free Wi-Fi, and a variety of espresso drinks—including a yummy maple latte—provide a local alternative to larger coffee chains. While seating is limited, large windows provide a nice perch for people watching.

**Bard Coffee,** 185 Middle St., Portland; (207) 899-4788; www .bardcoffee.com. Serving beans roasted by Brunswick-based Wicked Joe Coffee (whose owner is a partner in this business), this Old Port cafe specializes in single-origin coffees—beans imported directly from the region they were grown, which are not blended with other coffees. Single-origin selections range from Ethiopian to Columbian, and change frequently. Regular cups of the house blend are custom brewed to order in a French press. With fresh baked goods and free Wi-Fi.

**Coffee By Design,** 620 Congress St., Portland; (207) 772-5533; www.coffeebydesign.com. Originally opened in 1994, this funky coffeehouse in Portland's Arts District helped to usher in an urban renewal in the area. Handcrafted, microroasted coffee is available brewed and by the pound, as well as a selection of breakfast pastries, sweet snacks, and coffee-related gifts. Owners Mary Allen Lindemann and Alan Spear are dedicated to supporting sustainable farming, and many organic and fair trade–certified coffees are avail-able. The company now has **three additional locations:** 67 India St., Portland; (207) 780-6767; 95 Main St., Freeport (inside the L.L. Bean flagship store); (207) 865-2235; and 43 Washington Ave., Portland; (207) 879-2233 x202 (also home to the microroastery).

**Dean's Sweets,** 82 Middle St., Portland; (207) 899-3664; www .deanssweets.com. Chocolatier and former architect Dean Bingham hand dips each dark chocolate truffle in this sweet shop at the edge of the Old Port. Flavors range from rum to hot coffee (Italian roast coffee and cay-enne) to chocolate stout, and centers are made with 56 percent cocoa content. The tastes of Maine are highlighted in blueberry, maple, and needham truffles. No nuts are used in production, and many truffles are gluten- and dairy-free. See Dean's Sweets' recipe for **Maine "Needham" Dark Chocolate Truffles** on p. 38.

**Gorgeous Gelato,** 434 Fore St., Portland; (207) 699-4309; www .gorgeousgelato.com. As the name proclaims, owners Donato Giovine and Mariagrazia Zanardi make gorgeous, glorious gelato at this inviting Old Port shop. Flavors include familiar favorites like almond, pistachio, and chocolate, and more creative combinations like sour cherry, panna cotta, and rum chocolate. Also for sale are

# Dean's Sweets' Maine "Needham" Dark Chocolate Truffles

### Ganache:

2 cups heavy cream

21 ounces semisweet chocolate chips

7-ounce package of unsweetened coconut flakes

⅓ cup Cold River Vodka (p. 98)

### Enrobing:

2 pounds bittersweet chocolate (approximate), tempered (Note: Tempering chocolate is a process of heating and cooling chocolate to prepare it for enrobing.)

*Start by making the ganache. Heat the heavy cream to just below boiling in a heavy-bottomed saucepan. Pour most of the cream over the chocolate chips in a glass or metal bowl. Allow to sit for a couple minutes to melt the chocolate, then slowly mix to combine the chocolate and cream. Finally, mix in the remaining cream.*

*While the cream is heating, place the coconut in a food processor on high for about a minute, pulsing until fairly fine. Add the vodka and process several seconds more. It should look somewhat like mashed potato with a bit of texture.*

*Remove the coconut mixture from the food processor and add to the ganache. Mix thoroughly. Pour into a flat storage container and cover loosely with plastic wrap or a* lid. *Allow to come to room temperature. As it sits it will thicken and set. At this point you can simply wait for the natural thickening, or to hasten the process, place container in the refrigerator for several hours.*

*When cooled and thickened, scoop teaspoonfuls of ganache and form into balls by placing a second teaspoon on top. Place on a wax paper–covered baking sheet. It may take a bit of practice to figure out size, but balls should be about ¾-inch in diameter. When all are scooped, place baking sheet in freezer for 20 minutes to chill.*

*Remove tray from freezer, and with clean hands form into balls by rolling between palms. For a less messy technique, simply squeeze them a couple times between thumb and forefinger. This makes for a somewhat less-round truffle, but I think it's perfect.*

*When all truffles have been formed, gently melt the tempered chocolate, in a double boiler set over—but not touching—simmering water. Pick up a truffle ball from your baking sheet, drop into the tempered chocolate, flip over once or twice until completely coated, and scoop it out with a fork. Place the coated truffle on the baking sheet and go on to the next one. During this process the coating chocolate needs to be kept at about 88 to 90 degrees F. It will maintain its temperature longest in a heavy glass bowl, but you may still need to periodically return it to the microwave for an additional 30 second periods to keep it at the correct temperature.*

*As soon as the coating has set, they are ready to package or eat!*

*Makes 36 truffles.*

Recipe courtesy of Dean's Sweets (p. 37).

gelato pops and cakes, perfectly made espresso drinks, and Italian hot chocolate so thick you can nearly stand your spoon on end.

**Maine Mead Works,** 51 Washington Ave., Portland; (207) 773-6323; www.mainemeadworks.com. Surprisingly crisp and light, HoneyMaker Mead is crafted from local wildflower honey, and was created to "honor the honeybee and the environmental harmony it brings." Varieties include Dry Mead, Semi-Sweet Mead, Blueberry Mead, and Lavender Mead, among others. Available by the bottle at the Washington Avenue tasting room and from wine merchants across the state.

**Pastor Chuck Orchards,** Portland; (207) 773-1314; www.pastorchuckorchards.com. Begun with surplus apples from founder C. Waite Maclin's tiny orchard in Cushing, this small company offers organic apple butter, applesauce, and apple salsa. Maclin, a psychotherapist who is also an ordained Episcopal priest, named the business after a family nickname given to him by a cousin, and he donates 1 percent of all profits to community endeavors. Apple butter is sweet, spicy, and intense, while applesauce has a hint of tartness; both are available without added sugar. Sold at stores throughout Maine.

**158 Pickett Street Cafe,** 158 Benjamin W. Pickett St., South Portland; (207) 799-8998; $$. The modest exterior and thrift-store aesthetic of this beloved cafe belie the carefully crafted sandwiches, soups, and baked goods found on the menu. From the chewy, homemade bagels—excellent alone, even better as the base of an egg, cheese, and local ham sandwich—to soups and classic sandwiches accented with surprising condiments, each meal is hearty and nourishing to body and soul.

**555,** 555 Congress St., Portland; (207) 761-0555; www.five fifty-five.com; $$$$. The elegant atmosphere of this upscale res-taurant is underscored by chef-owner Steve Corry's inventive, ever-changing menu. Meals are created by the plate; start with small or green (or both), continue to savory, and move on to cheese or sweet. Combinations are intricate, but always work: Burgundian snails may come with lemon-caper butter, bronzed fennel, and an artichoke "turnover," while a pungent artisanal blue cheese may be matched with house-made Fig Newtons. A tasting menu provides more structure but takes away some of the fun. Staff is attentive and helpful, and, with advance notice, the chef is happy to work around food allergies and sensitivities. Open nightly and for Sunday brunch.

**Artemisia Cafe,** 61 Pleasant St., #109, Portland; (207) 761-0135; $$. The artsy atmosphere of this casual cafe is emphasized by its

location in a former bakery that now houses artists' studios. Paint-spattered regulars come in for take-out coffee and sandwiches, and chat with busy waitresses from a stool by the register. Sandwiches are supreme, and combinations like sweet potato, avocado, and sprouts on chewy whole-grain bread, and turkey, stuffing, and cranberry sauce never disappoint. House-made nonalcoholic coolers are refreshing, as are a variety of teas and Mexican hot (and cold) chocolate.

**Asmara,** 51 Oak St., Portland; (207) 253-5122; $$. One of Portland's hidden gems, this family-run Eritrean restaurant is as unassuming as it is delicious. A video of Eritrea plays in the corner, and regional maps line the walls of this small storefront behind the Portland Museum of Art. From the kitchen, large rounds of fresh *injera* bread emerge, topped with vegetable and meat stews and spiced to diners' preference, along with a house salad of lettuce and tomato in oil and vinegar. Silverware is optional, as food is traditionally scooped up with pieces of *injera*. Many vegetarian selections are available, and Asmara herself is happy to pop out of the kitchen and offer recommendations.

**Back Bay Grill,** 65 Portland St., Portland; (207) 772-8833; www .backbaygrill.com; $$$$. With a seasonally changing menu and a wine list that has received the Wine Spectator's Award of Excellence every year since 1999, this upscale eatery receives consistently rave reviews. Chef-owner Larry Matthews Jr. offers rich classics with a twist: filet mignon tartare comes with caper pesto, pasture-raised chicken comes with grilled figs and confit of brussels sprouts. Cap your meal with one of 20 available scotches.

**Bar Lola,** 100 Congress St., Portland; (207) 775-5652; www.bar lola.net; $$$. Open for dinner on Munjoy Hill, this understated restaurant serves a changing menu of small, medium, and large plates that reflects what's seasonally available and interesting to chefowner Guy Hernandez. Though not a wine bar, the restaurant's carefully chosen wine list makes it a great spot to linger over a bottle.

**The Bar of Chocolate Cafe,** 38 Wharf St.; (207) 773-6667; $$. Nestled on a cobbled street in the Old Port, this tiny cafe and dessert bar specializes in small plates and, as the name suggests, chocolate. Rich cakes—chocolate caramel with sea salt, flourless chocolate, *boca negra*—are available by the slice, and an evening rush for sweets and coffee, wine, or a cocktail (try the espresso martini) begins around 8 p.m.

**Bintliff's American Cafe,** 98 Portland St., Portland; (207) 774-0005; www.bintliffscafe.com; $$$. Behind a Greek Revival facade, this casual restaurant is known for its daily brunch, served from 7 a.m. to 2 p.m. Offerings range from classics like eggs Florentine and corned beef hash to dark-chocolate waffles and granolacrusted French toast, and specialty drinks include the Honeymoon, a mead-and-champagne cocktail, and the Lady Godiva, a combination of locally roasted coffee and liqueur. In warm weather, outdoor seating is available, and the restaurant is perfectly situated for a post-meal stroll in the rose gardens of nearby Deering Oaks Park.

**Boda,** 671 Congress St., Portland; (207) 347-7557; www.bodamaine .com; $$. The menu is "very Thai" and street-vendor inspired at this West End restaurant and skewer bar. Don't look for Americanized dishes like pad thai; pork belly skewers, fried taro sticks with *sriracha* sauce, and beef salad start the menu, while entrees range from tilapia with herbs in banana leaf to lamb *mussaman* curry. Drinks and a special late-night tapas and skewer menu are served until 1 a.m. every day.

**Bogusha's Polish Restaurant and Deli,** 825 Stevens Ave., Portland; (207) 878-9618; $$. Specializing in homemade pierogi, hearty stews, and traditional Polish dry sausages, this unassuming restaurant and market is a haven for Eastern European immigrants craving a taste of home. In the tiny kitchen, owner Bogusha Pawlaczyk cooks up stuffed cabbage and chewy, smoky kielbasa. Out front, shelves are filled with imported canned goods—from caviar to vegetable soup—kvass soda, and birthday cards in Polish and Russian.

**Bonobo,** 46 Pine St., Portland; (207) 347-8267; www.bonobopizza .com; $$. You'll know you've found this corner pizzeria in the West End when the smell of smoke perfumes the air and you see cords of wood stacked against its outer wall. The brick-oven pizza has a crisp crust, and while the menu is limited, its clever combinations range from Morocco (with spiced lamb sausage) to Marley (with jerk chicken sausage). Meats are antibiotic-, hormone-, and nitrate-free, and vegetables are sourced locally whenever possible. In the dining room, cozy nooks are perfect for conversation, and staff is friendly and efficient.

**Bresca,** 111 Middle St., Portland; (207) 772-1004; www.restaurant bresca.com; $$$$. This intimate restaurant in the Old Port takes its name from the Catalan word for "honeycomb," and like its totem bee, the restaurant is busy. Since opening in 2007, chef-owner Krista Kern Desjarlais has received national attention for her simple and elegant menu, which showcases local, seasonal ingredients in regionally inspired preparations from France and Italy, including fresh pastas and gnocchi. The dining room is small, and reservations are recommended. See Bresca's recipe for **Marinated Fried Smelts** on p. 46.

**Caiola's,** 58 Pine St., Portland; (207) 772-1110; www.caiolas.com; $$$. This cozy neighborhood restaurant in the historic West End combines a warm atmosphere with a well-considered menu. Chef Abby Harmon's variations on American comfort foods are peppered with surprises—Caesar salad is topped with spicy fried oysters, the excellent bacon cheeseburger comes with homemade Tater Tots—and local ingredients are showcased. The Sunday brunch menu is

# Marinated Fried Smelts

Tiny smelts, like the salmon they resemble, spend most of their lives at sea, making their way to fresh water only to breed. It's during this journey, in late winter and early spring, that many smelts veer off course and make their way to Maine's dinner tables. Just a few inches long, whole smelts are traditionally battered and fried and served by the pile.

At Portland's Bresca (see p. 45), chef Krista Kern Desjarlais puts a new twist on this classic. Her smelt can be eaten fresh from the frying pan and piping hot or can be chilled overnight in this delicate marinade. Either way, they're a winter treat.

## Pan-Fried Smelts

3 pounds smelts
Salt and pepper

6 tablespoons flour
Oil for frying (canola works well)

Clean the smelts. Cut off the fins. Wash and dry well. Sprinkle the fish with salt and pepper, then dip in the flour. Heat ¼-inch of oil until it shimmers. Fry fish on both sides in hot oil until golden brown. Let cool on a rack to keep them crisp. Serve with fried potatoes and pumpernickel bread.

## Marinated Fried Fish

(For 3 pounds of smelts or other fried fish)
1 cup water
6 bay leaves
8 peppercorns

1 teaspoon salt
1 carrot, thinly sliced
1 cup onion, sliced
1 cup vinegar

Bring the water to a boil. Add the spices, carrots, and onion rings. Simmer until carrots are soft and onions transparent. Add the vinegar. Cool. When mixture is lukewarm, pour the marinade over the fried fish. Chill overnight before serving.

Recipe courtesy of Bresca (p. 45).

extensive and satisfying, ranging from house-made Pop Tarts to a fried oyster po'boy. A private dining room and terrace can be reserved for parties.

**Cinque Terra,** 36 Wharf St., Portland; (207) 347-6154; www .cinqueterramaine.com; $$$$; and **Vignola,** 10 Dana St., Portland; (207) 772-1330; www.vignolamaine.com; $$$. Tucked down a narrow cobbled street in a historic ship chandlery in the Old Port, chef Lee Skawinski's crisp, upscale res-taurant Cinque Terra incor-porates local flavors into traditional Italian cuisine, offering a regu-larly changing dinner menu. Highlights include hand-cut pasta and local seafood—if grilled octopus is on the menu, it's not to be missed. Down the street, sister restaurant Vignola offers a more casual dining experience, including lunch and weekend brunch service—crispy trout with bacon and chocolate brioche French toast are special favorites. Produce for both restaurants is supplied by Grand View Farm, in Greene, Maine, which is owned by the proprietors.

**The Corner Room,** 110 Exchange St., Portland; (207) 879-4747; www.thefrontroomrestaurant.com; $$$. See the Front Room listing, p. 51.

**The Downtown Lounge,** 606 Congress St., Portland; (207) 773-1363; $$; and **Norm's Bar & Grill,** 617 Congress St., Portland; (207) 828-9944; $$. The pleasantly divey feel of this duo (including the clean but strangely situated bathroom at the Downtown Lounge) provides a nice counterpoint to the well-executed comfort food on each menu. Interesting takes on pub fare abound at both places, as do strong drinks and ample portions. The kitchen at the Downtown Lounge is open until 11 p.m.

**Duck Fat,** 43 Middle St., Portland; (207) 774-8080; www.duckfat.com; $$. This small sandwich shop, owned by chef Rob and Nancy Evans of nearby Hugo's (p. 54), gets its name from its signature dish: Belgian fries made with local potatoes and cooked to crisp, browned perfection in duck fat. Available with such dipping sauces as homemade truffle ketchup, garlic aioli, and Thai chili mayo, the fries are a meal in themselves. Even better, try them in *poutine*, a Franco-American delight that combines fries with cheese curds and hot gravy. The menu is rounded out by a selection of salads, pressed panini sandwiches—duck confit with kimchee and chili sauce is a surprising favorite—and soups. Beverages include sodas, teas, locally roasted coffee, beer, and wine. For dessert, artisanal gelato milk shakes and duck fat–fried beignets are a decadent treat.

**El Rayo,** 101 York St., Portland; (207) 780-8226; www.elrayo taqueria.com; $$. Housed in a renovated gas station at the edge of the working waterfront, this cheerful restaurant brings the flavors of Oaxaca to Maine. Bright colors, Latin music, communal tables, and a sprinkle of kitsch make every meal festive. Citrus and seafood figure prominently in the lively menu—don't miss the fish tacos and seviche. Fried plantains and smoky potato fritters are piping hot and a nice alternative to chips and salsa, which are also available. In warmer months, sit outdoors and watch the world go by with a glass of potent house sangria, a margarita, or a refreshing hibiscus cooler.

**Emilitsa,** 547 Congress St., Portland; (207) 221-0245; www.emilitsa .com; $$$. This upscale Greek restaurant in the downtown arts district offers a range of *mezethes* (small plates) and *megala plata* (large plates) and traditional Mediterranean preparations of Maine's fresh seafood. Stuffed grape leaves, moussaka, and spanakopita are on the menu, but there are surprises, as well: *gigantes sto fournou* (white beans baked with tomato and dill) or simple grilled lamb loin with tomatoes, feta, and lemony potatoes. Don't miss house-made baklava, packed with ground nuts and dripping with honey. Wines are Greek, but staff will guide you to the right pairing.

**Figa,** 249 Congress St., Portland; (207) 518-9400; www.figa restaurant.com; $$$$. Chef Lee Farrington's eclectic menu is fusion in the best sense, incorporating international flavors and techniques with locally sourced ingredients. Dishes are separated into "spoons" (small plates), "forks" (half portions), and "knives" (full entrees) and range from spicy, slow cooked wild boar *rendang* to salmon tandoori to a *brigadeiro,* a Brazilian home-made chocolate. Friendly waitstaff is happy to suggest pairings from an ample wine list. Seating is limited, and reservations are recommended.

**Flatbread,** 72 Commercial St., Portland; (207) 772-8777; www .flatbreadcompany.com; $$. Perched above the waterfront, with outdoor pier seating when weather permits, this relaxed restaurant is known as much for its commitment to the community as it is for its crisp, wood-fired pizzas. Every Tuesday is Benefit Night, when $3.50 of every flatbread sold is given to a local organization. And the pizza: Baked in a primitive oven in the center of the restaurant, flatbread pizzas are prepared with organic produce, free-range chicken, and nitrate-free meats. The house salad, dressed with berry vinaigrette and topped with an appealing mixture of toasted sesame seeds and *arame* seaweed, is not to be missed, nor is the wood-fired brownie.

**Fore Street,** 288 Fore St., Portland; (207) 775-2717; www.fore street.biz; $$$$. Since 1996, this Old Port restaurant has blazed the trail for dining that celebrates Maine's local, sustainably grown and harvested ingredients. Pioneering chef Sam Hayward, recipient of the James Beard Foundation's Best Chef: Northeast 2004 award, has been at the forefront of the city's food renaissance. He changes the menu daily to reflect what's in season, and puts into practice his belief that "good food travels the shortest distance between the farm and the table." The kitchen and its wood-burning oven, grill, and turnspit are visible to diners, and producers and foragers are listed by name on the menu. The full bar opens before dinner service. Reservations are recommended.

**The Front Room,** 73 Congress St., Portland; (207) 773-3366; and **The Grill Room,** 84 Exchange St., Portland; (207) 774-2333; and **The Corner Room,** 110 Exchange St., Portland; (207) 879-4747; www.thefrontroomrestaurant.com; $$$. Since opening the Front Room in Portland's hip Munjoy Hill neighborhood in 2005, chef Harding Lee Smith's ramped-up comfort food has received national attention and a devoted local following—weekend brunch lines can be out the door. His Old Port restaurant and bar, the Grill Room, features wood-fired meats and pizzas, and serves classic cocktails from its handcrafted bar. Down the street, his most recent offering, the Corner Room Kitchen & Bar, serves affordable, rustic, Italian-inspired food, including house-made pasta, in a space that was formerly the gallery of the Salt Institute for Documentary Studies.

**Full Belly Deli,** 1070 Brighton Ave., Portland; (207) 772-1227; $. Offering a little taste of NYC in Portland since 1987, this kosher-style deli serves classic sandwiches mounded with meat, like corned beef, hot pastrami, chopped liver, and tongue on rye, with half-sour pickles and potato salad on the side. Potato latkes, knishes, and noodle kugel are also on the menu of this no-frills eatery, as well as nontraditional fare like calzones and clam cakes (it's Maine, after all).

**Grace,** 15 Chestnut St., Portland; (207) 828-4422; www.restaurant grace.com; $$$. The grace is in the details at this elegant downtown restaurant, housed in the meticulously restored Chestnut Street Church. The Gothic Revival building, which dates from 1856, is on the National Register of Historic Places, and while it has been repurposed, the space retains the expansive floor plan and hallowed feel of a church. The pulpit has been transformed into an open kitchen, and seating is arranged lining the walls beneath the stained glass, around a central circular bar, and in the choir loft. Votive candles accent each table, menus open like hymnals, and napkins are ringed with the wire inner workings of an unsalvageable church organ. On the menu, cocktails are inspired (try the Holier Than Thou), and entrees change seasonally but always showcase offbeat regional ingredients (rutabaga "ramen," salsify *dulce de leche*). Desserts are, well, sinful.

**Green Elephant,** 608 Congress St., Portland; (207) 347-3111; www .greenelephantmaine.com; $$. In a cheerful, informal atmosphere, this Asian-inspired vegetarian bistro serves tasty, nutritious, and surprisingly filling meals, making it popular with students from nearby Maine College of Art. "Quick bites" include fried spring rolls and soy nuggets, and most entrees come with sides of mashed winter squash and brown rice. More than half the menu is vegan, and much is gluten-free.

**The Grill Room,** 84 Exchange St., Portland; (207) 774-2333; $$$. See the Front Room listing, p. 51.

**Hamdi Restuarant,** 30 Washington Ave., Portland; (207) 615-0023; $$. While several markets cater to southern Maine's large Somali population, this simple restaurant has broad appeal within the immigrant community and beyond. Though the decor is some-what spartan, the spicy beef, goat, and chicken stews are delicious and hearty, especially with a cup of sweetened tea or cardamom coffee. East African music adds to the ambience, as does a glimpse of the adjoining market that sells such staples as cooking oil, millet, and cornmeal.

**Hi Bombay,** 1 Pleasant St., Portland; (207) 772-8767; www .hibombay.com; $$. With Bollywood on the television, this family-owned north Indian restaurant offers a taste of south Asia in down-town Portland. Bay of Bengal seafood specialties use local fish, and the menu includes a broad range of vegetarian dishes. Delivery and catering are available.

**Hot Suppa,** 703 Congress St., Portland; (207) 871-5005; www.hot suppa.com; $$. This West End favorite, run by brothers Moses and Alec Sabina, aims to provide "simple, affordable food done right." In a Victorian building with high ceilings and original moldings that nicely complement the classic American fare, the restaurant serves breakfast and lunch daily, and dinner Tues through Sat. The menu includes Southern favorites and soul food—cornmeal-crusted catfish, gumbo, chicken and waffles—as well as quirky takes on regional dishes, like *foie gras poutine* and fried green tomatoes with smoked Maine scallops. Full bar and beer on tap.

**Hugo's,** 88 Middle St., Portland; (207) 774-8538; www.hugos .net; $$$$. This upscale restaurant at the edge of the Old Port is a haven for serious gourmands. Chef-owner Rob Evans, recipient of the James Beard Foundation's Best Chef: Northeast 2009 award, trained under famed chef Thomas Keller, and his exquisite creations combine the best of Maine's ingredients in inventive and beautifully presented dishes. The menu changes weekly, and plates are of similar sizes so diners can create their own tasting. The Chef's Blind Tasting Menu is special fun and brings out one's inner culinary detective: The menu isn't presented until the end of the meal.

**Little Seoul,** 90 Exchange St., Portland; (207) 699-4326; $$. Going beyond well-known staples like bibimbap and kimchee (both of which are done well here), this Old Port eatery introduces more adventurous Korean fare: beef tripe with vegetables and chili sauce, cooked sea snail and mixed greens salad, and traditional Korean sweet pumpkin soup. Japanese favorites like tempura and katsu are also on the menu, as well as a large sushi list and a few dishes that bridge the culinary gap—the Seoul roll is made with spicy tuna and kimchee.

**Local 188,** 685 Congress St., Portland; (207) 761-7909; www .local188.com; $$$. Founded in 1999 in a storefront at 188 Congress St., this Spanish-infused restaurant has been a West End hot spot for more than a decade. Several years ago, chef-owner Jay Villani moved to a new location across the street, which offers two bars— one full, one overlooking the open kitchen—comfy sofas, and a menu that incorporates warm North African spices. Free parking is a bonus. The decor is rich—deep colors and flattering light—and the food ranges from classic tapas and larger *raciónes* to an excellent brunch. Don't miss the house paella and sangria.

**Local Sprouts Cooperative Cafe,** 649 Congress St., Portland; (207) 899-3529; www.localsproutscooperative.com; $$. The mission of the Local Sprouts Cooperative is "to provide people in Maine with creative local and organic food and holistic learning through cooking food for our community." To that end, the cooperative's cafe was created as a community gathering space, transforming a disused college cafeteria into a fun, relaxed restaurant, decorated with bright mosaics in a curving floor plan. Great for families, there's a large kid's play kitchen separated by half walls.

The changing menu offers comfort food, salads, and freshly baked sweets, and profits go to the cooperative's community programs.

**Miyake Restaurant,** 129 Spring St., Portland; (207) 871-9170; www.restaurantmiyake.com; $$$; and **Pai Men Miyake,** 188 Congress Ave., Portland; (207) 541-9204; $$. Chef Masa Miyake's first restaurant, an acknowledged hole-in-the-wall with limited seating and a BYOB policy, raised the bar for Portland's sushi: A la carte dishes were jewels of fresh seafood—some of it harvested by the chef—and the *omakase* (chef's tasting) was a carefully assembled progression of up to seven delicate dishes. Pai Men Miyake, a noodle and sake bar, is a more casual experience, with heartier food, but the attention to detail is equally meticulous. Hot, rich broth, melting pork belly, and crunchy homemade kimchee are standouts—and don't miss the pork buns. Open every day at noon, it's a perfect antidote to a harsh winter, and a great restorative if you've over-indulged the night before.

**Norm's Bar & Grill,** 617 Congress St., Portland; (207) 828-9944; $$. See the Downtown Lounge listing, p. 48.

**Nosh Kitchen Bar,** 551 Congress St., Portland; (207) 553-2227; www.noshkitchenbar.com; $$. Though this urban eatery takes its name from the Yiddish word for snacking, their menu takes deli food to a new level, offering an extensive list of house-cured meats, homemade pickles, artisanal cheeses, and fresh-caught seafoods. Hearty sandwiches and fries—don't miss the bacon-dusted version with horseradish mayo—make a great lunch. For a late-night nosh, try small plates of charcuterie and other snacks. Turn to the knowledgeable staff for pairings from their large list of wines and beers.

**Old Port Sea Grill,** 93 Commercial St., Portland; (207) 879-6100; www.theoldportseagrill.com; $$$. The main event at this upscale Old Port eatery is an expansive marble raw bar, offering the city's largest selection of oysters on the half shell. Also on the menu are clams, crabs, mussels, and calamari, and entrees of local meat and fish. Wood-grilled seafood provides a flavorful, light alternative to fried, which is also available. The seasonal dessert menu includes gluten-free options, which are marked.

**Otto,** 576 Congress St., Portland; (207) 773-7099; www.otto portland.com; $. Under a black awning in busy downtown, this tiny pizzeria turns out traditional and regionally influenced oven-baked pies, sold whole and by the slice. Toppings range from eggplant, ricotta, and basil; and classic Margherita; to mashed potato, bacon, and scallion; and butternut squash, ricotta, and cranberry. Eat at the narrow counter, a handful of tables, or take a slice to go.

**Paciarino,** 468 Fore St., Portland; (207) 774-3500; www.paciarino .com; $$. Specializing in supple house-made pastas and rich, concentrated sauces, this Old Port restaurant and market serves classic Italian fare in a rustic environment. Chef-owners Fabiana De Savino and Enrico Barbiero moved to Maine from Milan just months before opening, and their menu reflects both their roots and their new home. Italian wines are available by the glass and the bottle, and pastas, sauces, and a selection of imported foods—all of which they use in the menu—are available in their store.

**Pai Men Miyake,** 188 Congress Ave., Portland; (207) 541-9204; $$$. See Miyake Restaurant listing, p. 56.

**Ribollita,** 41 Middle St., Portland; (207) 774-2972; www.ribollita maine.com; $$$. This cozy trattoria, in what was once the heart of Portland's Italian neighborhood, serves traditional Italian favorites, from hand-filled cannelloni to veal osso bucco to the restaurant's namesake dish, ribollita (Tuscan vegetable and bread soup). The staff is warm and knowledgeable about the extensive list of Italian wines. Twelve tables fill quickly, and reservations are recommended. Open for dinner, Mon through Sat.

**Silly's Restaurant,** 40 Washington Ave., Portland; (207) 772-0360; www.sillys.com; $$. Originally opened by the Nice sisters in 1988, this comfortable East End establishment has been serving  casual food in a cheerful, kitschy environment for more than 20 years. New management has preserved the menu, the feel, and the community activism of the restaurant. Menu includes salads, sandwiches, and cleverly named entrees—including a large selection of vegetarian and vegan offerings—as well as decadent desserts and great shakes (available with rice or soy milk).

**Sonny's,** 83 Exchange St., Portland; (207) 772-7774; www.sonnys portland.com; $$$. The staid mosaic tiles and heavy woodwork in the entryway of this historic former bank are livened up deeper in the restaurant by bright colors, swinging music, and paintings by co-owner Patrick Corrigan. Chef and co-owner Jay Villani (the pair are also behind Local 188, p. 55) brings Latin American and south-western influences to the menu, with fried plantains, empanadas, and grilled meats with chimichurri sauce. Cocktails—caipirinhas, vodka-spiked sangria, and combinations of Cava (a Spanish spar-kling wine) and muddled fruit—are tasty and fun. Deep couches, attentive waitstaff, and views of a small city park add to the charm.

**Street and Company,** 33 Wharf St., Portland; (207) 775-0887; www.streetandcompany.net; $$$$. For more than two decades, this upscale seafood restaurant in the Old Port has set the standard for fresh, beautifully prepared fish. The open kitchen, rustic brick walls, and copper-topped tables provide an engaging backdrop for the main event: seafood served broiled, grilled, in the pan, or with linguine. The menu leans to the Mediterranean, with "tastes" and appetizers that bring in the flavors of Spain and Italy. Seating is limited, and reservations are recommended.

**Vignola,** 10 Dana St., Portland; (207) 772-1330; www.vignola maine.com; $$$$. See Cinque Terra listing, p. 47.

**Aurora Provisions,** 64 Pine St., Portland; (207) 871-9060; www .auroraprovisions.com. This charming West End market and cafe promises "beautiful food for busy people," and it delivers: Cases full of freshly prepared foods and pastries, a selection of gourmet staples (imported sauces, crackers, and jams), and a well-chosen wine section are complemented by tasteful gifts that make perfect hostess presents. The cafe serves breakfast—don't miss the raspberry scones—and lunch, and the relaxed, kid-friendly atmosphere makes it a great place to meet friends for cocoa (with homemade marshmallows) and a "cowboy cookie." See Aurora Provisions' recipe for **Maple Bacon Baked Beans** on p. 61.

**Le Roux Kitchen,** 161 Commercial St., Portland; (207) 553-7665; www.lerouxkitchen.com. Offering everything from microrasps to home milk-shake makers, this Old Port kitchen shop is filled to the brim with gadgets, gifts, and gourmet treats. This is the place to go when in need of essential bakeware, enameled pots, and kitchen tools of all descriptions. The store's well-chosen edibles include a small wine section, a variety of handcrafted chocolates, and shelves of sea salts and infused olive oils.

# Maple Bacon Baked Beans

*Bean Suppah! Bean suppers, held in a church, grange hall, or outside around a rock-lined "bean hole" (a deep fire pit in which beans can be cooked overnight), are a New England tradition that dates to the Pilgrims and possibly further back to the Native Americans who lived in Maine long before Europeans arrived. These communal meals have adapted through the years but are marked by beans baked with molasses, onions, and salt pork, thick slices of brown bread slathered with butter, and, to cap the meal, an array of freshly baked pies. Bean suppers are a living tradition, and can be found year-round throughout the state. A calendar of upcoming bean suppers can be found at: www.beansuppah.org.*

*If you can't make it to the grange, pick up a can of B&M Baked Beans (made in Portland since 1867) or try this recipe, from Chef Rae Hebert at Portland's Aurora Provisions.*

**8 cups cannellini beans (preferably from the Beanery located at 988 Exeter Rd. in Exeter, Maine; 207-278-3572)**

**1½ pounds bacon, diced**

**1 large yellow onion, peeled and diced**

**½ teaspoon red chili flakes**

**¾ to 1 cup maple syrup (adjust to taste)**

**Sea salt and pepper to taste**

*Soak beans overnight. Cook bacon in stock pot until lightly crispy. Add onions to bacon fat. Cook until soft. Add chili flakes and drained beans. Add water to cover beans by three inches. Bring to a soft boil and cook, uncovered, over medium flame for 2½ to 3 hours, adding more water if they begin to stick. Beans should thicken nicely as they cook. Finish with maple syrup, salt, and pepper to taste.*

*Serves a crowd.*

Recipe courtesy of Chef Rae Hebert of Aurora Provisions (p. 60).

**Maple's Organics,** 14 Gary Maietta Pkwy., South Portland; (207) 899-3342; www.maplesorganics.com. The open floor plan of this certified-organic gelateria gives patrons a view of gelato in action. Owner Kristie Green uses local ingredients in artisanal gelatos and *sorbettos,* available by the scoop or the hand-packed pint. Each batch is started from scratch—no mixes or syrups—and flavors include house favorites like sea salt caramel and cardamom ginger, as well as changing seasonal offerings.

**Micucci Grocery Store,** 45 India St., Portland; (207) 775-1854. For more than 50 years, this Italian grocery has offered imported meats, cheeses, pastas, wines, and more. House-made bread and pizza has a cultish following—with good reason. The "luna bread" crust, sweet tomato sauce, and high-quality cheese ensure that there will be lines every lunch. A knowledgeable staff helps over-whelmed shoppers choose between prosciutto, capocollo, pancetta, and mortadella, while reasonable prices encourage you to try it all.

**Old Port Wine and Cigar Merchants,** 223 Commercial St., Portland; (207) 772-9463; www.oldportwine.com. Former wine dis-tributor Jacques de Villier's enthusiasm and unpretentious manner dispel any intimidation caused by the vast treasury of bottles in his Old Port shop. He and the educated staff are there to guide you to the right vintage, no matter the price—many of which are surprisingly reasonable. For cigar lovers, the walk-in humidor is also a marvel.

**Pat's Meat Market,** 484 Stevens Ave., Portland; (207) 772-3961; www.patsmeatmarket.com. Since 1918, this quintessential butcher shop has been selling cuts of meat and house-made sausage from its store in Portland's Deering neighborhood. The full-service market includes pantry staples and produce, but the main event is meat: from cold cuts to specialty steaks to fresh sausage by the pound. Prices are reasonable, and staff is knowledgeable and accommodating.

**The Public Market,** 28 Monument Sq., Portland; (207) 228-2056; www.publicmarkethouse.com. This indoor market at the edge of Monument Square is home to seven permanent vendors, a community kitchen, and changing "day tables" that sell a variety of Maine-made products. On the ground floor, **K. Horton Specialty Food** offers an impressive selection of local and imported cheeses; **Maine Beer & Beverage Co.** sells wines, beers and snacks; and **Big Sky Bread Company** bakes fresh breads, cookies, and pastries. Upstairs, restaurants share communal dining space and specialize in everything from soup to peanut butter and jelly (yes, the menu is all PB and J).

**Rabelais Books,** 86 Middle St., Portland; (207) 774-1044; www .rabelaisbooks.com. Thousands of books on food, wine, farming, and gardening can be found in this specialized independent bookshop.

Owners Don and Samantha Hoyt Lindgren bring their passion for gastronomy to the shop's collection of rare, out-of-print, and new books, and they are happy to offer recommendations to find the perfect tome. The shop hosts regular book signings, readings, and culinary events. See Rabelais Books's recipe for **Whole Wheat Sables** on p. 66.

**Rosemont Market & Bakery,** 580 Brighton Ave., Portland; (207) 774-8129; www.rosemontmarket.com. This classic corner grocery offers everything from fresh local produce and meats to fine wines and beer to prepared foods and sauces to take away. House-made artisanal breads and an excellent cheese counter make this a great stop for picnic supplies, while a section of natural cleaning products and staples like spices and whole free-range chickens (sourced locally from Maine-ly Poultry) allow for daily shopping. Owner John Naylor's knowledge and  enthusiasm make his recommendations hard to resist. **Other locations** at 88 Congress St., Portland; (207) 773-7888; and 96 Main St., Yarmouth; (207) 846-1234.

**Simply Scandinavian,** 469 Stevens Ave., Portland; (877) 874-6759; www.simplyscandinavianfoods.com. With products that range from salty licorice to pickled herring to *gjetost* (Norwegian caramelized goat cheese), this imported food shop is as colorful as the Scandinavian flags that flutter above its awning. A smorgasbord of condiments, cookies, and kitchen essentials line the shelves, and fresh baked goods like Swedish princess torte and Norwegian *kransekake* can be ordered.

**Soak Foot Sanctuary & Teahouse,** 30 City Center, Portland; (207) 879-7625. This tiny storefront in the heart of downtown offers tea-infused spa treatments in its lower level, and rare and organic teas by the cup and the ounce upstairs. The atmosphere is quiet and relaxing—a refuge in the center of the city. Small plates and specialty drinks such as Chai, smoothies, and *maté* lattes are also available.

**Sun Oriental Market,** 626 Congress St., Portland; (207) 772-8675. Products in this pan-Asian store range from Chinese canned lychee fruit to Korean sweet potato noodles to Indian fenugreek powder. Serving every corner of Portland's small Asian community, this small store offers a surprising range of frozen, dried, canned, and packaged products, as well as a few nonperishables like tea sets and the ubiquitous Hello Kitty gifts.

**Urban Farm Fermentory,** 200 Anderson St., Bay 4, Portland; (207) 653-7406; www.urbanfarmfermentory.com. Combining an urban "microfarm" with a community center for food and beverage fermentation, this once-neglected single-story warehouse in the East Bayside neighborhood has become a teaching facility, cider fermentory, apiary, source of infused honey, and staging area for a permaculture garden. There's a lot going on, from cider pressings

# Whole Wheat Sables

*Bookseller Samantha Hoyt Lindgren trained as a pastry chef at the Institute for Culinary Education and worked in bakeries in New York and Maine before she and husband Don Lindgren opened Portland's Rabelais, a bookstore specializing in "fine books on food and drink." Their shop is a hub of the food community, and Samantha often treats patrons to a plate of exquisite baked goods. In December, the store's annual cookie swap is a much anticipated event.*

*Samantha says, "Borrowed from Alice Medrich, this is one of my favorite butter cookies. Disarmingly simple and yet remarkably delicious. Nothing heavy or health-conscious here. Just a delicate buttery, nutty bite of cookie delight. Even better when made with Maine-grown whole wheat flour. Optional variations include adding chopped dried fruit such as cherries or currants, chopped toasted nuts such as hazelnuts or walnuts, or cacao nibs."*

1 cup (4.5 ounces) unbleached all-purpose flour

1 cup (4 ounces) whole wheat flour (can also use kamut or spelt flour)

8 ounces (2 sticks) unsalted butter at room temperature

½ (3.5 ounces) cup sugar ( I use organic cane sugar)

¼ teaspoon salt (I use sea salt)

1 teaspoon pure vanilla extract

Optional: ⅓ cup cacao nibs, chopped dried cherries, currants, or chopped toasted hazelnuts

*Combine the flours in a bowl.*

*In a standing mixer or a bowl with a handheld mixer or with a wooden spoon, beat the butter with the sugar, the salt, and the vanilla until smooth. Do not cream, you are not trying to beat in any leavening here.*

If you are using any of the additions, add them next, and mix until incorporated.

Add the flour and mix just until combined. Turn the dough out onto a flat surface and knead a few times.

There are two different ways to deal with the dough at this point.

You can roll it into a log (or logs) of a size of your choosing. Wrap the dough in either waxed paper or plastic wrap and nestle it into a tube from a roll of paper towels that you have cut in half lengthwise. This will keep the log round as it chills so your cookies will be fully round. When the dough is fully chilled, at least 2 hours although overnight is preferable (the logs also can be stored in the fridge for 3 days or in the freezer for up to 3 months before baking), preheat your oven to 350 degrees. Slice the dough into rounds ¼-inch thick and place on a lined cookie sheet 1½ inches apart. Bake for 10–14 minutes, rotating the pan(s) front to back and top to bottom halfway through the baking time. You want the cookies to be lightly browned around the edges. Cool on the sheets before removing.

If you have more time and feel like being more creative, you can roll the dough out ¼-inch thick between two sheets of waxed or parchment paper, or on a cool counter, trying not to use too much flour (which will make the dough tougher). Use cookie cutters to cut out shapes, trying to make the least amount of scraps possible. Bake in a 350 degree oven for about 10–14 minutes, rotating pans front to back and top to bottom halfway through the bake. You want your cookies to be lightly browned around the edges. Cool on the sheets before removing. The cookies will keep up to a month in an airtight container.

Yield: 4–5 dozen, depending on how you roll them out

Recipe courtesy of Rabelais Books (p. 63).

to swap meets to sauerkraut demonstrations. Consult their online events calendar for up-to-date schedules.

**Vervacious,** 227 Commercial St., Portland; (207) 221-3590; www .vervacious.com. With stylish packaging and inventive combinations, the "voyage inspired fancy foods" of this luxurious Old Port store make wonderful gifts. From Oaxacan Mole Roasting Rub to Sicilian Sumac Salt to Black Mission Fig Paste, flavors are concentrated and zesty on the palate. Don't miss the intense, lightly sweetened spiced cocoas.

**West End Deli and Catering,** 133 Spring St., Portland; (207) 874-6426; www.thewestenddeli.com. This tiny neighborhood market stocks morning essentials like coffee and the daily paper (as well as other essentials like soap) in their front grocery and serves soups, salads, and sandwiches from their deli counter. Sandwiches and deli platters are reasonably priced, and staff is friendly and helpful. An extensive catering menu goes beyond cold cuts, with such offerings as smoked trout mousse in cucumber cups and grilled Cornish game hens with fried black-pudding stuffing.

# Southern Maine

The most accessible region in the state, southern Maine is also the most visited, with tourists from near and far flocking to its sandy beaches, sparkling waters, and festive boardwalks. Daytrippers from Boston meet Quebecois in search of (relatively) warm southern waters at Old Orchard Beach, and shoppers hunting for bargains scour the outlets in Kittery and Freeport. Since the late 1800s, southern Maine has been a region of tourism, and many of the area's lobster shacks, saltwater-taffy shops, and ice-cream stands date from the first half of the 20th century. Here, you're in the heart of "Vacationland," a moniker officially added to Maine's license plates in 1936.

But southern Maine is also a region of elegance, and affluent summer communities in Kennebunkport—home of the Bush family compound—and Prouts Neck, among others, have inspired exquisite restaurants, like the White Barn Inn. Surrounded by lush gardens, Arrows, in Ogunquit, is a foodie destination, serving meals that come almost entirely from produce grown on the restaurant's property. And Stonewall Kitchens, in York, operates a cooking school and cafe in addition to creating its famed jams and sauces.

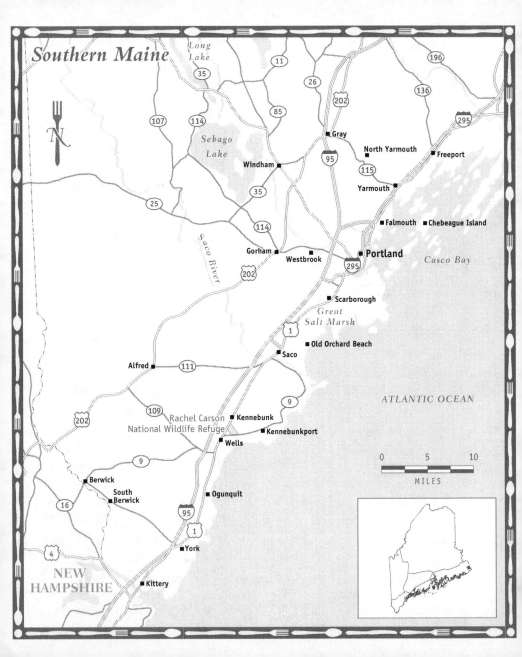

Away from the coast, the land is agricultural, and roughly painted signs point you to farm stands and pick-your-own strawberry fields. Cheesemakers tend herds of goats, young families pick up their winter CSA shares, and beekeepers check on the hives that edge their fields. Offering a microcosm of Maine's food culture, the southern region has it all, from fried clams and ice-cream sundaes to poached *foie gras* and crème brûlée. Bon appétit!

## Bakeries

**The Baker's Bench,** 33 Brackett St., Westbrook; (207) 856-7333. For more than 25 years, this cozy bake house has been serving homemade bread, chicken potpies, and buttery pastries, including their famed crème horns. Breakfast sandwiches are served on croissants, and hearty lunch sandwiches come on fresh bread (try the prairie wheat). Look for the bright yellow building, and you'll know you're there.

**Beach Pea Baking Co.,** 53 State Rd. (US 1), Kittery; (207) 439-3555; www.beachpeabaking.com. Housed in a renovated cottage, this growing bakery offers traditional European-style breads, pastries, cookies, and beautifully presented cakes (don't miss the almond chocolate ganache, or the cheesecake with passion fruit curd). A daily lunch menu includes fresh salads, soups, and sandwiches, which can be enjoyed at outdoor porch seating that offers a restful garden view.

## Made in Maine: Kate's Homemade Butter

The Patry family has been raising dairy cattle in Maine for four generations, but it's only been in the last 30 years that they've turned their full attention to butter. Since 1981, they've been making award-winning slow-churned butter in small batches at their Old Orchard Beach facility. Sweet and creamy on the palate, it's perfect on a warm muffin or slice of toast. Look for the box with the baby in a bandana. **Kate's Homemade Butter,** Old Orchard Beach; www.kateshomemadebutter.com.

**Bread and Roses,** 246 Main St., Ogunquit; (207) 646-4227; www .breadandroses.com. This beloved seasonal bakery often has lines out the door on summer weekends, when people queue for breakfast scones, cinnamon butter puffs—a cross between a doughnut and a muffin—and locally roasted coffee. Cakes, pies, pastries, and home-made breads are also available, as well as vegetarian lunch items, from sandwiches to fresh baked pizza. Open Apr through Nov, with an off-season mail-order company for those who need a winter fix.

**Clara's Cupcake Cafe,** 2 Beach St., York Beach; (207) 361-6300; www.clarascupcakes.com. From homemade old-fashioned dough-nuts (pastry chef Kristen Lawson's grandmother's recipe) to flaky dark-chocolate-filled croissants to the eponymous cupcakes, this bakery and cafe offers desserts to satisfy every sweet tooth. Open year-round for breakfast and lunch—service includes soup, which changes daily; there is limited seating. Special orders available, including holiday pies and gorgeous cakes.

**European Bakery and Tea Room,** 395 US 1, Falmouth; (207) 781-3541; www.europeanbakeryinc.com. Swiss-trained owner-baker Helen Budri is at the helm of this elegant tearoom, specializing in European pastries and tortes. A lovely spot for a cup of tea and an éclair—or a slice of heavenly Black Forest kirsch torte—the bakery also offers exquisite wedding cakes to order.

**Monkey Business Bakery,** 440 Main St., South Berwick; (207) 384-2383; www.monkeybusinessbakery.com. This sweet little bakery, adorned with the monkeys of its name, offers crisp breakfast croissants, filled Danish pastries (try the cheese), and monkey bread, made with a rich cinnamon-and-sugar pull-apart dough. Bakers Nicole Bouchard and Andrea Young have both received awards for their sculpted cakes, which are available, among other specialty cakes, to order. Stop by Sunday mornings for the weekly doughnut specials, made by co-owner Jake Bouchard, the only untrained pastry chef in the troupe, who usually stays out of the kitchen.

**When Pigs Fly Bakery,** 40 Brickyard Court, York; (207) 363-0612; and 447 US 1 (near Kittery Outlets), Kittery; (207) 439-3114; and 21 Main St., Freeport; (207) 865-6006; www.sendbread.com. Begun on a lark by owner and home baker Ron Siegel, this growing bread bakery now offers more than 25 types of classic and artisanal breads in its retail stores, and at shops and farmers' markets throughout the state. Breads can also be ordered for delivery through the mail, both finished and "par-baked"—partially cooked and then frozen, so you can bake a perfect loaf at home.

# Brewpubs & Microbreweries

**Federal Jack's Restaurant & Brew Pub,** 8 Western Ave., Kennebunk; (207) 967-4322; www.federaljacks.com. Offering "brew with a view" with seating overlooking the Kennebunk River, this restaurant and ale house takes its name from a schooner built in the city's historic shipyards and is the birthplace of Shipyard Brewing Company. Though the company has expanded, beer served in-house is still brewed on premises. Restaurant is family friendly, but you must be 21 to participate in free brewery tours.

**Run of the Mill Public House,** 100 Main St., Saco; (207) 571-9648; www.therunofthemill.net. In a renovated mill on the Saco River, this 14-barrel brewpub serves handcrafted, cleverly named lagers, ales, and stouts. Menu includes well-executed British-style pub fare like shepherd's pie, bangers and mash, and "drunken" pot roast (braised in beer), as well as sandwiches, soups, and chowders. With live music on Thursday and Saturday and open-mike night on Tuesday.

**Sebago Brewing Co.,** Brewpubs: 67 Portland Rd., Kennebunk; (207) 985-9855; and 201 Southborough Dr., Scarborough; (207) 874-BEER (2337); and 164 Middle St., Portland; (207) 879-ALES (2537); and 29 Elm St., Gorham; (207) 775-BEER (2337). Production brewery: 48 Sanford Dr., Gorham; (207) 856-2537 x100; www .sebagobrewing.com. With their own handcrafted ales on tap and a casual brew-house menu and atmosphere, restaurants offer large booths, Wi-Fi, and reservable meeting space. Tours of production brewery in Gorham are available upon request.

## Farm Stands

**Ahlquist Farm Stand,** 20 Small Pond Rd., Gorham; (207) 839-7813. This little farm stand is open daily in the summer with red raspberries and strawberries, and offers cut-your-own Christmas trees in November.

**Broadturn Farm,** 388 Broadturn Rd., Scarborough; (207) 233-1178; www.broadturnfarm.com. Farmers Stacy Brenner and John Bliss tend organic vegetables and fruits, cutting flowers, and assorted livestock on this charming diversified farm just outside of Portland. The lovely farm store carries their seasonal produce, as well as seedlings and potted herbs. With pick-your-own strawberries in late June. Open daily June through Oct.

**Chipman Farm Stand,** ME 26, Gray; (207) 657-4925; and US 302 in Raymond; (207) 655-2148. Selling produce from their farm in Poland Spring, this seasonal stand opens with spring asparagus and closes when the last cabbages and winter squash are gone. Baskets of veggies line the outer walls, and pies, local syrups and honeys, and fresh cider are sold inside. Strawberries are the farm's main crop, and they open for u-pick in June; for more information, call the "strawberry hotline" at (207) 998-2027.

**Rippling Waters Organic Farm,** 55 River Rd., Steep Falls/ Standish; (207) 642-5161; www.ripplingwaters.org. This community-minded, certified-organic farm on the picturesque banks of the Saco River offers vegetables, bedding plans, herbs, flowers, and perennials. Store is open year-round, though hours change seasonally.

**Snell Family Farm,** 1000 River Rd., Buxton; www.snellfamilyfarm .com. The Snell family has been farming in Buxton since 1926, and their business includes a CSA (community supported agriculture), stands at farmers' markets, seasonal u-pick berries and apples, and a farm stand. Farm stand is open daily from spring to fall, with limited hours through the winter.

## Farmers' Markets

**Cumberland Farmers' Market,** Mabel I. Wilson School parking lot on Tuttle Road, Cumberland. May through Oct, Sat, 8:30 a.m. to 12:30 p.m.

**Gray Farmers' Market,** behind former Town Hall on Shaker Road, Gray. May through Oct, Thurs, 2 p.m. to 6 p.m.

**Falmouth Farmers' Market,** US 1 and Depot Road, Falmouth; (207) 829-4159. May through Oct, Wed, 3 p.m. to 6 p.m.

**Freeport Farmers' Market,** L.L. Bean campus, Freeport. May through Oct, Fri, 3 p.m. to 7 p.m.

**Kennebunk Farmers' Market,** municipal parking lot off US 1, Kennebunk; (207) 646-5926. May through Oct, Sat 8 a.m. to noon.

**North Berwick Farmers' Market,** North Berwick; (207) 646-5926. May through Oct, Fri 3 p.m. to 6 p.m.

**Saco Farmers' Market,** Spring Street, Saco; (207) 929-5318. May through Oct, Wed and Sat, 7 a.m. to noon.

**Wells Farmers' Market,** Wells Town Hall parking lot on Sanford Road (ME 109),Wells; (207) 646-5926. May through Sept, Wed, 2 p.m. to 6 p.m.

**Westbrook Farmers' Market,** Riverbank Park, Westbrook; (207) 854-9105. May through Nov, Fri, 9 a.m. to 5 p.m.

**Yarmouth Farmers' Market,** Town Hall Green on Main Street, Yarmouth. May through Oct, Tues, 11 a.m. to 3 p.m.

**York—The Gateway Farmers' Market,** next to Stonewall Kitchen Factory, US 1 (Stonewall Lane), York; (207) 363-4422. June through Oct, Sat, 9 a.m. to noon.

## Lobster Shacks & Fishmongers

**Bayley's Lobster Pound,** Pine Point, 9 Ave. 6, Scarborough; (207) 883-4571 or (800) 932-6456; www.bayleys.com. Family owned and operated since 1915, this year-round lobster pound sells whole lobsters (live and cooked), fresh fish and shellfish, and take-out sandwiches, seafood salads, chowders, and stews. Open seven days a week, closed major holidays.

**Billy's Chowder House,** 216 Mile Rd., Wells; (207) 646-7558; www.billyschowderhouse.com. With views of the Rachel Carson Wildlife Refuge and Tidal Marsh, this seaside eatery has a classic menu: plenty of fried seafood, baked and broiled fish, boiled lobster, and rich seafood chowders. Closed Dec and Jan.

**Bob's Clam Hut,** 315 US 1, Kittery; (207) 439-4233; www.bobs clamhut.com. Since 1956, this landmark clam shack has been serving fried seafood by the basket, sandwich, roll, and dinner. Fried clams are the specialty, but oysters, bay scallops, shrimp, and haddock are also on the menu. Originally just for takeout, indoor and seasonal outdoor seating is now available. Open year-round.

**Bob's Seafood,** 901 Roosevelt Trail, Windham; (207) 893-2882; www.lobsters-shipped.com. At this "total seafood store" near Sebago Lake, fresh fish, live lobsters and shellfish, and precooked steamahs (steamed clams) and mussels are sold along with a menu of fried seafood, chowders, and lobster stew that are available by the pint and the quart. Open year-round.

**Day's Crabmeat and Lobster,** 1269 US 1, Yarmouth; (207) 846-3436; www.dayscrabmeatandlobster.com. This seasonal marsh-side lobster pound has been in business since the 1920s, when founders John and Charles Hilton began selling crabmeat and crabmeat rolls (lobster came later). The tradition continues with hand-picked crabmeat (don't miss the crab salad!), lobster rolls, and steamed clams. Orders are picked up at a take-out window, and seating is outdoors at picnic tables. Inside, pick your own live lobsters at the pound. Open May through Oct.

**Fishermen's Net,** 59c Portland Rd., Gray; (207) 657-3474; and 849 Forrest Ave., Portland; (207) 772-3565; and 93 State St., Presque Isle; (207) 762-3782; www.fishermensnet.com. This simple, unpretentious fishmonger sells fresh, locally caught fish, live lobster, and a small take-out menu of fried seafood, sandwiches, lobster rolls, and homemade chowder. Stuffed lobsters and prepared seafood can be ordered ahead to cook at home.

**Harraseeket Lunch & Lobster,** 36 North Main St., South Freeport; (207) 865-4888 (lunch) or (207) 865-3535 (lobster); www.harraseeketlunchandlobster.com. Owned and operated by the Coffin family for more than 40 years, this waterfront eatery's menu includes fried seafood by the pint, lobster rolls—chunks of succulent lobster on a toasted, buttered roll—and homemade desserts from family recipes. Outdoor seating offers views of fishing boats on the harbor—you can watch the day's catch come in as you eat. The lobster pound sells live and freshly cooked lobsters, steamers, corn on the cob, and more, including packing boxes and gel packs for traveling. Open May through Oct.

**Ken's Place,** 207 Pine Point Rd., Scarborough; (207) 883-6611. This seasonal seafood restaurant is famed for meaty clam cakes, plump fried scallops, crispy onion rings, and generous baskets of fried seafood. An institution since 1927, it's popular with locals. Indoor and outdoor seating; open from Apr through Oct.

**Linda Bean's Perfect Maine Lobster Roll,** 57 Main St., Freeport; (207) 865-1874; and 37 Exchange St., Portland; (207) 773-2469; www.lindabeansperfectmaine.com. Opened by Linda Bean, granddaughter of L. L. Bean, these casual restaurants are an extension of her efforts to conserve the working waterfront of the fishing villages of Downeast Maine. Serving Maine-caught seafood from the **Port Clyde Lobster Company** (p. 2), also owned by Bean, the menu's signature offering is its lobster roll, made with ¼ pound of claw meat and dressed with Bean's secret recipe of herbs, served on a buttered white or whole wheat roll, along with bread-and-butter pickles, freshly made coleslaw, and crisp kettle chips. Also on the menu are a variety of other seafood special-ties, including a lobster panini sandwich. The Old Port location in Portland is year-round, but Freeport is open from May through Dec. There are **seasonal locations** in Port Clyde (next to the Monhegan Ferry terminal; 207-372-1112), Rockland (346 Main St.; 207-593-9388), and Camden (11 Main St.; 207-230-7400).

**Mabel's Lobster Claw,** 124 Ocean Ave., Kennebunkport; (207) 967-2562. This homey restaurant, beloved by former president George W. Bush (who is a summer regular), serves classic seafood in a relaxed atmosphere. The menu includes creamy chowder, rolls full of sweet lobster meat, and the shore dinner—boiled lobster on steamers with clam broth and drawn butter. Finish it off with the justly famed peanut butter ice-cream pie. Open Apr through Oct.

**Nunan's Lobster Hut,** 9 Mills Rd., Kennebunkport; (207) 967-4362; www.nunanslobsterhut.com. Since 1953, the Nunan family has been running this seasonal lobster shack out of the same cheerful converted Cape Porpoise workshop in which it was founded. Lobstermen Richard and Keith Nunan serve their daily catch at the restaurant, while Keith's wife, Kim, bakes dessert pies according to her mother-in-law's famed recipes. Open May through Oct.

## *Food Happenings*

**June**

**Annual New Gloucester Strawberry Festival,** Congregational Church, 19 Gloucester Hill Rd., New Gloucester. Sponsored by the New Gloucester Historical Society, this one-day festival features fresh local strawberries, shortcake made with homemade biscuits, various baked goods, and the tunes of the Berry, Berry Good Band. Late June. Visit the town's website at www.newgloucester.com for more information.

**South Berwick Strawberry Festival,** 197 Main St., South Berwick; (207) 384-2882; www.southberwickstrawberryfestival.com. For more than 30 years, this annual one-day festival has celebrated the strawberry while raising money for community nonprofits. Festivities include a strawberry shortcake and cheesecake tent, a juried art fair, and live entertainment—past performers have included cloggers and a gospel choir. Always the last Saturday in June.

## July

**Maine Farm Day at Shaker Village,** 707 Shaker Rd., New Gloucester; (207) 926-4597; www.shaker.lib.me.us. Though farms are open statewide on Maine Farm Day, it's a special treat to visit the Sabbathday Lake Shaker Village, the last active Shaker community in the United States. Enjoy a barbecue, shop at the Shaker Store, and go on guided tours of the barns, gardens, and herb department. Admission is free. Held in late July.

**Yarmouth Clam Festival,** downtown Yarmouth; www.clamfestival .com. This annual weekend-long celebration of all things clam has been a Yarmouth tradition since 1965. Beginning with the kickoff parade down Main Street, the festival includes an arts and crafts fair, a kayak and canoe race, a firefighters' muster competition, the official Maine State Clam Shucking Contest, and, of course, plenty of clams to eat. A midway offers carnival rides. Always begins the third Friday in July.

## August

**Wells ChiliFest at Wells Harbor,** Wells; (207) 646-2451; www .wellschilifest.com. This annual chili cook-off is sanctioned by the International Chili Society, and winners can go on to compete at the World's Championship Chili Contest. Three varieties are judged—salsa, chili verde, and red chili—and participants also compete for a people's choice and showmanship award. Note: Enthusiasts can also attend the regional and state-wide cook-offs, held in September.

## September

**Maine Lakes Brew Fest,** 261 Point Sebago Rd., Casco; (207) 647-3472; www.mainelakesbrewfest.com. This early Oktoberfest celebrates Maine-crafted beers and wines in a one-day festival. Sample brews, listen to live music, and peruse the goods at a craft fair of local artisans. Must be 21.

## The Maine Ice Cream Trail

**B & R Dairy Bar,** 19 Portland Rd., Gray; (207) 657-4191. This tiny seasonal ice-cream store scoops hard- and soft-serve at a takeout window in the parking lot of a strip mall. Don't be put off by the scenery—the homemade ice cream is worth a stop. Flavors not to be missed include neon-blue cotton candy (really), rum raisin, and, late in the season, pumpkin. Open May through Oct.

**Brown's Old Fashioned Ice Cream,** 232 Nubble Rd., York; (207) 363-1277. This homey, seasonal stand offers more than 50 handmade ice-cream flavors, including the only-in-Maine classics Grapenut and Indian pudding. Lines for the take-out window can be long, but friendly and efficient staff keeps everyone moving along. Outdoor seating offers a view of the Isles of Shoals. Open May through Sept.

**Dairy Corner,** 612 US 1, Scarborough; (207) 883-6939; www .dairycornericecream.com. This ice-cream shop in a converted gas station serves hard-serve, soft-serve, and frozen yogurt from its take-out window, in addition to a small menu of "real food." Treats have clever names—Lion King (soft-serve with animal crackers), Nor'easters (flurries)—and service is quick and friendly. Open Apr through Oct.

**Garside's Ice Cream,** 320 Ferry Rd., Saco; (207) 283-0045. Since the 1950s, this seasonal ice-cream shop has been serving more than 40 flavors of homemade ice cream and sherbet from its take-out window. Hand-packed pints, quarts, and half gallons are also available. Open May through Oct.

**Hodgman's Frozen Custard,** 1108 Lewiston Rd., New Gloucester; (207) 926-3553. This old-fashioned roadside stop has been a local landmark since 1946, serving rich frozen custard—made with eggs as well as cream and sugar—and specialty treats from its take-out window. The flavor of the day is posted out front, so passing motorists can decide to stop (they usually do). Plain cones are treat enough, but sundaes are divine. Open May through Oct.

**The Ice Cream Dugout,** 3 Storm Dr., Windham; (207) 894-7769; www.icecreamdugout.com. From the child-sized "bunt" scoop to the decadent "triple play" banana split, this beloved baseball-themed seasonal stand hits a home run. Serving more than 50 flavors of Shain's of Maine ice cream, as well as their famous Sea Dog Biscuits (ice cream sandwiches named for Portland's AA baseball team, the Sea Dogs). If you're feeling especially partisan, try the Yankees Suck, a super-thick frappe. Open during baseball season.

**Mrs. & Me Ice Cream,** 400 US 1, Kittery; (207) 439-1141; www.mrsandme.net. Originally opened by newlyweds Luke and Hilda Wilson in 1948, this seasonal ice-cream shop has expanded since its early days, but it has stayed true to its spirit. It aims to offer something for everyone, and menu includes sugar-free and low-fat frozen treats, as well as 28 regular hard-serve flavors. Open May through Sept.

**Shaker Pond Ice Cream,** 148 Waterboro Rd., Alfred; (207) 459-5070; www.shakerpondicecream.com. Known for enormous portions and a fun Red Sox–themed decor, this parlor also does a wholesale business of its ice creams, frozen yogurts, and sorbets, available at groceries and restaurants throughout northern New England. Flavors include Payeur's Blueberry, made with nearby Payeur Farm's berries (See p. 121), Grapenut, and bubble gum. Open year-round, with limited winter hours.

**Sundaes at the Beach,** 231 Post Rd. (US 1), Wells; (207) 646-LICK; www.sundaesatthebeach.com. Serving homemade ice cream and Italian ices, this seasonal ice-cream shop's claim to fame is its sundae bar. They'll scoop your ice cream—choose from 45 flavors including cantaloupe, maple walnut, and Moose's Drool—and you can load it up with nuts, candy, and jimmies. A limited menu of soups and sandwiches is served daily. Open Apr through Oct.

**Toots,** 137 Walnut Hill Rd. (ME 115), North Yarmouth; (207) 829-3723; www.tootsicecream.net. Served out of a red caboose on the bucolic grounds of a working dairy farm, the ice cream at this seasonal stop is homemade and rich. Magnets with the day's flavors are posted on the side of the train car—don't miss Ladybug, Pig Pen, or Licorice—and seating is scattered around the farm at picnic tables and under a gazebo. A small petting zoo holds alpacas, goats, rabbits, and a draft horse. In the off-season, half gallons can be purchased at the Market at Pineland Farms (15 Farm View Dr.), in New Gloucester. Open May through Sept.

# Needhams: Potato and Chocolate, United at Last

The origins of this iconic Maine candy are a little murky, and the candy store where they were first cooked up has long been out of business, but most histories of the humble needham include a reference to a charismatic Evangelical preacher named George Needham and the date 1872. Whatever their inspiration, over the past century and a half needhams have become a holiday staple in many Maine homes, with mail-order businesses shipping them across the country and families perfecting their own recipes. At their core, needhams are a square of mashed potatoes, shredded coconut, butter, and a little vanilla, dipped in dark chocolate and occasionally sprinkled with coconut or chopped almonds (imagine a homespun cousin of Mounds and Almond Joy). Proportions vary by recipe, and sizes range from delicate to gargantuan. In an original twist on the classic, truffle-maker Dean Bingham, of Portland's **Dean's Sweets** (see p. 37), incorporates potatoes in liquid form: his needhams are spiked with **Cold River Vodka** (see p. 98), distilled from Maine potatoes.

**Village Scoop Ice Cream,** 226 York St., York; (207) 363-0100; and **The Ice Cream House,** 1300 US 1, Cape Neddick; (207) 363-5800; www.maineicecream.com. These seasonal parlors offer more than 50 flavors of rich (16 percent butterfat!) ice cream at each of their two locations. Waffle cones and bowls are made in-house, as are a variety of toppings. Open Apr through Oct.

## *Landmark Eateries*

**Cole Farms Restaurant,** 64 Lewiston Rd., Gray; (207) 657-4714; www.colefarms.com; $$. Serving honest food for more than 50 years, this homey diner's menu ranges from fried Maine shrimp and chowder to beef liver and boiled dinner. Everything is made in-house, from the salad dressing (available bottled) to the rolls to the perfectly battered onion rings. Waitresses are unfailingly cheerful, as are the teens who bus tables (a local rite of passage). Save room for homemade tapioca or Indian pudding. Open year-round.

**Congdon's Doughnut Shop,** 1090 Post Rd. (US 1), Wells; (207) 646-4219; www.congdons.com; $$. Dozens of doughnut flavors and "breakfast anytime" are the hallmarks of this casual family restaurant, first opened in 1955. Breakfast and lunch are served in the Pancake Room, while doughnuts are available at a counter and a drive-through. Still made from Nana Congdon's recipe, the doughnuts come crunchy with glaze, loaded with jimmies, and stuffed with crème—don't miss the maple crème and the honey cruller. A lunch menu of Maine favorites like baked-bean dinner and pot roast is also available. Open year-round.

**Don's Lunch,** 517 Main St., Westbrook; $. This mobile lunch truck has been serving "the Big One" (a double cheeseburger) since 1976 out of a converted RV parked at the edge of a lot on Main Street. Open year-round for lunch and dinner—and until 2 a.m. on summer weekends—the grill serves up hamburgers, hot dogs, clam-cake burgers, and grilled cheese, available with an array of condiments. A few picnic tables offer outdoor seating. Cash only.

**Dunston School Restaurant,** US 1, Scarborough; (207) 883-5261; www.dunstanschool.com; $$. From tray-holding lines at the buffet to the chalkboards that still cover the walls, this converted schoolhouse serves nostalgia with every plate. Serving breakfast, lunch, and dinner, meals are reminiscent of cafeteria fare, albeit homemade, with the option of a 1¼-pound boiled lobster, and all-you-can-eat desserts. Open year-round.

**Flo's,** US 1, Cape Neddick; www.floshotdogs.com; $. This tiny shop has been selling steamed hot dogs and zesty homemade relish since Florence Stacy first opened in 1959. Her daughter-in-law Gail now commands the counter, serving up small dogs (an adult appetite generally requires four) to the masses. The ordering system is specific: Ask for the number of dogs first, then wait to request toppings when asked. Regulars insist that all the dogs need are a slap of mayo, some zesty relish (now in bottles) and a sprinkle of celery salt, but other condiments are available. Summer lines are long, but happily, Flo's is open year-round. Open only for lunch from 11 a.m. to 3 p.m., and closed Wed.

**The Goldenrod,** 2 Railroad Ave., York Beach; (207) 363-2621; www.thegoldenrod.com; $$. Home of the famed Goldenrod Kisses, this candy store, soda fountain, and luncheonette has been making saltwater taffy by the beach since 1896. The candy is still made before patrons' eyes in copper kettles, though the 8 million pieces (50 tons!) made annually are now stretched by machine. Hot breakfast and sandwich lunch—old-fashioned fare from sliced turkey club to tuna melts to cream cheese and olive—are served at the attached luncheonette, as is homemade ice cream. Open Memorial Day through Columbus Day.

**Harmon's Lunch,** 144 Gray Rd., Falmouth; (207) 797-9857; $. This roadside burger joint has been serving sizzling burgers on buttered buns—with a healthy side of gruff attitude—since it opened in 1960. A posted sign reads YOU TAKE IT MY WAY, OR YOU DON'T GET A DAMN THING. Burgers are cooked medium and can be topped with cheese, grilled onions, mustard, and ketchup, but don't ask for tomato or lettuce. The menu also includes hot dogs and fries, served piping hot. Open for lunch, year-round.

**Jameson Tavern,** 115 Main St., Freeport; (207) 865-4196; www
.jamesontavern.com; $$$. This historic tavern, founded in 1801,
can be considered "the birthplace of Maine," as the papers giving
Maine independence from Massachusetts were signed in a meeting
room on its second floor. The town of Freeport has grown up around
it, and the tavern is now next door to the L.L. Bean flagship store,
making it popular with tourists looking for a place to rest after a day
of shopping. The restaurant includes a casual tavern, with a menu
of well-executed pub fare and seafood standards, and a more formal
dining room, with a cozy working fireplace and a menu of local
meats and seafood, including several lobster preparations. House-
roasted prime rib is served at dinner Thursday through Saturday.
With a full bar and seasonal outdoor seating on two patios.

**Maine Diner,** 2265 Post Rd. (US 1), Wells; (207) 646-4441; www
.mainediner.com; $$. This landmark diner, first opened in 1953 to
serve locals in the off-season, is now a major summer attraction,
serving more than 1,000 patrons daily in the high season in its two
cheerful blue-and-white dining rooms. Since brothers Miles and Dick
Henry bought the eatery in the 1980s, the menu has been expanded
to include new specialties as well as old standbys. Try the lobster
pie—their justly famed specialty of fresh lobster meat baked with
stuffing—or the Clam-O-Rama: clam chowder, fried clams, clam
strips, and a clam cake. Desserts are baked fresh, and beer and
wine are available. Hearty breakfast, from pancakes to Maine crab
Benedict, is served from 7 a.m. Open year-round.

**Palace Diner,** 18 Franklin St., Biddeford; (207) 283-8462; $. Maine's oldest diner, opened in 1927, once stayed open around the clock to feed hungry mill workers getting off each shift. Now, with the mills closed, this shiny former dining car is open only for breakfast, serving up fried eggs, crisp toast, and perfect pancakes to the dozen of patrons who sit elbow to elbow at the counter. Owner Kyle Quinn mans the griddle and makes everything to order while keeping up cheerful banter with regulars. Open for breakfast year-round, closed Sun.

**Pizza by Alex,** 93 Alfred St., Biddeford; (207) 283-0002; $$. This no-frills pizza parlor has been a local attraction since 1960. Open for lunch, dinner, and late-night snacking (till 11 p.m. during the week and midnight on weekends), the menu offers a single size of pizza—large enough for one hearty appetite, or two snackers—and an assortment of fountain drinks. Owner Andrew Mantis continues in his uncle Alex's tradition, serving standard toppings (the most exotic is Hawaiian) on a chewy crust that gets crisp around the edges. Try Ya Ya's Greek Pizza, with spinach, raw onions, and feta cheese, and the Alex Special, loaded with a bit of everything.

**Rapid Ray's,** Pepperell Square, 189 Main St., Saco; (207) 282-1847; www.rapidrays.biz; $. Meat cutter Renald "Ray" Camire started his business in 1953, selling hamburgers by night out of the back of a converted bread truck, and it wasn't until the mid-1980s that the takeout was stationary. The menu and the service haven't changed: Meat is still cut and ground on premises, two more generations of Camires work the counter, and grilled burgers and steamed hot dogs are sold plain and loaded, with fried onion rings, and milk or soda. Everything is takeout, but there's a wide window ledge so you can prop your order and dig in. Open lunch, dinner, and late night, year-round, closed major holidays.

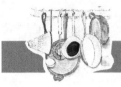

## Learn to Cook

**Immigrant Kitchens Project,** Freeport Community Center, 53 Depot St., Freeport; www.immigrantkitchens.com. Food writer and trained chef Lindsay Sterling turns her attention to global cooking, the subject of her regular column in the *Portland Phoenix,* in these monthly classes. Each session features recipes from area immigrants—from Swedish salmon to Sudanese stew—and all proceeds go to the Freeport Food Pantry. Check the website for upcoming classes.

**Kitchen and Cork,** 400 Expedition Dr., Suite A, Scarborough; (207) 885-5727; www.kitchenandcork.com. This premium kitchen store presents classes that range from hot appetizers to cookie decorating to wine tasting in the demonstration area of the shop, and are led by resident chef David Mollari. The shop specializes in high-end cookware. Products include Le Creuset pots, Emile Henry bakeware, Wusthof and Henckels knives, and a variety of cookbooks, locally roasted Carpe Diem coffees, Stonewall Kitchen jams, and assorted gadgetry. Check their website for monthly class schedule; contact the store to arrange private classes.

**Man with a Pan,** 2 Elsie Way, Scarborough; (207) 650-1404; www .manwithapan.com. Personal chef Jonathan Carr specializes in intimate in-home cooking demonstrations, as well as catering for small dinner parties. The "man with a pan" arrives with equipment and local ingredients, and cooks a customized meal on-site. Guests can linger and learn, or simply enjoy the meal.

**The Stone Turtle Baking and Cooking School,** 173 Howitt Rd., Lyman; (207) 324-7558; www.stoneturtlebaking.com. Opened by baker and former King Arthur Flour Company spokesman Michael Jubinsky and his pastry-chef wife Sandy after the couple "retired" in Maine, this rustic cooking school is focused on foods cooked in its "stone turtle," a wood-fired Le Panyol stone oven from France. Classes are offered several times a month and include intensive weekends as well as one-day workshops on topics that range from artisan loaves to pizza to hand-boiled bagels. Check their website for schedules.

**Stonewall Kitchens & Cooking School,** 2 Stonewall Lane, York; (877) 899-8363; www.stonewallkitchen.com. Held at the company headquarters of Stonewall Kitchens, this cooking school is an extension of the culinary curiosity that drove founders Jonathan King and Jim Stott to create their wildly successful specialty foods business. With classes taught by their own chefs and guest professionals, offerings include everything from comfort food to Korean cuisine, and are held at different times of day to accommodate every schedule. Classes fill quickly, so advance reservations are a must. Check their website for monthly schedules.

**Ten Apple Farm,** 241 Yarmouth Rd., Gray; (207) 657-7880; www .tenapplefarm.com. This small dairy-goat farm and apple orchard offers workshops in homesteading skills that range from basic cheesemaking and bread baking to fruit-tree pruning and poultry processing. Farmers Karl Schatz and Margaret Hathaway have learned on the go, and they enthusiastically share their experience. Workshop schedule is on the farm's website; private classes can be arranged.

## Made or Grown Here

**Blacksmith Winery,** 967 Quaker Ridge Rd., Casco; (207) 655-3292; www.blacksmithswinery.com. Crafting wines, ciders, and nonalcoholic sodas from grapes and locally grown fruits, this rural winery and tasting room near Sebago Lake is a charming spot to relax and sample the local flavor. Fruit wines include rhubarb and blueberry, which blend fruit with crisp white Vidal Blanc, and traditional wines include Chardonnay, Merlot, and Cabernet Sauvignon. Roughshod, a combination of brandy and Maine blueberries, and Casco Port, are among the many dessert wines, and Ice Wine and hard cider are seasonal treats. The tasting room is open year-round, serving complimentary flights of wine—a  range of samples for tasting and comparison—and bottles of new nonalcoholic grape soda. Families welcome, though you must be 21 to taste.

**Harbor Candy Shop,** 248 Main St., Ogunquit; (207) 646-8078 or (800) 331-5856; www.harborcandy.com. Since its founding by chocolatier George Sotiropoulos in 1956, this old-fashioned confectionary shop has been selling freshly made, luxurious chocolates by the piece or pound. Specialties include caramallows (caramel and homemade marshmallow dipped in chocolate), sugar plums, and chocolate-dipped glacéed fruit. Elegant samplers make great gifts and can be made with exclusively vegan candies.

**Len Libby Chocolate,** 419 US 1, Scarborough; (207) 883-4897; www.lenlibby.com. First opened in 1926, this chocolate and candy shop is famed for its fresh coconut needhams (see p. 88), solid chocolates and truffles, fudge, Bangor taffy, and above all, for Lenny,  the 1,700 pound, solid milk-chocolate moose that has stood in the entry way since 1997. Each winter, the shop hosts Candy Cane Day, at which visitors are taught to roll candy canes by hand, as the shop has been doing for more than 80 years. Open daily year-round, with extended holiday hours.

**Maine Distilleries,** 437 US 1, Freeport; (207) 865-4828. This small batch distillery uses Maine potatoes and water from the Cold River Aquifer to craft award-winning, super-premium Cold River Vodka, Cold River Blueberry Vodka, and Cold River Gin. Norwis round-white potatoes are grown using sustainable farming methods at Green Thumb Farm in Fryeburg, and spirits are triple-distilled in copper pot stills. Classic vodka is smooth and satiny, and blueberry is flavorful but not sweet. Gin is herby and botanical. Free tours offered year-round, generally between noon and 5 p.m. (call ahead).

**Prospect Hill Winery,** 318 Orrills Hill Rd., Lebanon; (207) 658-7817; www.prospectihillwines.com. This family-run winery grows five varietals of white grapes, and eight of red, producing wines made exclusively from their own grapes, a rarity in Maine. Light, fruity whites include their signature Elvira and Edelweiss, which is similar to a Reisling. Full-bodied reds like Chancellor and Frontenac have hints of fruit and a little bite. Open Sun 1 to 5 p.m., and by appointment for tastings and tours.

**Wilbur's of Maine Chocolates,** 174 Lower Main St., Freeport; (207) 865-4071 or (888) 762-5787; www.wilburs.com. The heavenly aroma of this family-owned and family-run confectioner is inviting, but it's the abundance of chocolate on display that makes patrons feel like, well, kids in a candy shop. Here you'll find chocolates of all kinds—shaped like seashells; filled with caramel, nougat, and crème; coating apples on sticks. In addition to sweets, owners Tom and Catherine Carty-Wilbur offer regular events, from book signings to dip-your-own-chocolate-covered-pretzel workshops, and tours of the chocolate factory. Open daily.

## *Restaurants*

**50 Local Restaurant,** 50 Main St., Kennebunk; (207) 985-0850; www.localkennebunk.com; $$$. Serving dinner and weekend brunch, this hip restaurant and bar offer a changing menu of French bistro foods with an American twist, from *moules frites* to grass-fed burgers. Chef-owners Merrilee Paul and David Ross are committed to using local ingredients, and producers are listed on a chalkboard in the dining room. The wine list is well chosen, with many vintages available by the glass, and house cocktails are fun and potent—try the Local Greyhound, with vodka, roasted grapefruit, and clementine. Open for dinner Tues through Sat and weekends for brunch.

**91 South Restaurant at PineCrest Inn,** 91 South St., Gorham; (207) 839-5843; www.pinecrestmaine.com; $$$. The intimate restaurant and wine bar at this snug inn require reservations, but the charm of the atmosphere is worth any hassle of advance planning. Chef Maureen Terry's changing menu brings an international flair to local ingredients—past entrees have paired lobster with couscous, and Maine shrimp cakes with lime cilantro aioli. Though it has only four stools, the wine bar stocks more than 110 bottles. Open for dinner Thurs, Fri, and Sat; reservations necessary.

**98 Provence,** 104 Shore Rd., Ogunquit; (207) 646-9898; www.98provence.com; $$$$. With its flagstone fireplace, bright cotton tablecloths, and collection of ceramic roosters, the country French decor of this seasonal restaurant perfectly matches its menu. Chef Pierre Gignac's menu changes three times a year to reflect what's seasonally available, but it's always full of seafood (try the anise-inflected fisherman's soup), and peppered with his own takes on French cooking. The summer menu includes skate wings and grilled duck, while fall offers the house cassoulet and roasted venison. A changing list of French wines complements the cuisine. Open Apr through Dec.

**Amore Breakfast,** 309 Shore Rd., Ogunquit; (207) 646-6661; www .amorebreakfast.com; $$. This breakfast hot spot opens at 7 a.m. to serve eggs, waffles, and French toast in its cheerful black-and-white checked storefront. Eggs come many ways, but the house specialties are variations on eggs Benedict—from asparagus and crab with dill hollandaise to Be Still My Heart, with poached eggs, bacon, and sausage atop German potato pancakes. Dark-roast and house-blend coffees are sold by the cup and the pound and are roasted by owner Leanne Cusimano's brother-in-law. For more espresso drinks and Amore gear, visit **Cafe Amore,** next door. Open Apr through Dec.

**Anneke Jans,** 60 Wallingford Sq., Kittery; (207) 439-0001; www .annekejans.net; $$$. With a changing menu that ranges from Pemaquid mussels to calves liver, this upscale bistro offers something for every palate, including a nightly vegetarian entree. Dessert is a must, from the smooth white-chocolate crème brûlée to the rich trifle parfait. The wine list is extensive, with more than 100 wines offered by the bottle, and attentive staff will help you find the perfect pairing. Open nightly for dinner.

**Arrows Restaurant,** 41 Berwick Rd., Ogunquit; (207) 361-1100; www.arrowsrestaurant.com; $$$$. This flagship restaurant of James Beard Award–winning chefs Mark Gaier and Clark Frasier was green before it was trendy. Since 1992, the restaurant's beautifully tended gardens have grown 90 percent of the produce served, while other ingredients are gathered and foraged in the surrounding woods. Cheeses and charcuterie are produced on premises, as well as breads and pastries. *Bon Appetit* rated the restaurant one of America's 10 most romantic, and the farmhouse and gardens can be rented for weddings. Open late April through late December. Reservations recommended.

**Azure Cafe,** 123 Main St., Freeport; (207) 865-1237; www.azure cafe.com; $$$. The seasonally changing menu is Italian inspired, and each plate meticulously arranged, at this elegant restaurant in the heart of Freeport. Entrees range from classics like veal Marsala to the house specialty, Sicilian-style cioppino, a plethora of seafood in spicy tomato broth. Potent cocktails and live jazz on weekends bring a vibrant energy, and a series of wine dinners pairing regional Italian wines and dishes has earned the restaurant an Award of Excellence from *Wine Spectator*. Seasonal outdoor seating and a less-formal lunch menu. Reservations recommended.

**Blue Elephant,** 12 Pepperell Sq., Saco; (207) 282-2100, www .blueelephantcatering.com; $$. Blue Elephant Catering is known for its attentive event planning and beautifully orchestrated weddings, and its cafe is at the heart of its business. Offering a simple breakfast and lunch menu Mon through Fri, fare ranges from Belgian waffles and ham-and-Swiss croissant to flaky vegetable tarts and daily soup. After hours, the cafe can also be reserved for private parties.

**Blue Sky on York Beach,** 2 Beach St., York Beach; (207) 363-0050; www.blueskyonyorkbeach.com; $$$. Located above **Clara's**

**Cupcake Cafe** (see p. 72) on the second floor of the renovated Atlantic House Hotel, this restaurant's warm, modern design is as inviting as the menu. Sit at a banquette or the food bar and start the evening with a signature cocktail—try the Skyberry margarita, spiked with jalapeños, cherries, and cranberries, or the blackberry caipirinha. The sophisticated menu includes oysters Rockefeller, lobster linguini Bolognese, wild salmon roulade, and several wood-fired pizzas. At brunch, don't miss the Frangelico French toast. Open daily for lunch and dinner, and for Sunday jazz brunch.

**Bruce's Burritos,** 438 US 1, Yarmouth; (207) 846-6330; www.brucesburritos.com; $$. The filling burritos at this colorful cafe are surprisingly healthy and inventive. Served on your choice of white or wheat tortilla, standard fillings include sweet potato and spinach and a daily tofu, in addition to spiced chicken, beef, and pork. Quesadillas, tacos, and chili are also available, as are condiments from mild salsa to fiery hot sauce. Get your own drinks from the cooler and sit inside or at painted picnic tables on the sidewalk. If blueberry salsa is the special, don't miss it.

**Chebeague Island Inn Restaurant,** 61 South Rd., Chebeague Island; (207) 846-5155; www.chebeagueislandinn.com; $$$$. With a diverse and changing menu that celebrates the flavors of the region, the restaurant of this celebrated 1880s inn is as much a destination as the island itself, which is located a leisurely ferry ride from Portland. Dinner is served nightly, with cocktails and an hors d'oeuvres menu from 2:30 p.m. Lunch is served on Fri and Sat, with brunch on Sun. Offerings range from lobster corn dogs to buffalo flank steak, and desserts are not to be missed (try the coriander-scented lemon curd). Reservations are recommended, especially in the busy summer season, even if you're a guest of the inn. Jackets are not required, but dress is generally smart.

**China Rose,** 23 Main St., Freeport; (207) 865-6886; $$. Though the Pine Tree State boasts an impressive array of fine Asian restaurants, there are relatively few Chinese in the bunch. This casual Szechuan-Mandarin-Hunan restaurant received statewide attention several years ago, when the owner's koi fish were seized by the state (though in an enclosed tank, they were considered an invasive species). The community rallied, the fish were returned, and customers became even more loyal. Offerings are well-done Americanized Chinese: hot and sour soup, General Tso's chicken, moo goo gai pan, and the like. Full bar includes cocktails and Scorpion Bowls. Open for lunch, dinner, and takeout, seven days a week.

**Chopstick Sushi,** 438 US 1, Yarmouth; (207) 846-8738; www.chopsticksushi.com; $$. The surprise of finding such fine Japanese and Korean cuisine in a coastal strip mall is almost as delightful as the food. Offerings start with appetizers such as agedashi tofu (deep-fried tofu served in a sweet dashi, sprinkled with bonita flakes) and *yakinasu* (grilled sliced eggplant served with soybean sauce), and entrees include katsu (deep-fried chicken or pork), udon soup, and grilled Korean beef *bulgoki*. Dozens of sushi, sashimi, and *maki* options are available by the piece and the platter—don't miss the alligator roll. A small dessert menu includes green-tea and red-bean ice creams, and banana tempura. Open for lunch and dinner, Mon through Sat, and dinner only on Sun.

**Clayton's Cafe,** 447 US 1, Yarmouth; (207) 846-1117, www.claytons cafe.com; $$. Serving scrumptious pastries, over-stuffed sandwiches, prepared salads, daily soup specials, and an assortment of entrees, this gourmet cafe is a popular take-out spot for boaters and picnickers. The lofty ceiling and warm natural wood of the interior is inviting, and ample indoor and seasonal outdoor seating is available. Drinks from the full espresso bar and bright penny candy from the wall of glass jars make a great afternoon pick-me-up. Open Mon through Sat.

**Conundrum Wine Bistro,** 117 US 1, Freeport; (207) 865-0303; $$$. Under the Big Wooden Indian (you'll know it when you see it), this intimate wine bar and bistro is some distance from the village center and is popular among locals for its deep wine list, bracing martinis, and a savory menu that ranges from light nibbles to full dinner. The atmosphere indoors has a solid, clubby feel, while seating on the covered outdoor patio is arranged around a warm woodstove and stays open in chilly months. Attentive staff is knowledgeable about the wines, and is happy to bring flights of several glasses for an impromptu tasting.

**The French Press Eatery,** 855 Main St., Westbrook; (207) 887-1040; www.thefrenchpresseatery.com; $$$. See the Frog and Turtle listing, below.

**The Frog and Turtle,** 3 Bridge St., Westbrook; (207) 591-4185; www.thefrogandturtle.com; $$; and **the French Press Eatery,** 855 Main St., Westbrook; (207) 887-1040; www.thefrenchpress eatery.com; $$. The gastro-pub fare, clever cocktails, and convivial atmosphere of the Frog and Turtle have made it a neighborhood favorite since it opened. There's a menu that brings touches of French-Canadian and Yankee flavors to traditional British pub food—a shepherd's pie crepe is popular, and the "Jalbert" burger, laden with bacon, blue cheese, mushrooms, mustard, and BBQ sauce, is divine. There is a great wine list, and drinks include the Swamp, a bubbling blend of spirits, juices, and dry ice. Sister restaurant the French Press Eatery specializes in good coffee, house-made doughnuts, and a lighter lunch of soups, salads, and sandwiches. Both restaurants closed Mon.

**The Harraseeket Inn,** 162 Main St., Freeport; (207) 865-9377; www.harraseeketinn.com; $$$. There are two dining options at this historic inn: the elegant Maine Dining Room and the more casual Broad Arrow Tavern. Crafting their menus with a commitment to supporting local agriculture, both kitchens serve a seasonally changing menu. In the dining room, try crispy quail with house-made bacon, poached Seckel pears, onion marmalade, and local York Hill panna cotta, or jumbo scallops with celery root, sliced almonds, golden raisins, and parsley foam. In the tavern, snack on wood-oven-roasted Maine mussels, a cup of award-winning lobster stew, or panko-crusted haddock. The tavern offers a luncheon buffet Monday through Saturday, while the dining room hosts Sunday lobster brunch (reservations highly recommended).

**Hurricane Restaurant,** 29 Dock Sq., Kennebunkport; (207) 967-9111; www.hurricanerestaurant.com; $$$$. This romantic restaurant, perched over the water and mentioned in the travel guide *The Best Places to Kiss in New England*, features an intimate atmosphere with river views from every table. The menu is eclectic, with offerings that range from a seafood bento box to Maine-lobster cobb salad to duck liver–mousse pâté with peppered fig jam and curried leeks, and all desserts on the changing menu are made in-house. Open Apr through Dec; reservations recommended.

**Joshua's,** 1637 Post Rd., Wells; (207) 646.3355; www.joshuas .biz; $$$. The realization of chef Joshua Mather's lifelong dream, this upscale restaurant is just miles from the farm on which he was raised. Serving produce from his family's Easter Orchard Farm, and breads and desserts baked on-site, the menu offers seasonal vegetables and a range of meats, from rack of lamb to pork tenderloin. Don't miss the duck pâté, or the simple sautéed mushrooms, perfectly caramelized with shallots and garlic. Reservations recommended. Open year-round, Tues through Sat, though closed for brief winter breaks.

**MC Perkins Cove,** 111 Perkins Cove Rd., Ogunquit; (207) 646-6263; www.mcperkinscove.com; $$$. This upscale American bistro was created by Mark Gaier and Clark Frasier, the team behind nearby Arrows (see p. 101), and the kitchen at this beachfront eatery uses produce from the same gardens. The menu and atmosphere are more casual, with offerings like Maine peekytoe crab cakes, onion rings, and Kobe beef burgers, but there are still elegant touches: lemon fennel salad with the fried haddock, house-cured gravlax with watercress, and the Grand Shellfish "Tower" to start any meal. A reasonably priced mid-week Date Night menu includes three courses and a bottle of wine, and weekly live music livens things up, even in the off-season. Open Wed through Sun. Closed for the month of Jan.

**Old Vines Wine Bar,** 173 Port Rd., Kennebunk; (207) 967-2310; www.oldvineswinebar.com; $$. In a converted barn, this relaxed, 36-seat wine bar offers light meals and a sophisticated wine list at its burnished tables and bar. Owner Mike Farrell cooked in several New York kitchens before deciding to slow his pace and relocate to Maine, and the atmosphere and menu reflect his unpretentious attitude. Open year-round; the off-season brings live jazz, experimental menu offerings, and frequent tastings.

**On the Marsh,** 46 Western Ave., Lower Village, Kennebunk; (207) 967-2299; www.onthemarsh.com; $$$$. With a romantic atmosphere of cozy tables, rich drapery, and—in warm weather—French doors that are opened onto lush gardens, this elegant restaurant serves dinner nightly and can be reserved for parties and culinary classes with chef Jeffery Savage. The menu verges on decadent, offering *foie gras* custard, oyster with champagne mignonette, and sea scallops with lobster-truffle risotto (not to be missed) on the savory side, and desserts like chèvre cheesecake with port-fig syrup and the aptly named Seduction by Chocolate. Open year-round, reservations recommended.

**Que Huong Restaurant,** 49 Main St., Biddeford; (207) 571-8050; www.quehuongbiddeford.com; $$. In the shadow of a disused mill at the edge of the Saco River, this unassuming restaurant serves Vietnamese classics like brothy pho, delicate bun (Asian vermicelli topped with spicy meat or stir-fried vegetables), and hearty *hu tieu mi* (thick egg noodles served with meat and vegetables). Start your meal with fresh spring rolls, and wash it all down with Vietnamese coffee or a bottle of Asian beer. Open Mon through Sat, dine in or take out.

**SeaGrass Bistro,** 305 US 1, Yarmouth; (207) 846-3885; www.sea grassbistro.com; $$$. Chef-owner Stephanie Brown's changing menu combines Asian, French, and Tuscan influences at this tasteful year-round restaurant. The atmosphere is warm and the service personalized. Patrons are encouraged to make off-menu requests, though the menu offers plenty of epicurean delights. Open Wed through Sat; reservations recommended.

**Stones Cafe and Bakery,** 424 Walnut Hill Rd. (ME 115), North Yarmouth; (207) 829-4640; www.stonescafeandbakery.com; $$. With fresh-baked cinnamon rolls and biscuits, dark-roast coffee, and an assortment of breakfast sides from the griddle, this home-spun cafe starts serving breakfast at 6:30 and keeps going through lunch. Sit at the counter or in a Formica booth and read the paper, listen in on local gossip, and enjoy a bottomless cuppa joe. Lunch includes daily salads, sandwiches, and daily soup. Bread, dinner rolls, and seasonal pies can be bought from the bakery. Open for breakfast and lunch Tues through Sun.

**Stonyfield Cafe,** 240 US 1, Falmouth; (207) 781-8889; www .stonyfieldcafe.com; $$. Gary Hirshberg, founder of Stonyfield Farm yogurt, began this cafe in 2001 to offer a delicious, quick, and healthy alternative to roadside fast food. Originally called O'Naturals, the cafe was renamed in 2010 but continues to

offer flatbread sandwiches, soups, salads, and smoothies, as well as tasty and nutri-tious kids' meals and, of course, Stonyfield yogurts. Ingredients are sustainably grown and sourced locally whenever possible, and weekly Community Nights give 10 percent of dinner sales to local nonprofits and schools. The casual atmosphere is family friendly (there's even a play area and train table). Open daily.

**Tulsi,** 2 Government St., Kittery; (207) 451-9511; www.tulsiindian restaurant.com; $$. Named for a "holy basil" popular in Ayurvedic healing, this inventive Indian restaurant brings the rich spices of Northern Indian and Mughlai cooking to the Maine coast. Chef Rajesh Mandekar's menu ranges from classics like chicken tikka masala to inventive dishes like tandoori salmon and *zaffrani jhinga*, tiger shrimp simmered in garlic and saffron cream sauce. The menu isn't extensive, but each dish is made with a deft hand. With a variety of vegetarian entrees and beverages that include lassis, well-chosen beers, and Chai. Open for dinner, closed Mon.

**The White Barn Inn,** 37 Beach Ave., Kennebunk Beach; (207) 967-2321; www.whitebarninn.com; $$$$. Housed in two restored 19th century barns, the atmosphere of this acclaimed restaurant is at once rustic and crisp: Table settings are immaculate, as is the service, and the menu is a changing, four-course prix fixe in the French tradition. Chef Jonathan Cartwright's menu combines local flavors with his own European culinary roots and features seafood and local game paired with creamy sauces, truffles, and caviar. Reservations are essential, and dining is formal; for men, a jacket is required, though tie is optional.

**Bessie's Farm Goods,** 33 Litchfield Rd., Freeport; (207) 865-9840; www.bessiesfarmgoods.com. Named for co-owner Kathy Heye's grandmother Bessie, this cafe, gift shop, and workshop space is the fruition of a long-held dream of Heye and partner Deede Montgomery, both retired middle-school teachers. Serving coffee and fresh baked goods on the open porch, the tidy shop sells seasonal vegetables, perennials and cut flowers, and idiosyncratic gifts (repurposed boat rockers, hand-spun yarns). Workshops range from kids' cooking classes to adult splint-basket-making. Open year-round.

**Bow Street Market,** 79 Bow St., Freeport; (207) 865-6631; www.bowstreetmarket.com. This family-owned-and-operated grocery has been a local landmark since 1946, providing fresh local produce, warm baked goods, and a full-service butcher counter that offers beef from nearby Wolfe's Neck Farm. Prepared entrees and sandwiches are made on-site, and a large liquor, wine, and beer section carries hundreds of bottles, including locally distilled Cold River Vodkas (see p. 98). Open seven days a week, at 6:30 a.m.

**Cape Porpoise Kitchen,** 1 Mills Rd., Kennebunkport; (207) 967-1150 or (800) 488-1150; www.capeporpoisekitchen.com. Behind its white clapboard exterior, this delightful market and caterer offers elegant prepared meals, artisanal cheeses and olives, wines, and a changing menu of sandwiches, specials, and desserts. A few tables indoors and out offer limited seating. Open daily from 7 a.m.

**The Cheese Iron,** 200 US 1, Scarborough; (207) 883-4057; www
.thecheeseiron.com. Taking its name and logo from an instru-
ment used to test cheeses for maturity, this purveyor of fine foods
offers wines, locally crafted microbrews, breads, chocolates, olives,
cured meats, and an extensive list of artisanal cheeses. Ripening
the cheeses to perfection in their climate-controlled cave, owner-
*affineurs* Jill Dutton and Vincent Maniaci happily guide patrons to
the perfect products for their palates. European-style sandwiches
and soups are served at lunch, and cheese and charcuterie platters
and gift baskets can be ordered.

**Cork and Barrel,** 204 US 1, Falmouth; (207) 781-7955; www
.mainecorkandbarrel.com. This genial wine and gift shop has its
roots in a popular seminar on enology and viticulture that German-
born owner Nik Koengeter, a cultural anthropologist turned winemaker, and his American wife Connie taught for many years in
Heidelberg. Stocking more than 1,200 wines and gifts that range
from candles to corkscrews, the shop is a perfect stop for hostess
gifts. Regular, free wine tastings aim to be fun and informative
without being "wine snobby."

**Freeport Cheese and Wine,** 178 Lower Main
St., Freeport; (207) 869-4048; www.fcandw
.blogspot.com. The walls of this specialty food
and wine shop are lined with hundreds of bottles,
and the cheese case is packed with lush wedges and
ripening wheels. Owner Eric Fullagar has tasted them

all, and only sells what he likes, preferring also to support small producers. He and his knowledgeable staff are happy to make recommendations and suggest pairings. Wine and cheese events are hosted frequently, including a regular wine tasting held the third Friday of each month.

**Freeport Knife and Kitchenware,** 181 Lower Main St., Freeport; (207) 865-0779 or (800) 646-9430; www.freeportknife.com. Billing itself as the "sharpest company in the state of Maine," this specialty shop carries an array of professional kitchen cutlery (and hunting and sporting knives), as well as sharpening equipment, knife blocks, heavy-duty magnetic kitchen tool bars, and assorted kitchenware. Sharpening services are also available, so you can bring in the dull knives of a summer rental and get back their edge.

**H.B. Provisions,** 15 Western Ave., Kennebunk; (207) 967-5762; www.hbprovisions.com. This quaint general store and deli sells everything from dry goods to hot lunch. Open 365 days a year in its renovated 137-year-old storefront, products include a selection of gifts from Maine, freshly baked breads, coffee by the cup and the bean, and more than 450 varieties of wine (all whites are refrigerated, for your convenience). Deli serves full breakfast and lunch, and is available for catering. Open year-round at 6 a.m.

**Hoggy's Market,** 771 Roosevelt Trail, Windham; (207) 892-9303; and 9 Westbrook St., Westbrook; (207) 887-7220; www.hoggys market.com. The cases of this old-fashioned meat market are filled with cuts of beef and pork, whole and marinated chicken, nine varieties of house-made sausage, and a selection of cold salads, deli cheeses, pickles, and marinades. Hot and cold sandwiches are available to order, and ice cream is sold by the scoop. Special orders can be placed in advance, including meat packages like Tammy's Cookout (hot dogs, beef patties, salads, and buns), and Nick's Tailgating Party (marinated meats, hamburger patties, sausage, shrimp, and a six-pack of beer).

**The Hop Shop,** 59 Portland Rd., Gray; (207) 657-5550 or (800) 252-5550; www.thehopshop.com. Owner and brewer Ed McDowell offers "goods for what ales ya'" in this home-brewing and wine-making supply shop. From starter kits for beginning brewers to an array of malts, hops, yeasts, extracts, and concentrates for masters, the shop is a hub for local enthusiasts, who converge to share their tales of ales and troubleshoot experimental batches with the resident brewmaster.

**Keys to the Kitchen,** 155 Port Rd., Kennebunk; (207) 967-4904; www.keystothekitchen.com. This charming kitchen shop has offered local and seasonal visitors expert kitchen advice for more than

20 years. They carry more than 600 gadgets, as well as high-end cookware, housewares, and cookbooks. Events include cooking and gadget demonstrations, as well as book signings.

**Leavitt & Sons,** 37 Depot Rd., Falmouth; (207) 781-3753; www .leavittandsons.com. This pleasant deli and market serves up prepared sandwiches and soups, a range of charcuterie and imported cheeses, an impressive list of more than 350 wines by the bottle, and a wide selection of beers, chosen by owner and former brewer Pete Leavitt. But what they're really known for is dinner to go. Their specialty chicken potpie, rich with meat and gravy, is available every day. Other made-from-scratch menu items change weekly.

**Le Creuset Factory Store,** 283 US 1, #4, Kittery; (207) 439-4811; www.lecreuset.com. Just off I-95 as you cross into Maine, the Kittery Outlets can be a crowded summer destination, but this orderly shop is worth the trip. Stocked with all manner of cookware, from the company's classic enameled cast-iron pots to teakettles, stoneware, kitchen utensils, textiles, and cookbooks. Helpful staff is on hand to explain gadgets and hunt for additional colors and sizes.

**Lois' Natural Marketplace,** 152 US 1, Scarborough; (207) 885-0602. This classic natural foods market has a little bit of everything: organic produce, groceries, freshly baked bread, vitamins, natural make-up and gift items. The in-store cafe serves up creative, vegan-friendly fare, and the sustainable ethos of the market includes products from 75 local farms.

**Medeo European Food and Deli,** 529 Main St., Westbrook; (207) 854-4020; www.medeoeuropean.com. Specializing in provisions from Eastern Europe, this pleasant shop was founded by Russian immigrant Lyubov Gorelov to serve her community and preserve a taste of her culture. Products include household staples and over-the-counter European medicines, imported candies and chocolates, cheeses and kefir, kielbasa, fish, and rabbit. Closed Sun and holidays.

**New Gloucester Village Store,** 405 Intervale Rd., New Gloucester; (207) 926-4224; www.ngvillagestore.com. In the heart of the Lower Village, this homey bakery, cafe, and grocer is housed in a late 19th-century building that has served as a community gathering spot for more than 100 years. Over the years, the space has held a grocer, the farmers' union, and hardware and dry goods shop, but it now offers brick-oven pizza, prepared foods, a hot daily special, wine and beer, fresh baked bread, and weekend bagels. Open daily, with sunny indoor and patio seating.

**Perkins & Perkins,** 478 Main St., Ogunquit; (207) 646-0288 or (877) 646-0288; www.perkinsandperkins.com. This gourmet food and wine shop offers imported cheeses, pâtés, more than 300 varieties of wine, and candy made on the premises, as well as their own line of bruschetta toppings, tapenades, marinades, rubs, and spreads. Gifts, from cheese boards to hand-painted wine glasses, line the walls, and the shop specializes in thoughtfully crafted gift baskets, combining fine foods and wines with complementary accessories.

**Pineland Farms Market,** 15 Farm View Dr., New Gloucester; (207) 688-4539; www.pinelandfarms.org. Located on the grounds of Pineland Farms, a 5,000-acre nonprofit farm, this year-round market is an indoor farm stand, selling cheese, meats, and produce from the farm, as well as their own jams, honey, and pickles, and local treats like Toots Ice Cream (see p. 87). Deli sandwiches are made to order, and hot meals from the same local ingredients can be found at nearby Dish Creative Cafe, also on the Pineland campus.

**Royal River Natural Foods,** 443 US 1, Freeport; (207) 865-0046; www.rrnf.com. Up the wooden steps and past plentiful flowers bursting from raised beds, this cozy natural-food shop offers local and organic produce, eco-friendly household goods, bulk foods and snacks, groceries, and organic and specialty wines. An in-store deli serves vegetarian soups and stews, and helpful staff is on hand for recommendations and guidance ("How do I work the peanut butter machine?").

**Smiling Hill Farm Dairy and Market,** 781 County Rd., Westbrook; (207) 775-4818 or (800) 743-7463, www.smilinghill .com. Operated by the Knight family since the 1700s, this 500-

acre dairy farm sells a complete selection of their products at their on-farm store. Milk bottled on-site in returnable glass bottles, homemade ice cream, and award-winning artisanal cheeses crafted by their Silvery Moon  Creamery are available, as well as local meats and eggs. In summer, goats nuzzle up to patrons at the petting farm. Don't miss flavored orange crème milk, coffee milk, and seasonal eggnog. Open year-round.

**Vic and Whit's Sandwich Shop,** 206 Main St., Saco; (207) 284-6701. Under a broad red awning, this comfortable shop has been around since 1972 and carries a large variety of wines and beers—from fine imported bottles to local microbrews. Owner and former Saco mayor Mark Johnston is as eager to talk town history as wine ratings, which can make for an entertaining visit. Soup and sandwiches served daily.

## *Pick Your Own*

**Brackett Orchards,** 224 Sokokis Ave., Limington; (207) 637-2580; www.brackettsorchards.com. Apples, early September to late October.

**Dole Orchards,** Doles Ridge Road, Limington; (207) 793-4409; www.dolesorchard.com. Strawberries, tart cherries, raspberries, blueberries, apples, and plums, available seasonally from mid-June to early October.

**Gillespie Farms,** 725 Mayall Rd., New Gloucester; (207) 657-2877. Strawberries and shelling peas, mid-June to July.

**Giles's Family Farm at Notre Dame,** US 202, Alfred; (207) 324-2944. Apples, Labor Day to mid-October.

**Hammond Farms,** 180 Old North Berwick Rd., Lyman; (207) 985-2550. Apples, late August to late October.

**Hansel's Orchard,** 44 Sweetser Rd., North Yarmouth; (207) 829-6136; www.hansels orchard.com. Apples; open weekends from early September to late October.

**Kelly Orchards,** 1881 ME 109/Sanborn Rd., Acton; (207) 636-1601. Blueberries, peaches, and apples, early August to November.

**Lavigne Strawberry Farm,** Whichers Mill Road, Sanford; (207) 324-5497. Strawberries, late June to early July.

**Libby and Son U-Pick,** 86 Sawyer Mountain Rd., Limerick; (207) 793-4749; www.libbysonupicks.com. Highbush blueberries and apples, mid-August to October.

**McDougal Orchards,** 201 Hanson's Ridge Rd., Springvale; (207) 324-5054; www .mcdougalorchards.com. Apples, early August to late October. Nectarines, peaches, plums, pears, and raspberries sold at the farm stand.

**Payeur Farm,** Otis Allen Road, Alfred; (207) 324-3200. Blueberries, late July through August.

**Pine View Orchard,** 17 Sunset Lane, Berwick; (207) 698-5891. Apples, September to the first week in October.

**Randall Orchards,** Randall Road, Standish; (207) 642-3500. Apples, peaches, pumpkins, and squash, late August through mid-November.

**Raven Hill Orchard,** 255 Ossipee Hill Rd., East Waterboro; (207) 247-4455; www.ravenhillorchard.com. Organic apples, August through December. Cider, picked produce, and organic baked goods at the stand.

**Romac Orchard,** H Road, Acton; (207) 636-3247; www.romac orchards.freeservers.com. Apples, August through October.

**Spiller Farm,** 85 Spiller Farm Lane, Wells; (207) 985-2575; www
.spillerfarm.com. Strawberries, raspberries, blueberries, and apples,
seasonally available mid-June through October.

**Sweetser's Apple Barrel and Orchards,** 19 Blanchard Rd.,
Cumberland Center; (207) 829-3074; www.maineapple.com. Apples,
August through October.

**Thompson's Orchard,** 276 Gloucester Hill Rd., New Gloucester;
(207) 926-4738; www.thompsonsorchard.com. Apples, Labor Day to
Christmas Eve.

# Western Maine

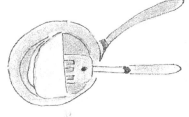

With grand lakes, steep slopes, and fragrant woods, the western mountain region offers year-round attractions. Around Memorial Day the smells of grilling meat begin to waft over Sebago, Kezar, and Long Lakes as people open their "camps" (summer lake houses) and move in for the season. Mornings begin with the cry of the loons and the quiet dip of canoe paddles over the glassy water, and on holiday weekends in the heat of summer, the air is alive with the gleeful splashes of families at play.

At the far west of the region, the Appalachian Trail crosses into the state from New Hampshire just north of White Mountains National Park and meanders through the many peaks of Grafton Notch State Park, crossing the tributaries into Rangeley Lake before heading north through the Bigelow Range. Rustic cabins are maintained along the length of the trail by the Maine Huts and Trails System, offering shelter to hikers out for a few days and those conquering the entire route, who usually arrive in Maine by late summer. Near the trail, the town of Rangeley is a popular spot with hikers, who often wander into the village in search of a hot meal.

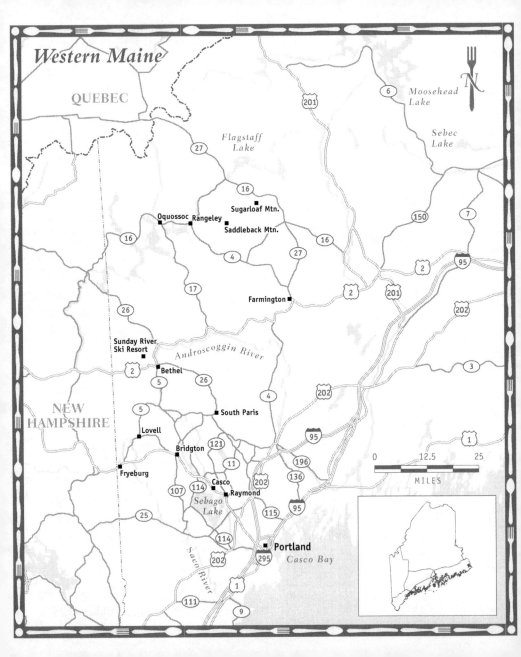

# Western Maine

QUEBEC

Moosehead Lake

Sebec Lake

Flagstaff Lake

Sugarloaf Mtn.

Oquossoc Rangeley

Saddleback Mtn.

Farmington

NEW HAMPSHIRE

Sunday River Ski Resort

Androscoggin River

Bethel

South Paris

Lovell

Bridgton

Fryeburg

Casco

Raymond

Sebago Lake

Saco River

Portland

Casco Bay

0    12.5    25

MILES

As temperatures cool, fall brings spectacular changing of the leaves, and the many maples turn the mountains into brilliant mosaics of scarlet, rust, and gold. It's a great spot for leaf peeping, and the farm stands that dot the rural roads are filled with bottles of maple syrup as well as late produce and apples by the bushel.

In winter the ski slopes at Sugarloaf and Saddleback Mountain sparkle with powder, and the surrounding towns are blanketed sweetly with snow. This is the region's true high season, and between November and April, thousands of skiers and snowboarders head to Carrabassett Valley and the Rangeley Lakes region.

In addition to outdoor recreation, western Maine is home to a vibrant cultural community. The Western Maine Cultural Alliance promotes the arts and folk studies, and the small towns of Lovell and Bethel are known for their dynamic arts scenes. South Paris is home to Celebration Barn, the school of performance art and mime founded by famed mime, the late Tony Montanaro. Located along the Little Androscoggin River, South Paris is also the site of the Paris Manufacturing Company, founded in 1861, which supplied sledges for Admiral Robert Peary's expedition to the North Pole and made the iconic Flexible Flyer children's sleds. Admiral Peary's home in Fryeburg is now a museum.

Away from the mountains, the land is agricultural, and diversi-fied farms and apple orchards are tucked between rolling acres of pasture. Each fall the Fryeburg Fair, the state's largest agricultural celebration and the final fair of the season, brings hundreds of farmers, thousands of animals, and tens of thousands of visitors to the fairgrounds.

The food culture here is casual, geared toward the outdoorsy vibe of visitors and locals alike. Though the food may be elegant, the atmosphere is generally relaxed. Brewpubs abound, as do great spots for a hearty breakfast and small community markets where you can put together a picnic or pick up some smokin' good barbecue.

## *Bakeries*

**Marta's Bakery,** 684 Valley Rd. (ME 35), North Waterford; (207) 583-2250; www.martasbakery.com. Owner-baker Marta Cistecky's creations draw on her Czech roots—she came to the United States from Prague in 1983—and her menu includes traditional Eastern European favorites like rich *vanocka* and stollen breads, strudels, and seasonal bûche de Noël, as well as delicious pies, tarts, pound cakes, tortes, and cheesecakes (try the chocolate bourbon). Gorgeous wedding cakes are available to order, and pound cakes and cinnamon buns can be shipped. Open seasonally, hours vary.

**The Orange Cat,** 329 Main St., Kingfield; (207) 265-2860; www.orangecatcafe.com. Housed in the historic Old Brick Castle building, this lively bakery and cafe is full of vibrant colors and energy, as well as fresh baked goods and thick sandwiches. Sweet treats range from rich cupcakes to whoopie pies filled with luscious cream, and sandwiches include several vegetarian offerings and can be ordered with daily soup or salad. Serving Carrabassett coffees (p.

137) and espresso drinks as well as smoothies. With free Wi-Fi. Open daily year-round, though hours vary by season.

## Brewpubs & Microbreweries

**Bray's Brew Pub and Eatery,** 678 Roosevelt Trail, Naples; (207) 693-6806; www.braysbrewpub.com. In a restored Victorian farmhouse, this micro-microbrewery serves up its own ales, crafted in the converted barn out back. From the light Brandy Pond Blonde Ale to the malty Pleasant Mountain Porter, brews are named for local landmarks and are served by the pint. Food nicely matches the ales: chowders and chili, lobster stew with brandy, and hearty grilled meats, seafood, and pastas.

**Ebenezer's Pub and Restaurant,** 44 Allen Rd., Lovell; (207) 925-3200; www.ebenezerspub.net. Rated the number-one beer bar in the world by *BeerAdvocate* magazine for five years running, this cozy tavern, nestled in the mountains, keeps more than 35 mostly Belgian beers on tap, and has another 1,000 bottled beers of various vintages in its expansive cellar. The food leans to juicy Angus burgers, thick sandwiches, and Belgian-style *frites,* but there are some surprises: Succulent *moules frites* are cooked with beer in traditional mussel pots, and stuffed sole is filled with scallops and crabmeat and napped with Newburg sauce.

**The Granary Brewpub,** 147 Pleasant St., Farmington; (207) 779-0710; www.thegranarybrewpub.com. This low-key pub keeps 12 beers on tap, including half a dozen Maine microbrews. The atmosphere is casual, and unless one of New England's teams is playing on the bar's flat-screen TVs, it's a quiet place for a beer and a bite. The menu serves standard pub fare—thick burgers, milk-marinated pork chops, grilled rib eye steak—as well as more stimulating entrees like smoked salmon Alfredo and chicken with chorizo and tortellini. Indoor and seasonal outdoor seating; open daily.

**The Jolly Drayman at the Briar Lea Inn,** 150 Mayville Rd., Bethel; (207) 824-4717; www.briarleainn.com. Serving cask-conditioned ale, single-malt whiskeys, and English-style pub food, this cozy tavern brings the British Isles to the mountains of Maine. Local and imported ales, lagers, porters, and stouts are on tap, as well as a few hard ciders from the United Kingdom. Some large-bottle beers are available, too, as is a small but well-chosen list of wines. Dig into some bangers and mash or a hearty Cornish pasty of steak, potatoes, turnips, and rutabaga in a flaky crust; check out the British beer memorabilia on the walls; and hum a few bars of "God Save the Queen" before heading back to the slopes. Open year-round.

**Sunday River Brew Pub,** 29 Sunday River Rd., Bethel; (207) 824-4ALE (4253); www.sundayriverbrewpub.com. Serving Sunday

River ales by brewer Stewart Mason, this pub has the feel of a mountain chalet, with exposed beams, warm wood floors, and a stone fireplace. An outdoor deck is open seasonally, and in winter, skiers and snowshoers play pool and thaw by the fire. The menu ranges from edamame to short ribs, with an extensive list of sandwiches and burgers. Lobster fritters are a greasy treat; follow them with a Cajun-style Black and Bleu burger and a pint of hoppy IPA.

## Farm Stands

**Harris Farm,** 280 Buzzell Rd., Dayton; (207) 499-2678; www.harrisfarm.com. Three generations of the Harris family have grown up on this 500-acre diversified farm, which raises dairy and beef cattle, hard red spring wheat (for bread), and seasonal vegetables in a landscape of lush, rolling hills. Natural beef and veal, sun-warmed vegetables, and lovely glass bottles of the farm's milk are available at the farm store. In winter, the farm opens 40 kilometers of cross-country ski trails and its toasty warming hut, which offers skiers soups, chili, and baked goods around the woodstove. Open year-round; hours change seasonally.

**Harvest Hill Farms,** 840 Bakerstown Rd., Poland; (207) 998-5485; www.harvesthillfarms.com. Selling warm pies and crusty breads, pasture-raised meat, and Maine-made products in addition to seasonal produce from their fields, this year-round farm stand

## SWITCHEL: TRADITIONAL HAY-MAKER'S PUNCH

Popular with colonial settlers, who may have imported the recipe from the West Indies, switchel or hay-maker's punch is a refreshing, thirst-quenching drink that was often brought out to the fields during haying. Recipes vary throughout New England, but in Maine it's generally made from apple cider vinegar, maple syrup or honey, water, and a little ginger. Quantities are mixed to taste, and are served at room temperature (or, if you're being historically accurate, left out to be heated by the sun).

serves up a little bit of everything. Housed in the first floor of a converted clapboard farmhouse, there's a deli counter with a mix of Boar's Head meats and their own house-cured hams and free-range turkey and chicken, and a pizza oven turning out signature square pizzas on dough made from scratch each morning. Hours change seasonally; in the summer, visit the petting barn next door while you wait for take-out orders.

**Weston's Farm Stand,** 48 River St., Fryeburg; (207) 935-2567; www.westonsfarm.com. Since patriarch Ephraim Weston bought 46 acres of land in 1799, this 1,000-acre family farm straddling the

Saco River, has practiced sustainable agriculture. Over the years, the family has shifted from a predominately livestock business to a small dairy to its current incarnation, raising vegetables on 60 acres of diversified fields and in five heated greenhouses. The farm stand carries an abundance of veggies, melons, and cut flowers in season, pasture-raised Angus beef from nearby Peppermint Fields Farm, holiday wreaths and Christmas trees, and maple syrup tapped from their trees and boiled down in their sugar house. Open year-round.

 ## Farmers' Markets

**Bethel Farmers' Market,** Bethel Health Center parking lot, ME 26, Bethel; (207) 824-2230. May through Oct, Sat, 9 a.m. to noon.

**Bridgton Farmers' Market,** Depot Street in front of Community Center, Bridgton; (207) 998-2196; www.bridgtonfarmersmarket .com. May through Sept, Sat, 8 a.m. to 1 p.m.

**Farmington–Sandy River Farmers' Market,** Front Street, Farmington; (207) 778-3115. May through Oct, Fri, 9 a.m. to 2 p.m.

**Lovell Farmers' Market,** ME 5 by the Wicked Good Store, Lovell; (207) 452-2772. May through Oct, Wed, 9 a.m. to 1 p.m.

**Naples Farmers' Market,** Naples Village Green, Naples; (207) 452-2772. May through Sept, Thurs, 8 a.m. to 1 p.m.

**Norway Farmers' Market,** corner of 419 Main and Deering Streets, Norway; (207) 674-5903. May through Oct, Thurs, 2 p.m. to 6 p.m.

## Food Happenings

### July

**Oquossoc Strawberry Festival,** Oquossoc Park, Carry Road; Oquossoc; (207) 864-5364. Celebrate all things strawberry at this daylong festival. Shortcakes are topped with sweet berries, and home-baked pies are chock-full of fruit. Crafts and gifts are also for sale.

### August

**Wilton Blueberry Festival,** Main Street, Wilton; (207) 778-4726; www.wiltonbbf.com. Pick your own berries, enjoy a blueberry pancake breakfast cooked by the area Lion's Club, buy a few juicy pies, and taste entries to the "blueberry cook-off" at this weekend family festival, held at the height of blueberry season in early August. Festivities include crafts and quilt shows, a firefighters' muster, and tours of the Wilton Historical Society. The weekend is capped by a fireworks display.

## September

**Cornish Apple Festival,** US 5, Cornish; (207) 625-4993; www .cornish-maine.org. For more than 20 years, this one-day festival has celebrated the season's apples with bushels of fruit, freshly pressed cider, and other delights. Festivities include a 5K road race, a crafts sale, and performances by local musicians.

## October

**Fryeburg Fair,** Fairgrounds, Fryeburg; (207) 935-3268; www .fryeburgfair.com. The largest fair in the state, and the last of the season, this mammoth agricultural festival has been going since 1851, when a few local farmers got together for an eight-day "Blue Ribbon Classic." The fair is now a Pine State institution, offering six days of harness racing, a farm museum, and the largest steer and oxen show in the world. The smell of frying food hits you miles away, and the stalls offer everything from fried dough to falafel. But the fair is truly a celebration of agriculture, with livestock judging, 4-H competitions, and

daily pig scrambles: The school kid who catches the greased pig gets to take it home.

**Great Western Maine Chili Cook-Off,** Waterford; (207) 647-3472. Held in the town square, directly following the Waterford Fall Foliage fun run, this annual cook-off invites restaurants, nonprofits, and regular folks to team up and compete for the honor of being named the Greatest Chili Cook in western Maine. Entries range from vegetarian to bison, mild to blazing, and participants run the gamut from librarians to town officers—firefighters usually make a good showing.

## The Maine Ice Cream Trail

**Lakeside Dairy Bar,** US 302, Naples; (207) 693-3090. From a yellow counter perched at the edge of Sebago Lake, this popular ice-cream shack serves dozens of flavors, admirably managing the crowds that swarm in midseason. A few chairs offer seating, but most patrons mill around, enjoying their treats on the go. Open May through Sept.

**The Mosquito,** 1333 Roosevelt Trail, Raymond; (207) 655-2899. Taking its name from pests at the marsh out back, this seasonal parlor makes homemade, quirkily named ice cream and treats on-site. Indoor seating keeps you bite-free, but the intrepid can sit on a bench out back and swat between licks. Open May through Oct.

# One-Pie® New England Pumpkin Pie

*The One-Pie® Canning Company in West Paris has been packing pumpkin and squash in western Maine since the late nineteenth century. The pumpkin pie recipe printed on the can is a holiday favorite with generations of Mainers, who stock up on cans of One-Pie® well in advance of Thanksgiving.*

**1 can One-Pie® Pumpkin (15 ounces)**

**1 tablespoon cornstarch**

**½ teaspoon cinnamon**

**½ teaspoon ginger**

**½ teaspoon nutmeg**

**½ teaspoon salt (scant)**

**1½ tablespoons butter (melted)**

**1½ cups milk or one 12-ounce can of evaporated milk**

**1 cup sugar**

**⅛ cup molasses**

**2 eggs (beaten)**

**Lemon juice (optional)**

**one 9-inch pie crust, unbaked**

*Sift sugar, cornstarch, salt, cinnamon, ginger, and nutmeg together. Mix this with contents of one can One-Pie® pumpkin. Add beaten eggs, melted butter, molasses, and milk. Add a dash of lemon juice (if desired). Line a 9-inch pie plate, pour in contents. Preheat oven and bake at 450 degrees for 15 minutes. Then reduce temperature to 350 degrees and continue to bake for 50 minutes.*

*Serves 6–8.*

Recipe courtesy of the One-Pie® Canning Company.

**Raymond's Frozen Custard,** 857 Roosevelt Trail, Casco; (207) 655-1116. The flavors are somewhat limited at this seasonal stand—8 to 10 on a given day—but the homemade, hard-scoop custard is smooth, creamy, and rich with egg yolks. Vanilla and chocolate are always on the menu, while special flavors like peach Melba, white chocolate mocha, and grasshopper (mint and chocolate) rotate through. Open May through Oct.

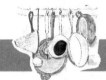

## Learn to Cook

**Cafe DiCocoa,** 125 Main St., Bethel; (207) 824-5282; www.cafedicocoa.com. Chef Cathi DiCocco serves up healthy, vegetarian (and many vegan) baked goods and light meals in this cheerful cafe and market. In winter, she hosts a Gentle Dining Series, taking guests around the world in a 12-week culinary tour that features weekly 5-course meals showcasing regional flavors—and customs and music—from Morocco to Mexico (by reservation only). In summer, the cafe becomes a cooking school, offering tasting workshops, seminars, community soup kitchens, and a summer cooking camp for kids. Classes and store hours change seasonally and are listed on the website.

**Carrabassett Coffee Company,** ME 27, Kingfield; (888) 292-BEAN; www.carrabassettcoffee.com. Roasting beans in the Carrabassett River Valley, a stone's throw from Sugarloaf ski resort, this microroastery sources beans from around the world but specializes in certified-organic and single-source coffees. Their wholesale business supplies beans to businesses around the state, and the roastery owns and operates two cafes: **Java Joe's at Sugarloaf** (207-237-3330) and **Java Joe's Corner Cafe** at the corner of Main and Church Streets, Farmington (207-779-1000).

## *Restaurants*

**Brian's Bistro,** 25 Hartford St., Rumford; (207) 364-3300; www .brians-bistro.com; $$. The lush colors and upscale feel of this lively restaurant are unexpected in the struggling mill town of Rumford, where the bistro occupies the street level of an old hotel from the town's bustling heyday. Chef-owner Brian Nichols's menu is eclectic, ranging from thick burgers to chicken saltimbocca, and it nods to the Mediterranean with a range of pastas and pizzas. With a full bar, beers on tap, and wines by the glass and bottle. Open Tues through Sat.

**Cho-Sun,** 141 Main St., Bethel; (207) 824-7370; www.chosun restaurant.com; $$. Bringing the flavors of her native South Korea to the mountains of Maine, Pok Sun Lane opened this lovely restaurant in 2002. The menu includes Korean classics like beef, chicken, or pork *bulgoki* (thinly sliced marinated meat with rice and kimchee), L.A. Bulcalbi (spicy beef short ribs), and bibimbap (meat and vegetable salad on rice), as well as dishes that incorporate Maine seafood like the hearty cham-pong soup with pork, shrimp, calamari, scallops, and mussels. If the charming East-meets-West decor strikes your fancy, visit the owner's antique and house-wares shop, **Pok Sun Emporium** (130 Main Street), just down the street. Also with Japanese entrees. Reservations recommended.

**Chute's Cafe,** 333 US 302, Casco; (207) 655-7111; $$. Known for its skillet breakfasts—hobo hash, farmers hash—and warm baked goods, this unpretentious diner serves comforting breakfast and lunch from 6 a.m. to 1 p.m. daily. Lunch includes barbeque—try the pulled pork, or one of two styles of ribs—home-baked beans, sandwiches, burgers, and hot dogs. Staff is attentive and friendly, and the homey atmosphere is winning. Open year-round.

**The Clipper Merchant Tea House,** 58 Main St., Limerick; (207) 793-3500; www.clippermerchant.com; $$. This darling tearoom, in the historic 1830 J. M. Morse House, serves luncheon and high tea in one of four charmingly restored dining rooms, replete with period furnishings, fresh flowers, and delicate china. Offering pots of more than 80 loose teas, as well as refreshing lavender lemonade, the teahouse serves tea sandwiches, fresh scones with Devon cream and homemade lemon curd, small desserts, and light salads. Favorite teas can be bought by the ounce, as well. Open 11 a.m. to 4 p.m., Wed through Sat.

**Frye's Leap General Store and Cafe,** Frye Island; (207) 655-4256; www.fryesleap.com; $$. Serving the summer community of Frye Island and boaters on Sebago Lake, this quaint shop and restaurant offers groceries, gifts, and casual dining on a deck overlooking the water. Whether you need laundry detergent or a lobster quesadilla, if you're on Frye Island, this is the place for you. The menu is solid and satisfying, offering sandwiches—the apricot-almond chicken is a treat—salads, and a few pasta entrees, as well as specialty pizzas. Takeout available. Open Memorial Day through Labor Day.

**The Gingerbread House,** ME 4, Oquossoc; (207) 864-3602; www .gingerbreadhouserestaurant.net; $$$. In a quaint house that once served as the local post office, this year-round restaurant specializes in hearty meals and sweet treats at the old-fashioned ice-cream parlor, in operation since the 1950s. Chef Dean Szablewski's menus incorporate the best of the region—try the venison sausage—with clever nods to more exotic flavors; the entree North and South, for example, refers not to the Civil War, but to the northern Thai spices that grace a pan-seared South Pacific barramundi. Open year-round for breakfast, lunch, and dinner.

**Homestead Kitchen, Bar & Bakery,** 186 Broadway, Farmington; (207) 778-6162; www.homesteadbakery.com; $$. Since 1982, this upscale eatery in the heart of downtown has offered elegant fare in a comfortable environment. Open all day, the kitchen opens with hearty breakfasts—fluffy pancakes, French toast with house-made bread, egg burritos, and the popular UMF Scramble (eggs, ham, bacon, home fries, and vegetables topped with cheddar). Lunch and dinner menus range from pub food to steak with truffle butter, and include a variety of tapas, which can be sampled by the fireplace with a drink from the full bar. Muffins, pastries, and desserts are made on-site, and whole pies and cakes can be ordered. Open daily for breakfast and lunch, dinner Tues through Sat.

**Krista's Restaurant,** 2 Main St., Cornish; (207) 625-3600; www .kristasrestaurant.com; $$. Serving hearty, eclectic fare in a cheerful dining room overlooking the river, this popular family-run eatery began as a catering business and has grown into a local landmark. The menu ranges from weekend breakfast of stuffed French toast to dinner entrees of salmon spiked with citrus, and steaks done to a turn. Reservations recommended, especially for dinner. Open Thurs through Sun year-round, except for a short break in March.

**One Stanley Avenue,** 1 Stanley Ave., Kingfield; (207) 265-5541; www.stanleyavenue.com; $$$. Since 1972 this sweet restaurant, housed in a Victorian bed-and-breakfast, has served dinners that feature the unique flavors of Maine's woods and mountains: fiddlehead ferns, juniper berries, rhubarb, crab apples, locally foraged mushrooms, and hemlock (yes, you read that right). Meals are hearty and inventive, ranging from beef-and-chestnut pie to roast duck with rhubarb glaze to sweetbreads with applejack and chives. Open for dinner, Tues through Sun, mid-December to mid-April. Reservations essential.

**The Oxford House Inn** and **Jonathan's at the OHI,** 548 Main St., Fryeburg; (207) 935-3442 or (800) 261-7206; www.oxfordhouseinn .com; $$$. The 50-seat dining room and granite-walled basement pub of this historic 1913 inn are a foodie destination, serving an inventive menu that changes seasonally. Chef-innkeeper Jonathan Spak's creations run from acclaimed bison short ribs—braised until they're meltingly tender and served in a sweet grilled-onion broth— to lobster mac 'n' cheese with shaved truffles and tempura green beans. In the lower-level pub, the atmosphere is casual, and the menu sticks to pub favorites with a twist: Barbecue wings come with green goddess dressing, sweet potato fries are dressed with Cajun remoulade. Open year-round, reservations recommended.

**The Restaurant at Center Lovell Inn,** ME 5, Center Lovell; (207) 925-1575; www.centerlovellinn.com; $$$. With views of Kezar Lake and the White Mountains, this 1805 country inn offers dinner nightly—by a crackling fire in winter and on the screened porch in summer. The menu offers elegant fare, from creamy coquilles St. Jacques to earthy pan-seared Muscovy duck breast enlivened by tangy sour-cherry and Zinfandel glaze. Attire is casual, but reservations are required. Open mid-May through Oct, and Dec through Mar.

**Rosie's Lovell Village Store & Restaurant,** 234 Main St., Lovell; (207) 925-1255; $$. In a little cream-colored clapboard building, this quaint market and restaurant is a community meeting spot and convenience store, serving homemade breakfast and lunch all day, as well as pizzas once the ovens are fired up. The motto of the friendly staff is written on the menu: "It's never too late for breakfast, it's never too early for lunch." Pancakes are light and fluffy, sandwiches are made to order, and pies are always homemade. Fans of Stephen King: He has a home in the area and Rosie's is rumored to be one of his favorite spots.

**Route 2 Diner,** 1371 US 2, Rumford Center; (207) 364-7777; www .route2diner.com; $$. Serving fresh baked breads, local produce and meats, and bison meat from Beech Hill Bison Farm in Waterford, this no-frills diner makes food the old fashioned way. Corned beef hash is homemade, as are soups, chowders, and chilis. Burgers— bison or beef—come with a pile of hot fries and a side of fresh slaw. Open for breakfast and lunch. Hours change seasonally; closed Tues in winter.

**Soup for You,** 222 Broadway, Farmington; (207) 779-0799; $. With its long menu posted above the busy counter, this popular lunch spot can be overwhelming at peak hours. Six soups rotate daily—the cafe's name is a nod to *Seinfeld*'s "Soup Nazi"—and the three dozen sandwiches on offer include a large variety of vegetarian and vegan creations. Coffee, tea, and myriad espresso drinks include soy options (rare in these parts) and fuel the studies of students at the nearby university. Cash only.

## Specialty Stores & Markets

**Good Food Store,** US 2, Bethel; (207) 824-3754; www.good foodbethel; and **Smokin' Good BBQ;** (207) 824-4PIG; www.smokingoodbarbecue.com. In a clapboard house, this gourmet grocer specializes in locally grown organic produce, bulk spices, fine wines, imported cheeses, and pantry essentials. Fresh baked goods and hot and cold lunches are available through the day, as well as prepared "heat and eat" meals. In the parking lot, it's a different story: Order succulent, hardwood-smoked barbecue from the window of the battered orange trailer, nicknamed "Graceland," and sneak away to enjoy it with a pile of napkins at hand. Rubbed with their own blend of spices and paired with homemade beans, coleslaw, and corn bread, ribs come by the slab, chickens are whole or half, and pulled pork and beef brisket melt on the tongue. Open year-round; in winter look for the bellowing smoker among the snowdrifts.

**The Good Life Market,** 1297 Roosevelt Trail, Raymond; (207) 655-1196; www.thegoodlifemarket.com. This family-owned specialty store is known for its excellent wine selection—considered the best in the Rangeley Lakes region, with more than 600 bottles, curated by owner Walt Manchester—as well as fine prepared foods, a deli counter, and a new microroastery, Swift River Roasters. Take-out catering and gift baskets of Maine products can be ordered, and occasional cooking classes (taught by Walt's wife, Linda) and wine tastings are held on-site. Open year-round.

**Hungry Hollow Country Store,** 28 Bethel Rd., West Paris; (207) 674-3012. Reminding patrons of their grandma's kitchen, this cozy store in a converted old farmhouse serves chicken pies, a daily soup, and fresh baked breads, cookies, and treats. Take-out entrees are available, and there's a single small table where you can enjoy a cup of soup or a sandwich. Open year-round, seven days a week, 7 a.m. to 5 p.m.

**Smokin' Good BBQ,** US 2, Bethel; (207) 824-4PIG; www .smokingoodbarbecue.com. See the Good Food Store listing above.

**Wicked Good Store,** ME 5, Lovell; (207) 925-3090. Yes, it's a convenience store that sells gasoline and diesel, firewood, snowmobile spark plugs, and maps, as well as wine, beer, cheeses, and snacks to area travelers. But at their small restaurant—23 seats at a counter and booths—they serve surprisingly good home-cooked soups, pies, cakes, and pudding, and a hearty breakfast popular among locals. Open year-round, seven days a week, 6 a.m. to 8 p.m.

## Pick Your Own

**Apple Acres Farm,** 365 Durgintown Rd., South Hiram; (207) 625-4777; www.appleacresfarm.com. Apples, mid-August through October. Famed homemade Apple Crackle snacks available at the farm store year-round.

**Blueberry Hill Farm,** Dallas Hill Road, Rangeley; (207) 864-5647. Wild blueberries, late July through early September.

**Douglas Hill Orchard,** 42 Orchard Rd., Sebago; (207) 787-2745. Apples, early September through late October.

**Five Fields Farm,** ME 107, South Bridgton; (207) 647-2425; www .fivefieldsski.com. Apples, late August through November.

**Meadow Brook Farm,** 727 Webbs Mills Rd. (ME 85), Raymond; (207) 627-7009. Apples; open weekends, early September through late October.

**Morrison Hill Orchard,** Morrison Hill Road, Farmington; (207) 778-4945. Strawberries, June. Apples, August through October.

**Wilton Blueberry Farm,** East Wilton; (207) 645-2128. Blueberries, mid-July through late September.

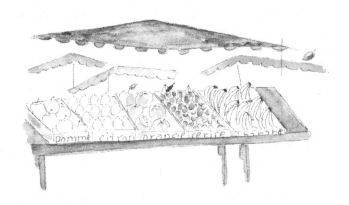

# Mid-Coast Maine

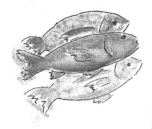

With quaint fishing villages nestled among its harbors and inlets, the mid-coast presents Maine at its most picturesque. Restored 18th- and 19th-century homes, built by sea captains and marked with historical plaques, are tucked down seaside lanes, their gardens teeming with flowers from spring to fall. Yachts and schooners dock in the marinas, bobbing in the glinting water through the summer; beyond them, wooded and rocky islands dot the bays. The area is known for its seafood—lobsters are caught in the waters of Muscongus Bay, oysters are cultivated in the mouth of the deep Damariscotta River, and haddock, cod, and other fin fish are brought in with every day's catch. Fishing families have been here for centuries, and many mailboxes sport the same names as the coves they're on.

The history of the region, however, predates the arrival of Europeans by millennia—Native Americans settled here as long ago as 200 BC. At the mouth of the Damariscotta, remnants of earlier cultures are visible in the deep mounds of oyster shells at the Whaleback Shell Midden, last added to by the Abenaki Indians a thousand years ago, and now an archeological site and state park.

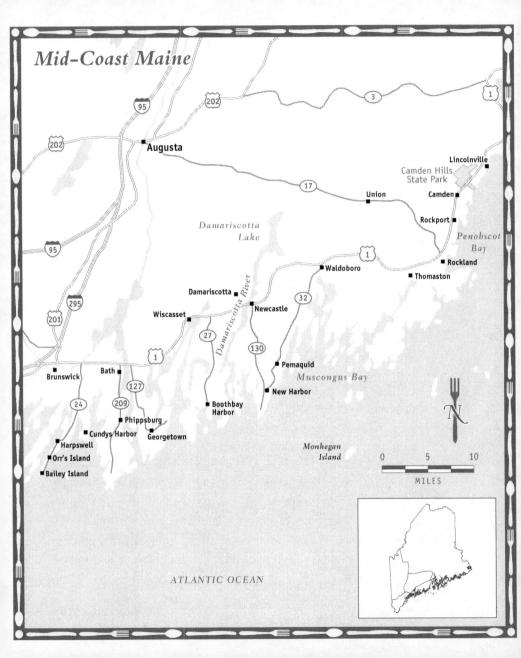

# Mid-Coast Maine

Augusta

Lincolnville

Camden Hills State Park

Camden

Rockport

Union

*Penobscot Bay*

*Damariscotta Lake*

Rockland

Thomaston

Waldoboro

Damariscotta

*Damariscotta River*

Newcastle

Wiscasset

Pemaquid

*Muscongus Bay*

New Harbor

Brunswick

Bath

Boothbay Harbor

Phippsburg

Georgetown

Harpswell

Orr's Island

Bailey Island

Cundys Harbor

*Monhegan Island*

0    5    10

MILES

N

*ATLANTIC OCEAN*

European settlers recognized the region's beauty, abundant seafood, and perfect situation for maritime pursuits: Beginning in the 18th century, tall ships were crafted at shipyards throughout the mid-coast, and the Bath Iron Works continues to build vessels for the US Navy to this day. In Bath, the Maine Maritime Museum chronicles the history of the area, while on the water, students from the Maine Maritime Academy in Castine refine their skills.

The bucolic beauty of the mid-coast has drawn artists—from painters to poets—to the region for more than a century, and cultural highlights include the Farnsworth Art Museum and Wyeth Center in Rockland, the historic Camden Opera House, and the Boothbay Opera House in Boothbay Harbor. In Rockport, the Maine Media Workshops (formerly Maine Photographic Workshops) offer residential instruction in photography, filmmaking, and multimedia design.

The town of Brunswick, since 1794 the home of Bowdoin College, is in many ways the intellectual hub of the mid-coast. The alma mater of President Franklin Pierce, Henry Wadsworth Longfellow, Nathaniel Hawthorne, Maine hero Joshua Lawrence Chamberlain, and Arctic explorer Admiral Robert Peary, Bowdoin hosts lectures and cultural events throughout the academic year. Other attractions in Brunswick include Frontier Cafe + Cinema + Gallery, a venue for independent films, discussions, and art exhibits, and the Joshua L. Chamberlain Museum, across from the college, which was Chamberlain's home and now presents exhibits about his remarkable life as a Civil War general, president of Bowdoin College, and governor of Maine.

# A Brief Guide to Maine Oysters

Maine's mid-coast provides ideal conditions for the cultivation of plump, briny oysters. A few are exported down the coast, but many are from small producers who make just enough to satisfy the state. Below is a brief guide to the oysters of the region:

**Bagaduce:** from the Bagaduce River; lovely alabaster shells, plump, meaty oysters

**Belons:** from the Damariscotta River; large flat shell, crisp, coppery oyster that almost fizzes in the mouth

**Flying Point:** from the waters near Yarmouth; large, with a mild, light flavor

**Gay Islands:** from the deep open waters near Cushing Harbor; briny and intense

**Glidden Point:** from the deep waters (40 feet deep) of the Damariscotta; rich, dense, briny

While the mid-coast is known primarily for its seafaring and aquaculture—the majority of Maine's oysters are gathered here—it is also a region of avid gardening and some of the earliest farm-to-table restaurants in the state. The Coastal Maine Botanical Gardens, in Boothbay, are both beautiful and instructive, and exhibits include a model kitchen garden and a dynamic children's garden. At Bowdoin College, the dining service operates an organic garden that supplies

**Little Bay:** technically from the Little Bay, New Hampshire, waters near Eliot, Maine; small, full meat, salty, with a crisp, sweet finish

**North Haven:** from North Haven; large, high salinity, available year-round

**Oak Points:** from Harrington; briny, exceptionally uniform size

**Pemaquids:** from the Damariscotta River; briny, firm, even a little tart

**Taunton Bay Oyster:** from waters near Acadia National Park; deep cupped, salty, with a metallic finish

**Wawenauk:** from Hog Island in the Damariscotta River; plump, deep cupped, briny

**Wiley Points:** from Damariscotta River Estuary; clean, smooth shelled, large and light

**Winter Points:** from Mill Cove, West Bath; thick shelled, meaty, almost a hint of sweetness

produce to the kitchens and is tended in part by the student Organic Garden Club. All along the coast, a growing number of restaurants are receiving national recognition for their commitments to farm-to-table dining, and chefs like Primo's Melissa Kelly change their menus daily to reflect what's in season. The mid-coast was the site of Maine's first Slow Food convivium, and that movement's ethos of slowing down to savor life is a good fit with the region.

The seafood here is stupendous, and seasonal lobster shacks can be found in every town, serving up lobsters boiled in seawater and heaping plates of steamed clams. Just as easily, you'll find Italian restaurants hand rolling their pastas, bakeries fragrant with buttery breakfast treats, and roadside stands scooping cones of hand-churned ice cream. This is Maine at its most iconic, and its most delicious.

## Bakeries

**Atlantic Baking Company,** 351 Main St., Rockland; (207) 596-0505; www.atlanticbakingco.com. The yeasty perfume of this bread and pastry bakery, across the street from the Farnsworth Museum, is enough to make the whole town hungry. Baking crusty breads with unbleached, unbromated flours, and buttery croissants, cookies, brownies, and breakfast treats, ABC—as the bakery is affectionately called—is dedicated to scratch baking and exceptional customer care. Sandwiches, salads, and two daily soups are offered at lunch time, to eat in or take out. Hours change seasonally.

**Mae's Cafe and Bakery,** 160 Centre St., Bath; (207) 442-8577; www.maescafeandbakery.com. Artfully decorated cakes, warm cinnamon buns, and pillowy dinner rolls are just a few of the many offerings at this homey bakery and cafe. In a renovated home with large windows and lots of natural light, the cafe serves hot break-

## MAINE: HOME OF THE DOUGHNUT

In 1847, Captain Hanson Gregory of Camden had an inspiration at sea: the fried cakes and "twisters" he ate aboard the lime trading ship on which he served were often crisp on the outer edges, but raw and doughy inside. What if they cut a hole in the center to encourage even frying? In his words, quoted from a 1916 interview with the *Washington Post,* "I took the cover off the ship's tin pepper box, and—I cut into the middle of that doughnut the first hole ever seen by mortal eyes!" Upon his return to Maine, he showed his mother, and the rest is history. A plaque in Rockport marks the place of Captain Gregory's birth and notes his achievement.

fast and lunch all day. The bakery provides breads and treats, and specializes in cakes for events and weddings. Open seven days a week, 8 a.m. to 3 p.m. (bakery open until 4 p.m.).

**Wild Oats Bakery & Cafe,** Tontine Mall, 149 Maine St., Brunswick; (207) 725-6287; www.wildoatsbakery.com. Gooey pecan rolls, hot cross buns, muffins, and flaky croissants start the menu at this Brunswick landmark. Fresh homemade breads and pies cool on racks behind the counter, and cakes fill the cases. Sandwiches, soups, and quiche are available for lunch—to eat in and take out—and the cafe also sells prepared meals, frozen entrees, and casseroles to heat at home. Open seven days a week, closed Sun in Jan.

**The Willow Bake Shoppe,** 1084 Commercial St., Rockport; (207) 596-0564. Set back a little from the road on a wide swath of lawn, this unassuming shop is famed for fresh, old-fashioned doughnuts sold hot in a brown paper sack. Pumpkins are a seasonal favorite, but they're all wonderful. Open 6 a.m. to noon. Cash only.

## *Brewpubs & Microbreweries*

**Badger Cafe and Pub,** 289 Common Rd., Union; (207) 785-3336; www.badgercafeandpub.com. In a historic building on the Union Common, this casual cafe and pub serves hearty food and dozens of beers on tap. Brews are chosen carefully, and range from hoppy local Dogfish IPA to chocolaty Meantime Coffee Porter from England, with a fair number of Belgian beers in the mix. The menu is comforting: crispy buttermilk fried chicken; thick, grilled pork chops Normandy; and the Barnyard Burger, a burger of ground beef, pork, and lamb topped with greens, a fried egg, and goat cheese— the whole farm in each bite. Ingredients are sourced locally when possible. Open Wed through Sun.

**Billy's Tavern,** 1 Starr St., Thomaston; (207) 354-1177; www.billys tavern.com. This traditional Irish pub offers the largest selection of single malt and Irish whisky in Maine, as well as pints of beer, oysters on the half shell, and a menu that leans toward the British Isles—though the house specialty, Mussels Normandie, is decidedly

French. On the weekends, stop in for a pot of tea and the Full Irish Breakfast: eggs, bacon, Irish bangers, black pudding, baked beans, tomato, home fries, toast, and jam. Stick around on Sunday for the weekly old-time music jam, from 3 p.m. to 6 p.m. Open daily.

**Joshua's Tavern,** 123 Maine St., Brunswick; (207) 725-7981; www .joshuastavern.com Named for hero Joshua Lawrence Chamberlain—Civil War general, Bowdoin College president, governor of Maine—this spirited pub celebrates the "Soul of the Lion" in all it has to offer, from its 20th Maine Regiment Chili to Chamberlain's Signature Plates (though it's doubtful that General Chamberlain ever sampled a grilled Reuben sandwich). With 21 beers on tap (including, of course, Shipyard's Chamberlain Pale Ale), and 21 wines by the glass, it's a local favorite.

## OTHER MID-COAST BEERS TO TRY

Though these microbreweries aren't open for tours, the beer hails from the mid-coast and is well worth a drink.

**Andrew's Brewing Company:** Try the Northern Brown Ale and English Pale Ale. Both are so tasty they were included in a gift basket of Maine's microbrews that was sent to President Obama.

**Belfast Bay Brewing Company:** Don't miss the dark copper Lobster Ale, or the award-winning McGovern's Oatmeal Stout.

**Sheepscot Valley Brewing Company:** Try the full-bodied Pemaquid Ale.

**King Eider's Pub,** 2 Elm St., Damariscotta; (207) 563-6008; www .kingeiderspub.com. Known for their luscious crab cakes—fresh-picked lumps of crabmeat sautéed and dressed with homemade tartar sauce—and the plump Damariscotta River oysters they get daily from Dodge Cove Marine Farm and shuck to order. This comfy pub serves local and imported beers on tap from mugs hung on low beams above the bar, as well as a wide range of bottled brews. Organic hard cider and 18.7-ounce "Victorian Pint" bottles of beer from Samuel Smith brewery in Yorkshire, England, are a special treat. With a full bar and a menu that combines pub classics like steak and ale pie and lighter fare like Mediterranean lentil cakes. Open daily for lunch and dinner.

**The Lion's Pride,** 112 Pleasant St., Brunswick; (207) 373-1840. Set in a strip mall next to a Dunkin' Donuts, this beer bar looks a little plain from the outside, but step in and you'll find one of the premier taverns in the state. Proprietor Chris Lively, who also owns the renowned **Ebenezer's Pub** in Lovell (see p. 127), brings 35 taps and more than 100 well-chosen bottles to the bar, as well as an offbeat menu that includes lamb lollipops and Thai shrimp. While you're there, check out the tap handles, each made from stained glass by a local artist.

**Marshall Wharf Brewing Company/Three Tides,** 2 Pinchy Lane, Belfast; (207) 338-1707; www.marshallwharf.com. Above the water on Marshall Wharf, this brewery and bar serves its own funkily named craft beers—Doktor Dunklesweizen, Umlaut Kolsch, Chaos Chaos Russian Imperial Stout—as well as a dozen or so other brews and a small menu of tapas. Pair Pemaquid Oyster Stout with half a dozen, or snack on crabmeat quesadillas with a pale ale. Open evenings, Tues through Sat.

**Montsweag Roadhouse,** 942 US 1, Woolwich; (207) 443-6563; www.montsweagroadhouse.com. Combine live music, homemade bar food, and a few pool tables, and you get this lively roadhouse. Popular among locals, there are dart boards, foosball, and Thursday open-mic nights; regulars join the Mug Club. Food is solidly good, with fresh seafood, juicy burgers, and creamy chowder and dressings made on-site. Open daily, 11 a.m to 1 a.m.

## Farm Stands

**Agricola Farms Country Store,** ME 17 at Clary Hill Road, Union; (207) 785-4018. More store than stand, this shop carries seasonal vegetables, cut flowers, potted perennials, cuts of natural lamb, wool yarn, and tanned sheepskins—all from the diversified 117-acre farm of owners Mark Hedrich and Linda Rose. Local cheese, jams, and Maine-made specialty foods are also for sale. Open May through Dec.

**Appleton Ridge Flower & Vegetable Farm,** 145 Appleton Ridge Rd., Appleton.; (207) 975-6995. Certified-organic vegetables, herbs, perennials, and cut flowers grown by farmer John Fromer, who also lectures about gardening. Open seasonally.

**Beth's Farm Market,** 1986 Western Rd., Warren; (207) 273-3695; www.bethsfarmmarket.com. Fruits and vegetables span the seasons, from spring rhubarb to winter rutabaga, and everything in between. The in-store bakery has expanded to include a variety of baked treats. In early summer, don't miss the heavenly strawberry shortcake. Open May through Dec, seven days a week.

## Farmers' Markets

**Bath Farmers' Market,** Waterfront Park, Commercial Street, Bath; www.bathfarmersmarket.com. Summer market: May through Oct, Sat, 8:30 a.m. to noon. Winter market: Bath United Church of Christ, 150 Congress Ave., Bath, Nov through Apr, first and third Sat, 9 a.m. to noon.

**Belfast Farmers' Market,** Lower Main Street, Belfast; (207) 478-4803. May through Nov, Tues, 3 p.m. to 6 p.m., and Fri, 9 a.m. to 1 p.m.

**Boothbay Farmers' Market,** ME 27, Boothbay Harbor; (207) 737-8834. June through Aug, Thurs, 9 a.m. to noon.

**Brunswick Farmers' Market,** Main Street, Brunswick; (207) 666-3116. May through Nov, Tues and Fri, 8 a.m. to 3 p.m.

**Camden Farmers' Market,** behind the Knox Mill, Camden; (207) 568-3201; www.camdenfarmersmarket .org. May through Oct, Sat, 9 a.m. to noon, and Wed, 3:30 p.m. to 6 p.m.

**Crystal Springs Farmers' Market,** 277 Pleasant Hill Rd., Brunswick; (207) 729-1112; www.crystal springcsa.com. May through Oct, Sat. 8:30 a.m. to 12:30 p.m.

**Damariscotta Area Farmers' Market,** US 1 and Belvedere Road, Damariscotta; (207) 549-5112. June through Aug, Mon, 9 a.m. to noon; May through Oct, Fri, 9 a.m. to noon.

**Deer Isle/Stonington Farmers' Market,** Congregational Church parking lot, Deer Isle; (207) 326-4741. May through Oct, Fri, 10 a.m. to noon.

**Islesboro Cooperative Farmers' Market,** Main Road, Islesboro; (207) 722-3303. June through Sept, Thurs, 9 a.m. to 1 p.m.

**Rockland Farmers' Market,** Public Landing, Rockland; (207) 691-0502. May through Oct, Thurs, 9 a.m. to 1 p.m.

**Woolwich Farmers' Market,** Nequassett Park, Woolwich; (207) 442-7298. May through end of season, Fri, 8:30 a.m. to 1 p.m.

## Lobster Shacks & Fishmongers

**Bayview Lobster Restaurant,** 16 Bayview Landing, Camden; (207) 236-2005; www.bayviewlobster.com. Antique wooden lobster traps line the harbor deck, and faded fishing nets wrap around the banisters at this classic waterfront lobster restaurant. Since outgrowing the shack and moving to a winterized space several years ago, the eatery has begun staying open year-round, offering chowders, fried seafood by the pint, and dinners of fried and baked seafood and, of course, steamed lobster. Lobster and crab rolls are especially light, with mounds of chilled, fresh meat on toasted buns, and butter or mayonnaise served on the side.

**Boothbay Lobster Wharf,** 97 Atlantic Ave., Boothbay Harbor; (207) 633-4900 or (800) 996-1740; www.boothbaylobsterwharf .com. At this working lobster pound and seafood wholesaler, you can watch the workings of the waterfront while enjoying lunch at a picnic table on the deck. The seasonal restaurant is no-frills—order your chowder, fried seafood, or lobster under one striped awning, pick it up from the window under another—but the food is as fresh as can be. The year-round fish market sells the daily catch, as well as mussels, cherrystones, clams, and oysters, and cooked lobster, crab, and shrimp.

**Cooks' Lobster House,** 68 Garrison Cove Rd., Bailey Island; (207) 833-2818; www.cookslobster.com. With splendid views of the water from its well-worn glossy pine booths and outdoor tables made from old cable spools, this landmark lobster house, in business since 1955, offers an iconic Maine experience (so iconic, in fact, that the restaurant was used some years back in a Visa commercial). Menu includes clams dug on the island at low tide, seafood bought on the nearby wharf, and, of course, lobster. Groups are accommodated, and lobster bakes on the beach can be arranged in warmer months. Open year-round.

**Five Islands Lobster Company,** 1447 Five Islands Rd., Georgetown; (207) 371-2990; www.fiveislandslobster.com. Choose your live lobster in the red building (helpfully marked LOBSTERS), and it will be cooked to order, with corn or potatoes, while you listen to the gulls on this picturesque dock. Fried seafood—deemed the best fried clams in Maine by *DownEast* magazine—onion rings and burgers are ordered while you wait from the Love Nest Grill, and the whole meal can be eaten outdoors on the dock's weathered blue tables. The lobster here is said to be extra sweet because it comes from deep, cold waters; it tastes even better because the spot is so beautiful. Bring your own wine or beer. Hours change seasonally; open seven days a week in summer.

**Gilmore's Seafood,** 129 Court St., Bath; (207) 443-5231 or (800) 849-9667; www.gilmoreseafood.com. Serving Bath since it was founded by Lefty Gilmore in 1958, this unpretentious wholesale and retail fish market is a local institution. Selling everything from Maine rock crabs and fresh cusk to finnan haddie and salted, sun-dried pollack, the market is full service—mongers know their fish and are likely to throw in a cooking suggestion with your order. Live lobsters are brought in by the shop's boat, *Rebel,* and can be shipped. The shop also operates a small take-out business of pre-pared seafood.

**Glidden Point Oyster Co.,** 707 River Rd., Edgecomb; (207) 633-0767; www.oysterfarm.com. A child-size wetsuit drips over the banister, and if no one's around, you choose your own oysters and put money into an honor-system cashbox at this family-owned sea farm, whose name comes from a nearby Native American archeological site of heaped oyster shells and artifacts. The oysters themselves are plump and firm, briny yet sweet, and harvested sustainably. The Sea Farm Store stocks oyster essentials like shucking tools, as well as oysters, steamers, and littleneck clams. Open year-round, 8 a.m. to 8 p.m.

**Hawkes' Lobster,** Cundy's Harbor, Harpswell; (207) 721-0472; www.hawkeslobster.com. Selling live lobsters and nautically themed gifts and antiques, this tiny lobster pound sits in a sea-weathered shop above the harbor. It's a family business, and Gary and Sue Hawkes sell lobsters caught by their two sons and two brothers, as well as a bit of local history: Sue's family has lived and fished in the area since the 1700s.

**Morse Lobster Shack,** 18 Bath Rd., Brunswick; (207) 725-2886. Follow the yellow chaser lights to this classic drive-in, pull your car under the flat-roofed canopy and enjoy lobster dinners and rolls, grilled crab 'n' cheese, or fish and chips, at the counter or delivered by car-side service. The menu includes all the favorites, plus a few extras like the fried oyster roll, heaped with crunchy nuggets of sweet meat. Live lobsters, steamers, and fresh haddock can also be picked up to make at home. Open daily, year-round.

**Muscongus Bay Lobster,** Town Lodge Rd., Round Pond; (207) 529-2251; www.mainefreshlobster.com. Lobsters come into the buying station at one end of the pier, and at the other, they go out on plates, steaming scarlet, with a side of corn. The menu at this traditional lobster shack is limited, but what it serves, it serves well. Lobsters, crabs, and clams are steamed, corn is boiled, and oysters are raw. Sides of chips, drawn butter, cocktail sauce, and lemon are available, and picnic-style dining is BYOB. Lobster and crab rolls are made with freshly picked meat and come on a locally baked white or wheat roll. Live lobsters, crabs, and clams are also sold by the pound.

**Sea Basket,** 303 Bath Rd., Wiscasset; (207) 882-6581; www
.seabasket.com. With five types of chowder and fried seafood by
the basket, this classic roadside cafe is just what it seems: tidy
and friendly with good, fresh food. Chowders are full of meat and
creamy without being too heavy, fried seafood is crisp and not
overly greasy, and homemade coleslaw has a refreshing bite. Closed
Tues.

**Shaw's Fish and Lobster Wharf,** 129 ME 32, New Harbor; (207)
677-2200. This beautifully situated lobster pound sits on the water,
with seating in the indoor dining room and on the open deck with
a wonderful view of the working waterfront. Inside, it's no frills—
place your order at one end of the wooden counter and pick it up
at the other—but there's a full bar, a rarity at lobster shacks. On a
beautiful midsummer day, the wait can be daunting, but the food is
fresh and the portions are generous—lobster rolls virtually explode
with meat. Open daily mid-May to mid-October.

**Simpson's Oceanfresh Seafood,** 690 Bath Rd., Wiscasset; (207)
882-9667. Owner Scott Simpson, a former fisherman, sells only the
freshest seafood in this meticulous shop. Lobsters and clams can be
cooked to order if you call before 4:30, but this is the spot for the
catch of the day, delivered with a smile. Open daily, 8 a.m. to 6 p.m.

**Waterman's Beach Lobster,** 343 Waterman's Beach Rd., South
Thomaston; (207) 596-7819 or (207) 594-7518; www.watermans
beachlobster.com. This beautifully situated lobster shack was the

winner of a James Beard Foundation America's Regional Classics Award in 2001, and it's easy to see why: Peacock-blue picnic tables sit above the ocean on an outdoor deck, each table bearing blue mason jars filled with fresh flowers. Steamed lobsters and clams are served from massive enameled pots, seafood rolls are made with freshly picked meat from that day's catch, and luscious rhubarb, berry, and lemon sponge pies are baked from family recipes. The view of Muscle Ridge Channel is filled with working fishing boats, shorebirds, seals, and an ocean breeze. Open Wed through Sun, mid-June to September.

**Young's Lobster Pound,** 4 Mitchell St., Belfast; (207) 338-1160. Enter the barn red building and the clean smell of brine welcomes you. Here, everyone's got one thing on their mind: lobsters. Choose hard-shell or soft-shell (in season) from the large tanks, and staff will weigh them, and, if you'd like, cook them in seawater for no extra charge. Crabs, clams, and mussels are also available by the pound, and they'll steam them, too. Pick up your order at the long stainless steel counter, throw in some chips and hot corn, and you're good to go. With seasonal outside seating at picnic tables by the water's edge.

# Food Happenings

**April**

**Fishermen's Festival,** Boothbay Harbor; (207) 633-6280. This weekend of fishy festivities begins with the Miss Shrimp Pageant and ends with a traditional blessing of the fleet. Events include a codfish relay, lobster-trap hauling, dory bailing, and lobster-crate running. A fish fry and plenty of chowder feed the crowd.

**June**

**Taste of Brunswick,** Town Green, Maine Street, Brunswick; (207) 729-4439; www.tasteofbrunswick.com. Sample the flavors of the best eateries in town while cheering on their waitstaff in the waiter's race at this one-day benefit for the Mid Coast Hunger Prevention Program. More than 20 area restaurants donate their time and talent, and live bluegrass, jazz, and rockabilly music keeps everyone moving.

**August**

**Maine Lobster Festival,** Harbor Park, Rockland; www.mainelobster festival.com. For more than 60 years, this five-day crustacean celebration has drawn crowds to the seaside town of Rockland. Festivities range from childrens' lobster-eating contests to the coronation of the Maine Sea Goddess. Tents display arts and crafts, live music fills the air, and more than 20,000 pounds of lobster are pulled from the sea, cooked on the shore, and served with drawn Cabot butter.

## September

**Annual Pemaquid Oyster Festival,** Schooner Landing, Damariscotta; (207) 380-9912. More than 10,000 oysters are consumed in this free one-day celebration on the working waterfront where Pemaquid oysters are cultivated. Festivities include a shucking contest, oyster poetry, live music, and, of course, oysters by the dozen, still glistening with brine as they're harvested from the Damariscotta River.

## October

**Brunswick Blues and BBQ Bash,** Town Green, Maine Street, Brunswick; (207) 729-4439. The smell of wood smoke curls through the town as local teams bring out their rubs and sauces on this one-day festival. 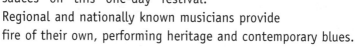 Regional and nationally known musicians provide fire of their own, performing heritage and contemporary blues.

**Damariscotta Pumpkinfest and Regatta,** Damariscotta; www.damariscottapumpkinfest.com. While the edibles are limited to a pumpkin dessert bake-off and a pie-eating contest, this week-long festival is a celebration of the squash. Events include a giant pumpkin weigh-in, pumpkin carving, pumpkin parade, and "chunking," in which pumpkins are shot from cannons into Salt Bay. The regatta consists of brave souls using hollowed giant pumpkins as boats—some with paddles, others with attached motors. (Yes, there are photos on their website.)

**Vinfest,** 367 Youngtown Rd., Lincolnville; (207) 763-4478. Two days of grape stomping, homemade-wine competitions, wine tastings, and delectable catered snacks in the vineyards of host **Cellardoor Winery** (p. 176). Live music accompanies the festivities, and participants can tour the wine cellars and shop at local farm stands. The intrepid can even take hot-air balloon rides over the vines and the lush coastal fields.

## The Maine Ice Cream Trail

**Dorman's Dairy Dream,** 189 New County Rd., Thomaston; (207) 594-4195. Since 1951, this beloved family-owned ice-cream business has been serving homemade ice cream from its shingled shack. Lines can be long, but they're worth it for the goods: Favorites include creamy ginger, rich buttercrunch, and raspberry chocolate chip. Open end of April through beginning of October.

**Island Cow Ice Cream,** Main Street, Stonington. From a sunny yellow stand, with the day's flavors scrawled in marker on a sheet of paper tacked by the window, rich scoops of homemade ice cream are dispensed to the masses. Flavors are classics—rum raisin, straw-berry, maple walnut—and scoops are generous.  The cows in question are part of a small herd, each with a name, and are rumored to listen to Bach in the barn. Open seasonally.

**Riverhouse Ice Cream,** 19 Mechanic St., Camden; (207) 236-0500. This sherbet-colored ice-cream stand rests perched at the end of the Riverhouse Hotel's footbridge, which bursts with flowers and is illuminated by twinkling white lights on summer evenings. The stand sells many flavors of locally made hard- and soft-serve ice cream and treats, as well as frozen yogurt and smoothies. Outdoor tables are a great place to sit with a cone and watch the seagulls. Open seasonally, 11 a.m. to 8 p.m.

**Round Top Ice Cream Stand and Factory,** 526 Main St., Damariscotta; (207) 563-5307. Offering more than 60 flavors, the "super premium" ice cream (15 percent butterfat!) made on-site is served at restaurants throughout the mid-coast. Flavors change throughout the season, but dozens are available each day. Listed on handwritten signs above the counter, they range from rocky road to cherry vanilla to Indian pudding (only offered in the fall). Open early April through Columbus Day.

## Swan's Way Catering

No discussion of the coastal food scene is complete without a mention of **Stacy Glassman** and her impeccable catering company, **Swan's Way.** Like Portland's **Sam Hayward (Fore Street,** see p. 50) and Ogunquit's **Mark Gaier** and **Clark Frasier** (**Arrow's,** see p. 101), Glassman has been creating elegant meals from local, organically grown, sometimes off-beat ingredients for decades. Begun in 1980 as a restaurant in Camden, Swan's Way has evolved into a catering business, and Glassman is renowned for her aesthetic imagination, attention to detail, and ability to transform any space in a matter of hours. Her latest venture, **Dolcelinos,** are gelato sandwiches, an indulgent frozen treat that combines crisp cookies with rich gelato—try the chili-spiked Coco-Aztec and the light ginger-lemon—sold at specialty markets throughout the state. **Swan's Way Catering,** Camden; (207) 763-3996; www.cateringmaine.com

**Thorndike Creamery,** 385 Main St., Rockland; (207) 594-4126. As much a cafe as a creamery, this year-round ice-cream parlor also serves thin-crust pizzas, sandwiches, and homemade soups. The ice cream itself is Gifford's, sold by the friendly, hipster staff in scoops and sweet treats like frappes, floats, and sundaes. Open year-round.

**Bristol Diner,** 1267 Bristol Rd. (ME 130), Bristol Mills; (207) 563-8000; $$. For more than 40 years, this cheerful diner has been at the heart of the village of Bristol Mills. Beneath the Moxie signs and memorabilia that line the turquoise walls, enjoy homemade doughnuts (try a plain dipped in Nutella), biscuits with sausage gravy, or the signature Bristol Cristo: ham, Swiss, and eggs between slices of French toast. Open for breakfast and lunch, Tues through Sun; closed Mon.

**Brunswick Diner,** 101½ Pleasant St., Brunswick; (207) 721-1134; $$. This tiny red train car has been serving diner delights to locals and Bowdoin students since 1946. Yes, it can be cramped at peak hours—weekend breakfasts are especially so—and yes, the food is classic diner fare with a few Maine embellishments (lobster and crab rolls). Still, a seat at the counter with a bottomless cup of coffee and a wisecracking waitress can be just the thing. Open daily, 24-hour service on Fri and Sat.

**Darby's Restaurant and Pub,** 155 High St., Belfast; (207) 338-2339; www.darbysrestaurant.com; $$. First opened in 1865, this landmark pub has been in operation continuously ever since. The tin ceilings and antique bar are original to the building, and they lend the place a quaint, old-fashioned feel. The menu is homemade pub fare with a few surprises: pad thai and a Buddha bowl offer a nice alternative to buffalo wings. Two doors down from the Colonial

Theatre, it's a natural choice for dinner and a movie. Open daily for breakfast, lunch, and dinner.

**Dolphin Marina and Restaurant,** Basin Point Road, Harpswell; (207) 833-6000; www.dolphinmarinaandrestaurant.com; $$. Perched over Pott's Harbor at the tip of Basin Point, this restaurant and marina have offered home-cooked meals, mooring, and spectacular views of Casco Bay to travelers since 1966. Recently, this family-owned business undertook a major redesign of the marina to make it environmentally friendly, and it's been certified a "Clean Marina" by the Maine Marine Trades Association. The food is fresh from the sea, and entrees come with a warm blueberry muffin. Open May 1 to Oct 31.

**Fat Boy Drive In,** 111 Bath Rd., Brunswick; (207) 729-9431; $$. LIGHTS ON FOR SERVICE reads a sign under the white-and-aquamarine awning of this drive-in burger joint. Royal Burger in a Basket, Fat Boy Whopper Burger, fried clams, and the signature BLT with Canadian bacon are on the menu, illuminated at strategic spots between the stalls. The lobster roll is heavy on the mayo but perked up by a dusting of cayenne and paprika, and frappes are almost too thick to use a straw. Enjoy it all from the tray they hook over your window, and revisit a simpler time. Open seasonally.

**Frosty's Donut and Coffee Shop,** 54 Maine St., Brunswick; (207) 729-4258; $. Religious pictures and quotations line the walls, and the smell of sugar hangs in the air at the mom-and-pop doughnut shop, a throwback to another time. For more than four decades, Bob and June Frost have been opening at 3 a.m. to help local fishermen start their days off right, with a cup of coffee and a glazed twist (made from Maine-produced potato flour) or a perfectly chewy doughnut. They're so good, they're usually sold out by 10 a.m. Closed weekends. Really.

**Larson's Lunch Box,** 430 Upper Main St., Damariscotta; (207) 653-5755; www.larsonslunchbox.com; $. Since 1962, this seasonal lunch stand has served up grilled burgers and sandwiches, soups and chowders, and local comfort foods like American chop suey. Crab and lobster rolls are among the most generous, and everything is reasonably priced. Sit at one of the outdoor tables, or take a picnic to Pemaquid Point. Open Apr to Oct, closed Wed. Cash only.

**Red's Eats,** 41 Water St., Wiscasset; (207) 882-6128; $$. On beautiful afternoons in the peak season, lines for this iconic lobster shack get so long that they extend over the Wiscasset Bridge, next to the cars backed up along US 1. It's no wonder: Whole tails and mounds of rosy lobster meat bulge from each buttery roll, zucchini and onion rings are hand battered and fried to a crisp golden brown, and sweet, juicy clams tumble from their baskets. Red's has been a summer institution since 1954—loved by locals and tourists alike. Outdoor seating is shaded and overlooks the water. Open mid-April to mid-October.

**Wasses Hot Dogs,** 2 North Main St., Rockland; (207) 594-7472; $. This classic hot dog stand has been frying franks for decades. Order at the window and peer inside at the dogs, lined up along the griddle, with a mound of chopped onions frying alongside, all waiting to be stuffed in a fluffy bun. For an extra 30 cents, dogs can be dressed with bacon, cheese, chili, or kraut. With outdoor seating and drinks from the cooler. Closed Sun.

## *Learn to Cook*

**Appleton Creamery,** 780 Gurney Town Rd., Appleton; www.appleton creamery.com. Award-winning cheesemaker Caitlin Owen Hunter demonstrates what she's learned in more than 20 years making handcrafted goat's milk cheeses. One- and two-day workshops in her small cheese room are intimate—limited to five participants—and include basic Home Cheese Making, Goat Cheese 101, and more advanced classes that work with mixed milk and specific cheese types, for those who want to take their hobby to the next level. Class schedule is listed on the dairy's website.

**The Hartstone Inn,** 41 Elm St., Camden; (800) 788-4823; www .hartstoneinn.com. Chef-owner Michael Salmon cooked around the country and the world before settling in this charming bed-and-breakfast in the heart of Camden. The inn's dining room is open to the public for luxurious five-course dinners (reservations essential).

In the off-season, from November to May, chef Michael invites you into the kitchen for one-on-one instruction and personalized cooking classes. Details on the inn's website.

## Made or Grown Here

**Bohemian Coffee House and Gelateria,** 4 Railroad Ave., Brunswick; (207) 725-9095; www.bohemiancoffeehouse.com. The house-roasted beans are consistently rated among the mid-coast's best at this cheerful coffeehouse and cafe. Serving daily soup, they also offer homemade gelatos and sorbettos in a variety of flavors that range from light limoncello and watermelon to rich blood orange to piquant chocolate chili. Among locals, they're also known for community mindedness: The store hosts an annual Thanksgiving feast that raises funds for the library. Look for their green lizard logo on everything from aprons ("Caffeinate the cook") to race cars (which they sponsor). Open daily.

**Breakwater Vineyards and Farm,** 35 Ash Point Dr., Owls Head; (207) 594-1721; www .breakwatervineyards.com. Named for the mile-long breakwater that buffers Rockland's harbor, this coastal vineyard and winery donates a portion of their profits to the restoration fund for the town's historic lighthouse. On 32 acres, this relatively new vineyard is growing more than 2,000 grapevines to produce their Rielsing, Chardonnays (oaked and unoaked), and a Pinot Noir. Call ahead to arrange tours and tastings.

**Cellardoor Winery,** 367 Youngstown Rd., Lincolnville; (207) 763-4478; www.mainewine.com. Offering reds, whites, and dessert wines, this established vineyard is beautifully situated in the hills above Camden Harbor. Wines are made in a restored post-and-beam barn, and tastings are held both at the vineyard and at the Villa (at the intersection of Routes 90 and 1 in Rockport), known to locals as the Yellow House, which serves as a second, year-round wine and gift shop. Both locations host events and classes throughout the season; vineyard tours are available by appointment.

**Gelato Fiasco,** 74 Maine St., Brunswick; (207) 607-4002; www .gelatofiasco.com. Serving a changing list of 30 of their more than 600 flavors daily, this beloved *gelateria* uses local milk and premium ingredients to craft flavors that range from Chinese five-spice and chocolate-chipotle to Italian eggnog and Junior Mint (modeled on the movie candy). Sorbettos include lemon, coconut, and seasonal cranberry. The goods are scooped at the flagship store in Brunswick but are available by the pint around the state.

**Mitchell & Savage Maple Farm,** 485 West Burrough Rd., Bowdoin; (207) 353-4090; www.mainemaplekitchen.net. Members of the Mitchell family have worked this small, horse-powered farm for 11 generations and currently tap 700 maple trees to make 125 to 150 gallons of maple syrup each year. Their prize-winning maple candy, maple walnuts (a special treat!), and maple butter are sold, along with their syrup, at mid-coast farmers' markets.

**Morse's Sauerkraut and European Deli,** 3856 Washington Rd., North Waldoboro; (207) 832-5569, www.morsessauerkraut.com. Since Virgil Morse delivered his first barrel of pickled cabbage to the Waldoboro general store in 1910, Morse's kraut has been an area staple each autumn. Now made year-round, this *"krauterie"* and deli offers classic cabbage and all-natural mustard pickles, as well as imported German specialty foods, from spaetzle to sausage. The attached **Kraut Haus** restaurant expands the Teutonic offerings with homemade sauerbraten, schnitzel, borscht, and their signature Reuben sandwich. Open for breakfast (puffed German apple pancakes!), Thurs through Sun, and lunch daily. Closed Wed.

**Oyster Creek Mushroom Co.,** 61 Standpipe Rd., Damariscotta; (207) 563-1076; www.oyster creekmushroom.com. On their small wooded farm, Candice and Dan Heydon have been cultivating exquisite shitake mushrooms for more than two decades. In addition, they are purveyors of locally foraged wild mushrooms, offering both fresh and dried porcini, oyster, chanterelle, black trumpet, hen, chicken of the woods, and morel mushrooms. The Heydons can be found at farmers' markets throughout the region, and they welcome visitors to the farm. Tours by appointment.

**Oyster River Winegrowers,** 929 Oyster River Rd., Warren; (207) 273-2998; www.oysterriverwinegrowers.com. Inspired by the aromatic white wines of Germany, Austria, and Alsace, winemaker Brian Smith is cultivating Vidal Blanc, Traminette, and LaCrescent white grapevines using organic and biodynamic methods to create his estate-grown wines. He's also released a crisp, fragrant Villager White and a Merlot-based Villager Red. Open May to Oct, Fri through Sun, and by appointment.

**Perry's Nut House,** 45 Searsport Ave., Belfast; (207) 338-1630; www.perrysnuthouse.com. Offering "nuts, curiosities and fudge" since I. L. Perry first sold a bumper crop of Georgia pecans in 1927, this Maine institution is packed with sweets and oddities. Python skins and stuffed gorillas have given way to novelty gag gifts, but the funhouse mirror still delights old and young, and the fudge is thick, rich, and sweet. Sample the seasonal flavors, but don't miss the classics: chocolate, peanut butter, and penuche. Open Apr through Dec, hours vary.

**Rock City Coffee Roasters,** 252 Main St., Rockland; (207) 594-5688; and **Rock City Books and Coffee,** 328 Main St., Rockland; (207) 594-4123; www.rockcitycoffee.com. Owners Susanne Ward and Patrick Reilley founded this local landmark as a bookshop and cafe in 1992, and began roasting their own coffee because they couldn't find locally

roasted beans. The small-batch coffee took off, winning national awards and a loyal local following, and the business now includes a wholesale division and two coffee shops (including the original, which continues to sell books). The company supports sustainable and organic farming methods and is committed to building community in the mid-coast and beyond. Open daily.

**Savage Oakes Vineyard and Winery,** 174 Bartlett Hill Rd., Union; (207) 785-5261 or (207) 785-2828; www.savageoakes.com. Part of a diversified farm that includes blueberry barrens and a herd of Belted Galloway cattle, this vineyard and winery has been in production for just a few years but routinely sells out of its most popular vintages. Owner-vintners Elmer and Holly Savage began with a sweet blueberry dessert wine, and offerings have expanded to include the only port made from Maine-grown grapes, as well as a variety of dry reds and whites. Open by appointment.

**State of Maine Cheese Company,** 461 Commercial St. (US 1), Rockport; (207) 236-8895 or (800) 762-8895; www.cheese-me.com. Making fine cheeses from local cow's milk for almost 30 years, this cheese company and shop offers several cheddars, plain and flavored Jack, Welsh Caerphilly, Colby, and more. Cheeses are available at groceries throughout the state and at the retail store in Rockport. Open daily.

**Sweetgrass Farm Winery and Distillery,** 347 Carroll Rd., Union; (207) 785-3024; www.sweetgrasswinery.com. Award-winning wines and spirits are made on this working farm, where sheep graze the pastures and visitors are invited to explore trails that overlook the Medomak River valley. Informal daily tastings are held of grape and fruit wines, ports, and a variety of spirits that include smooth Back River Gin, rich Three Crow Rum, and Maple Smash Liqueur. Don't miss handcrafted bitters—blueberry and cranberry add a dash of Maine to any cocktail. Open daily, May to Dec.

## Restaurants

**Amalfi,** 421 Main St., Rockland; (207) 596-0012; www.amalfion thewater.com; $$$. The menu hints at the Mediterranean while drawing out the flavors of local cold-water seafood at this upscale waterfront bistro. Diners have views of the water on the outdoor patio; inside, the kitchen is open and the granite bar curls around a bank of shaved ice mounded with oysters and clams. Highlights include rich paella, mussels several ways, and an Asian-infused scallop seviche with citrus, rice wine, and black sesame seeds. The wine list is extensive, and a new on-site microbrewery, **Shag Rock Brewing Company,** offers beer by the pint. Open daily for lunch and dinner, closed Sun.

**Anchor Inn,** Anchor Inn Road, Round Pond; (207) 529-5584; www .anchorinnrestaurant.com; $$$. See **Damariscotta River Grill** listing, p. 185.

**Bell the Cat,** 1 Belmont Ave., Suite E, Belfast; (207) 338-2084; $$. This lunch stop is famed throughout the region for its thick, inventive sandwiches served on Borealis breads (see p. 14) and packed with fresh vegetables and flavorful meats and cheeses. Ranging from basic, perfectly done egg salad to Off Main Street—olive cream cheese, avocado, tomato, and melted provolone on a toasted bagel—the offerings are tasty and satisfying. Soups change daily and are available in three sizes; salads are abundant and come with homemade croutons. If you're feeling decadent, try a shake. Open daily.

**Boynton-McKay Food Company,** 30 Main St., Camden; (207) 236-2465; www.boynton-mckay.com; $$. In a historic 1893 apothecary shop whose remedies and tinctures still line the walls, this breakfast and lunch cafe is a local favorite, and reproductions of the lion lithograph that hangs above the soda fountain are so popular that they're now sold at the restaurant ($12). Serving breakfast all day and soups, sandwiches, and a changing "grab and go" take-out menu, specialties include famed fluffy buttermilk pancakes and homemade granola, which is sold by the bowl and the pound. Open daily, but closed Mon in the off-season.

**Brevetto Kitchen and Wine Bar,** 43 Mechanic St., Camden; (207) 230-0111; www.brevettokitchen.com; $$. This modern Italian bistro and wine bar is filled with antique gadgetry—the name means "patent," and the decor is full of inventions from another era. Far from being cluttered, the menu is simple and elegant, incorporating Spanish and French influences as well as Italian, and offering a range of tapas, pastas, and main courses like bouillabaisse, steak with rosemary *frites,* and pan-seared haddock on a bed of risotto. With more than 20 wines by the glass and a full bar. Open nightly, year-round.

**The Brown Bag,** 606 Main St., Rockland; (207) 596-6372; www .thebrownbagrockland.com; $$. Serving breakfast, lunch, and a variety of baked goods, this Rockland institution is known for its sandwiches, from the Brown Bag Pocket served at breakfast (whole wheat pita stuffed with scrambled eggs and cheese) to the lunch-time Gobbler (turkey, stuffing, and cranberry sauce). All are served on freshly baked bread, and turkey for sandwiches is roasted daily. Round out the meal with a peanut butter cookie or a whoopie pie, and you're ready to picnic. Open for breakfast and lunch, Mon through Sat.

**The Cabin Restaurant,** 552 Washington St., Bath; (207) 443-6224; www.cabinpizza.com; $$. Beneath its sea-weathered sign, this casual restaurant is styled like the belly of a ship, with warm wood paneling on the ceiling and booths tucked snuggly against the walls. It's known for pizza—a crust that's at once crisp and chewy, generous handfuls of cheese, and toppings that range from standards like sausage and Canadian bacon, to calamari, shrimp, and clams.

Sandwiches and pasta are also available, but pizza's the main attraction. Serving a range of local beers by the bottle and on tap, and a few wines by the glass and carafe. Open daily for lunch and dinner.

**Cafe Miranda,** 15 Oak St., Rockland; (207) 594-2034; www .cafemiranda.com; $$$. Named for chef-owner Kerry Altiero's family dog, this relaxed restaurant bills itself as "Rockland's only multicultural restaurant." With a commitment to sustainability that goes a step beyond—the chef even grows and harvests the wood for the oven—the menu incorporates locally produced ingredients in dishes that range from chicken livers with bacon to Thai calamari. Friendly and low key, children are welcome. Open nightly for dinner.

**Chase's Daily,** 96 Main St., Belfast; (207) 338-0555; $$. To many, this cozy vegetarian restaurant, bakery, and farm stand represents perfection. Run by the entire Chase family—Addison and Penny and their daughters Meghan and Phoebe—the restaurant offers homey dishes created from the vegetables grown on their nearby farm in Freedom. Surplus veggies are sold in the back room and are piled beautifully in old wooden crates and galvanized tin buckets, a presentation that nicely picks up the old wood and exposed brick of the building. Fresh-cut flowers (also available for sale in the back) grace the tables, and the smells of the daily specials—which range from pizza to galette to fried rice—perfume the space. Breads, pies, and baked treats fill the counter, and virtually fly out the door. Open for breakfast, lunch, and weekend dinners, closed Mon. Call ahead for hours.

**Clementine Restaurant,** 44 Maine St., Brunswick; (207) 721-9800; www.clementinemaine.com; $$$. Husband and wife Dana and Nancy Robicheaw bring an elegantly simple aesthetic to the menu and atmosphere of this lovely restaurant. Chef Dana's menu changes seasonally, but often includes French classics like country pork pâté with pistachios, Dijon cream, and cornichons, and confit leg of chicken with seasonal vegetables and a nutty frisée salad. The wine list is gratifyingly extensive (Nancy trained under master sommelier Roger Dagorn at New York's Chanterelle Restaurant), and the cocktails are first rate. Open for dinner Tues through Sat.

**Coastal Maine Botanical Gardens' Kitchen Garden Cafe,** 132 Botanical Garden Dr., Boothbay; www.mainegardens.org; $$. With a curving wall of windows that overlooks the splendid botanical gardens, the ambience at this cafe is restful and calming. The food, made from vegetables, herbs, and edible flowers harvested from the Burpee Kitchen Garden, is fresh and light, with a regularly changing menu. A seasonal dinner series features some of Maine's best chefs, and lunch and snacks are served daily. Open May through mid-October.

**Conte's 1894 Restaurant,** 148 South Main St., Rockland; $$$. There's no phone or posted menu at this local landmark, nearly hidden beneath piled nets and dangling lobster crates, but to the hardy souls who duck in, there are treasures to be had. Offering seafood like no other in the mid-coast, what comes out of the kitchen is fresh, fragrant, and nearly spills from the simple plates: garlicky lobster and shrimp on a bed of fresh linguine, sausage and whole lobster napped with spicy tomato sauce. NO FRY, NO CARDS, NO KETCHUP reads a sign by the door. Open for dinner year-round, in winter the dining room is heated by a single pot-bellied stove, so plan to bundle up. Cash only.

**The Cupboard Cafe,** 137 Huddle Rd., New Harbor; (207) 677-3911; www.thecupboardcafe.com; $$. Housed in a log cabin, this comfortable cafe serves breakfast and lunch year-round, offering fresh bread, stacked sandwiches, and steaming bowls of haddock chowder. But it's "the buns" that bring in the masses: gooey pecan buns, buttery and dripping with caramel, and fluffy cinnamon buns, generously glazed with sweet icing. These sweet treats are so popular that they can now be ordered online and by phone, but nothing beats them warm from the oven. Open for breakfast and lunch, Tues through Sat, and for breakfast on Sun.

**Damariscotta River Grill,** 155 Main St., Damariscotta; (207) 563-2992; www.damariscottarivergrill.com; $$$; and **Anchor Inn,** Anchor Inn Road, Round Pond; (207) 529-5584; www.anchorinn restaurant.com; $$$. At the year-round Damariscotta River Grill, the husband-and-wife team of chef Rick Hirsch and Jean Kerrigan serve upscale comfort food, from Steak & Cakes—grilled rib eye paired with lobster cakes—to lobster strudel, a combination of fresh picked lobster meat and mascarpone wrapped in phyllo. Sunday brunch is a treat—try the quinoa cakes Benedict or the bananas Foster pancakes, flambéed at the table. Sister restaurant, the seasonal Anchor Inn, has a more casual menu of traditional broiled and baked seafood, with a few twists, like the yellowfin tuna with curried coconut-peanut sauce. At both restaurants, the food is fresh and the service is welcoming. Damariscotta River Grill: open daily for lunch, dinner, and Sunday brunch. Anchor Inn: open seasonally for lunch and dinner.

**The Edge Restaurant at the Inn at Ocean's Edge,** 24 Stonecoast Rd., Lincolnville; (207) 236-4430; www.diningattheedge.com; $$$$. Chef Bryan Dame's menu is full of surprises at this gracious restaurant with views of Penobscot Bay. The menu changes daily to reflect what's seasonally available, but imaginative offerings range from Day Boat Halibut with lobster brandade, black trumpet mushrooms, and candied olives, to lemon and leek risotto with bitter chocolate. The bar at the adjacent **Tantalus Lounge** shares the kitchen and turns out perfect snack foods like simple radishes with sea salt and anchovy butter, and a heavenly lobster roll with tarragon and bacon mayonnaise. Open nightly for dinner, May to Oct.

**El Camino,** 15 Cushing St., Brunswick; (207) 725-8228; www .elcaminomaine.com; $$. On a quiet side street near the river, this windowless cream-brick building gives little clue to the vibrancy inside, save a red lantern hanging above the entrance. Indoors, the walls are vivid pumpkin and decorated with shiny hubcaps and bright Mexican posters, and banquettes are red vinyl. The kitsch ends with the decor—the menu is Mexican with a local twist, starting with homemade flour tortilla chips, the smoky roasted-tomato house salsa, and spicy guacamole, and offering daily specials and quesadillas, chile rellenos, and soft tacos filled with seasonal vegetables and a choice of steak, chicken, tiny Maine shrimp, haddock, or the popular chorizo and potato. House limeade has a splash of coconut milk, and cocktails—especially the cleverly named riffs on margaritas—are divine. Open for dinner, Tues through Sat.

**Francine,** 55 Chestnut St., Camden; (207) 230-0083; www.francine bistro.com; $$$. Acclaimed chef Brian Hill shuns fads and gimmickry, instead serving classic French brasserie food that distinguishes the menu at this tasteful bistro. The menu changes daily, but regular items include perfectly done steak frites, with garlic fries to sop up the rosy juices, and dry-roasted mussels that are concentrated jewels topped with a little butter and a grind of sea salt. Reservations recommended. Open for dinner, Tues through Sat.

**Frontier Cafe + Cinema + Gallery,** 14 Maine St., Mill 3, Fort Andross, Brunswick; (207) 725-5222; www.explorefrontier.com; $$. This innovative cafe, cinema, and gallery space in the rehabilitated Fort Andross mill serves a changing menu of soups, sandwiches, salads, and "mezeplates," made from locally sourced ingredients.

The larger "marketplates" are arranged around regional flavors: The French plate combines ham, Brie, and house-made pâté with classic accompaniments, while the Middle Eastern brings together feta, dolmas, olives, dates, hummus, and pita. Meals and snacks can be eaten in the cafe or brought into the cinema, which shows independent and globally minded films, as well as hosting live events, from folk music to belly dancing to book signings. Open for breakfast, lunch, and dinner daily, closed Sun.

**Henry and Marty Restaurant,** 61 Maine St., Brunswick; (207) 721-9141; www.henryandmarty.com; $$$. From its menu to its decor, this cheerful restaurant finds the balance between playfulness and restraint. While the butter-yellow walls are covered with funky artwork, tables in the tastefully appointed dining room are covered in white linens. On the seasonally changing menu, pumpkin ravioli sit beside Korean tacos, tastier than they sound: a combination of pulled beef, house-made kimchee, sour cream, herbs, and Ko Chu Chung sauce on grilled corn tortillas. Ingredients are sourced locally, and waitstaff will cheerfully rattle off the origins of your meal. With many vegetarian, vegan, and gluten-free offerings. Open for dinner, Tues through Sun.

**Home Kitchen Cafe,** 650 Main St., Rockland; (207) 596-2449; www.homekitchencafe.com; $$. Inside its homey green-clapboard exterior, the colors are as warm as the Southwest-leaning menu at this comfortable cafe. Breakfast—including sticky buns and baked goods made at the **Cupboard Cafe** (see p. 185) by chef-owner

James Hatch's dad—is served all day, and offerings range from the house-specialty huevos rancheros (eggs poached in salsa on handmade corn tortillas) to seven variations on eggs Benedict, served on toast points or polenta. Sandwiches and half-pound burgers are on the lunch menu, as are wonderful fish tacos. Open daily for breakfast and lunch.

**In Good Company,** 415 Main St., Rockland; (207) 593-9110; www.ingoodcompany.com; $$$. Housed in an old bank—the vault now serves as wine cellar—this restaurant and wine bar is renowned for its warm atmosphere, extensive wine list, and changing menu. Chef-owner Melody Wolfertz works alone in the open kitchen, creating each plate to order and smoothly turning them over to her enthusiastic waitstaff. Desserts are a treat (try the crème brûlée), and the kitchen is one of few in town that stays open late. Open Tues through Sun for dinner and small plates.

***J. & E. Riggin* Schooner,** docked in Rockland; (800) 869-0604; www.mainewindjammer.com; $$$$. You have to book a trip on this historic schooner to enjoy a meal on board, but if you do, your adventure will be culinary as well as seafaring. Chef and co-captain Annie Mahle cooks on a cast-iron woodstove in the belly of the ship, turning out fresh bread and baked goods, hearty breakfasts, and improbably intricate meals, from earthy turkey confit with root vegetables to curried lamb and lentil stew. Trips booked from May to October.

**Lily Bistro,** 421 Main St., Rockland; (207) 594-4141; www.lily bistromaine.com; $$$. Chefs Lynette Mosher and Robert Krajewski have been collaborating since they first met in the culinary program at Johnson & Wales University, and now they share the kitchen in this intimate country French restaurant, where the changing menu is written on a strip of chalkboard that wraps around the bar. The menu is small, but everything is homemade, from the sourdough bread leavened with a 50-year-old starter that Krajewski tends, to the venison sausage, pork *rillettes,* and rustic country pâté that round the charcuterie offerings. Sustainably harvested seafood includes offbeat fish like fluke, and a range of small plates includes a daily quiche, potato gratin, and soup du jour. Open for dinner Thurs through Mon.

**Long Grain,** 31 Elm St., Camden; (207) 236-9001; $. Serving "Asian home cooked & street foods," this tiny restaurant offers a changing list of Japanese, Korean, Thai, and Vietnamese dishes. Steamed pork buns are tender and meaty, and the pad thai is generally considered to be the best north of Portland. The restaurant is casual, but since seating is limited, reservations are recommended. With a full bar.

**Natalie's at Camden Harbour Inn,** 83 Bayview St., Camden; (207) 236-4200 or (800) 236-4266; www.nataliesrestaurant.com; $$$$. The vivid red-and-white palette of the dining room and bar at this elegant hotel gives the restaurant a brasserie feel. Sit in stuffed chairs beneath fringed cherry-red lamps, and gaze out over the harbor and distant mountains while sipping a crisp cocktail or a glass from their deep list of wines. The menu starts with oysters and an anise-scented lobster bisque, spiked with tarragon and Pernod. Artfully composed entrees include the ubiquitous lobster—here enlivened with curry—as well as pasture-raised meats and local seafood. Open for dinner nightly.

**No. 10 Water at the Captain Daniel Stone Inn,** 10 Water St., Brunswick; (207) 373-1824; www.captaindanielstone.com; $$$. The expansive dining room of this elegantly appointed inn centers on the massive fireplace around which rustic tables are arranged. Like the atmosphere, chef Troy Mains's menu is both stylish and cozy: Lobster hash, portabella mushroom fries with truffle aioli, and braised chicken with olives and herbs are menu highlights. For dessert, don't miss the maple crème brûlée. Open for dinner Tues to Sat, and for Sunday brunch.

**Paolina's Way,** 10 Bayview Landing, Camden; (207) 230-0555; www.paolinasway.com; $$. Named for chef-owner Christina Sidoti's beloved grandmother, this Italian trattoria keeps the original

Paolina's culinary spirit alive. Organic produce is grown at the restaurant's own Well Fed Farm in nearby Searsport, and each afternoon the chef drives out to walk through the fields and choose from glossy chard, scarlet carrots, and violet heirloom tomatoes for the evening's menu. Offerings include pastas, meat and vegetable lasagnas, and wood-fired pizzas—Maine shrimp is a surprising delight. For dessert, pair your espresso with homemade tiramisu or a crisp and creamy cannoli. Call ahead for gluten-free pizzas and pasta. Open year-round, though hours change seasonally.

**Pemaquid Point Restaurant at the Bradley Inn,** 3063 Bristol Rd., New Harbor; (207) 677-3749; www.bradleyinn.com; $$$$. The elegant dining room at this charming inn has received national acclaim for its warm atmosphere and finely prepared meals. Open to the public as well as guests, the luxurious menu features local Pemaquid oysters (the inn is at the tip of the Pemaquid peninsula), house-cured charcuterie, locally foraged mushrooms, and pasture-raised meats. Pairings are inventive—shaved *foie gras* is served with wild arugula and fig syrup, roasted duck leg is complemented by minted peas and poached rhubarb—and plates are composed with a delicate hand. The more casual **Chartroom Tavern** has a full bar and is frequented by hotel guests, restaurant patrons, and locals. Reservations recommended.

**Primo Restaurant,** 2 South Main St., Rockland; (207) 596-0770; www.primorestaurant.com; $$$$. James Beard Award–winning chef Melissa Kelly cooked at restaurants around the world before settling in coastal Maine and founding this beautiful restaurant with partner and baker Price Kushner. In a restored Victorian home at the top of a hill, this was one of the first farm-to-table restaurants in the region, crafting a Mediterranean-infused menu from vegetables and herbs grown in their gardens, and meat from heritage Tamworth pigs who are fattened on table scraps. Chef Kelly studied with Alice Waters at Chez Panisse, and her tenure there is reflected in her style, at once elegant and simple, encouraging the flavor of each ingredient to come through. Dinner is served in three seasons, from early spring until the end of December. Reservations are essential.

**Richard's Restaurant,** 115 Maine St., Brunswick; (207) 729-9673; www.richardsgermanamericancuisine.com; $$. Steins line the paneled walls, and the menu is heavy with sausage, potatoes, and kraut at this local mainstay. Ask about the *hausgemachtes* (house specialties) or choose from *weinbergschnecken*—snails in garlic butter—strudel, and a range of schnitzels, and wash it down with a glass of Reisling or Gewüstraminer, or a stein of Hefeweizen. Open daily for lunch and dinner, closed Sun.

**Robinhood Free Meetinghouse,** 210 Robinhood Rd., Georgetown; (207) 371-2188; www.robinhood-meetinghouse.com; $$$$. High-backed pews remain in this carefully restored 1855 church, but the sumptuous menu is anything but austere. Known for the flaky cream-cheese biscuits that come by the basket to each table (and which are now available for order), this elegant restaurant serves a changing menu of fine food that's complex and surprising. Chef Michael Gagne's creations range from Citrus Mint Côtelettes of Lamb with roasted sweet potatoes, Swiss chard, mint sherry sauce, and curry reduction, to sautéed shrimp with smoked tomato cream, crisp andouille sausage, wild mushrooms, basil, and angel hair pasta. Desserts are varied, but the house-made honey ice cream is a must. Open nightly for dinner in the summer season, and Thurs through Sat from mid-October through mid-May.

**Shepherd's Pie,** Main Street, Rockport; (207) 236-8500; $$. The dark wood bar, abundant wild flowers, and flickering votive candles of this casual pub-style restaurant are a world away from the coast's traditional seafood restaurants. Here, chef Brian Hill (also of Camden's **Francine,** see p. 187) has crafted a menu of upscale comfort foods: tacos teaming with fried clams, pork belly sand-wiches that melt on the tongue, and, of course, a hearty shepherd's pie. Bartenders are at the top of their game, turning out inventive cocktails and cheerful conversation, no matter how crowded the bar. Open nightly for dinner and drinks.

**Solo Bistro,** 128 Front St., Bath; (207) 443-3373, www.solobistro .com; $$$. The contemporary design of this upscale eatery offers a counterpoint to its location in historic downtown Bath, and it's a marriage that's reflected in the menu. Classic offerings are given modern touches: Scallops are crusted with fennel and semolina, spice-rubbed steak is glazed with aged tamari. Wines are carefully chosen by owner Will Neilson, and desserts, made in-house, include milk chocolate mousse and tangy cheesecake. Open for dinner, Mon through Sat.

**Squire Tarbox Inn,** 1181 Main Rd., Westport Island; (207) 882-7693; www.squiretarboxinn.com; $$$$. Chef and innkeeper Mario De Pietro brings his Swiss background and classical training to this quaint, historic island inn. Formerly a pastry chef at New York's Four Seasons and general manager of all the restaurants in Rockefeller Center (among other posts), chef De Pietro's culinary style is elegant, and dinner offerings range from tender rack of lamb with fresh mint sauce to slow-roasted duckling with wild rice and red cabbage. Vegetables come from the inn's own organic farm, worked by the owners' son Kyle. The intimate restaurant retains the warm wood and low-ceilinged charm of the colonial buildings. In the off-season, cooking classes and retreats are offered, and Thursday nights bring Swiss fondue and raclette. Reservations essential.

**Suzuki's Sushi Bar,** 419 Main St., Rockland; (207) 596-7447; www.suzukisushi.com; $$. The calm that radiates through this stylish sushi restaurant is mirrored by the menu: fresh seafood, brought in hours before and arranged with precision on each plate. Chef-owner Keiko Suzuki Steinberger commands the kitchen, which is entirely staffed by women and is considered by many to turn out the best sushi in the region. Dishes are made with predominately local ingredients—including unusual bycatch like mini octopus and whelk that she buys off fishermen on her way to work—and the kitchen has neither a grill nor a fryer, preferring to poach, steam, or serve raw. Open for dinner Tues through Sat.

## Specialty Stores & Markets

**Bath Natural Market,** 36 Centre St., Bath; (207) 442-8012; www .bathnaturalmarket.com. This classic natural foods market, behind a brick storefront in historic downtown, offers fresh organic produce, breads, spices, bulk grains, local dairy products, and more. Specialties include a wide selection of organic wines and dried wild mushrooms from **Oyster Creek Mushroom farm** in nearby Damariscotta (see p. 177). Open daily.

**Belfast Co-Op,** 123 High St., Belfast; (207) 338-2532; http:// belfast.coop. Maine's oldest and largest food co-op, with more than 3,000 member-owners, has grown and expanded many times since it opened its storefront in 1976. Open to both members and non-members, the co-op offers a market of natural foods and local and organic groceries (try the treats by local wholesale bakery, Let Them Eat Cake), a cafe, and resources for healthy living. Monthly wine tastings are held in the market, as are a series of cooking classes that emphasize nutritious eating. Open daily.

**Black Sheep Wine Shop,** 105 Mountain Rd., Harpswell; (207) 725-9284; www.blacksheepwine.com. Owners Jen and John VerPlanck consider themselves "professional wine scouts" and are always on the lookout for great-tasting wines to offer customers in their tiny seaside shop. More than 600 bottles line the walls, from hard-to-find small production wines and Maine fruit wines to organic and biodynamic offerings. Specialty beers and fine chocolates are available, and the VerPlancks share their extensive knowledge in monthly tastings and wine appreciation classes. Open year-round, closed Sun.

---

## NEED A COFFEE FIX?

They may not be roasting their own beans, but these independent coffee shops make a mean cuppa joe.

**Cafe Crème,** 56 Front St., Bath; (207) 443-6454

**Little Dog Coffee Shop,** 87 Maine St., Brunswick; (207) 721-9500, www.littledog coffee.com

**North Cottage Coffee,** 77 Main St., Damariscotta; (207) 563-7779; www.northcottagecoffee.com

**Maine Coast Book Shop and Cafe,** 158 Main St., Damariscotta; (207) 563-3370; www.mainecoastbookshop.com

---

**Camden Bagel Cafe,** 25 Mechanic St., #11, Camden; (207) 236-2661; www.camdenbagelcafe.com. Paneled with warm wood and flooded with natural light, this spacious cafe bakes chewy, hand-stretched and hand-boiled bagels and buttery muffins several times each day. Cream cheese is made on-site—try the horseradish bacon—and sandwiches and soups are offered at lunchtime. The malty smell of bagels and the ever-smiling staff encourage lingering over coffee and the paper. Look for the bagel mounted over the awning and you'll know you're there. Open daily for breakfast and lunch.

**Camden Deli,** 37 Main St., Camden; (207) 236-8343; www.camden deli.com. Serving breakfast, lunch, and light dinner year-round, this inviting cafe offers more than 40 specialty sandwiches to eat in or out, all served with chips and a pickle. Breakfast ranges from burritos to omelets, and a coffee bar makes espresso drinks all day. If you eat there, sit on the lovely upstairs deck, overlooking the harbor falls and the working waterfront. Now serving beer and wine. Open daily.

**Farmers Fare,** ME 90 and Cross Street, Rockport; (207) 236-3273; www.farmersfare.com. This cavernous year-round indoor farm market, butcher shop, bakery, and cafe was built to mirror the size and shape of a barn, and its exposed hemlock and pine woodwork is sturdy and welcoming. Local produce is displayed in woven baskets with its farm of origin clearly marked, and Maine-made goods are stacked beautifully on tables in the open space. At the cafe, breakfast sandwiches, lunches, deli items, and baked goods are available to eat at tables, on the wraparound porch, or to take out. Open year-round, closed Sun.

**Five Islands Farm,** 1375 Five Islands Rd., Georgetown; (207) 371-9383; www.fiveislandsfarm.com. Inside the weathered clapboard of this tiny shop is a treasure trove of artisanal cheeses, fine wines, pasture-raised meats and eggs, specialty foods, and more. Selling everything from locally roasted Wicked Joe Coffee to raw Glidden Point oysters (see **Glidden Point Oyster Co.** on p. 162), this market has provisions for every adventure. Owner Heidi Klingelhofer seeks the best Maine has to offer and is committed to stocking local goods. Products are beautifully displayed, and in summer and spring, visitors are greeted by tables of potted annuals, perennials, and garden ornaments. Open May to late December.

**French and Brawn Marketplace,** 1 Elm St., Camden; (207) 236-3361; www.frenchandbrawn.com. This friendly, full-service corner grocery offers custom-butchered meats, a full deli counter, fresh baked goods, prepared entrees, produce, beers and wines, and live and cooked lobsters. Staff is exceptionally helpful, and delivery is available. Open daily.

**L. P. Bisson and Sons Meat Market & Farm,** 112 Meadow Rd., Topsham; (207) 725-7215. Selling cuts of beef and veal and homemade sausage from their own cattle, and hormone- and antibiotic-free pasture-raised pork and chicken from local farms, this family business has been a local landmark and carnivore's paradise for three generations. Hand-stuffed kielbasa, bacon, ham, and pork chops are smoked on-site, and meat pies and pork head cheese are also made at the shop. Closed Sun.

**The Market Basket,** 223 Commercial St., Rockport; (207) 236-4371; www.marketbasketrockportme.blogspot.com. This European-style specialty-foods market sells imported olive oils, artisanal cheeses, fine chocolates, and more. A changing list of fresh breads is made daily, sandwiches and prepared entrees are available from well-stocked cases, and staff can help you choose from a large array of wines and beers. Gorgeous wedding cakes and beautiful gift baskets are a specialty, as are homey chocolate-dipped peanut butter balls. Open daily.

**Megunticook Market,** 2 Gould St., Camden; (207) 236-3537; www.megunticookmarket.com. For more than 100 years, this country market has been known for thick steaks, ample roasts, and a variety of custom-cut meats. Its current owner, Lani Temple, has expanded the offerings to include local and imported cheeses, an impressive wine section, fresh-caught seafood, organic produce, locally roasted coffee, and scratch baked pastries and pies. Sandwiches, pizza by the slice, and prepared foods are sold in the deli, along with Boar's Head sliced meats and cheeses. Open daily.

**Morning Glory Natural Foods,** 60 Maine St., Brunswick; (207) 729-0546. Since 1981, this natural foods store has offered local and organic produce, products, and more. Under the awnings of its corner storefront, the market is filled with fresh fruits and vegetables, a wide selection of organic wines, and Maine-made products from raw honey and milk to lacto-fermented kimchee and locally made tempeh. A large selection of body products and gifts perfume the store with calming scents of essential oils. Open daily.

**North Creek Farm,** 24 Sebasco Rd., Phippsburg; (207) 389-1341; www.northcreekfarm.org. This gorgeous saltwater farm is at its peak in the midsummer, when the display gardens are lush and the roses are in bloom. An on-site plant nursery specializes in roses—owner Suzy Verrier has written two books on the subject—and the store offers everything from the farm's fresh eggs and organic produce to fair-traded imports, wines and beers, natural meats, and exotic cooking ingredients. The cafe serves lunch to be eaten indoors or taken on a picnic around the grounds. Open daily, year-round.

**Now You're Cooking,** 49 Front St., Bath; (207) 443-1402; www.acooksemporium.com. The encyclopedic collection of cookware in this rambling store—it occupies the first floor of an entire city block—ranges from copper pots to citrus zesters to cleaning supplies and more. Housewares, cookbooks, and assorted gadgetry are stacked to the ceiling, and owners Michael and Betsy Fear are knowledgeable about every item—they test new products, conduct regular demonstrations and cooking classes, and hold monthly guided tastings of their extensive inventory of wines and beers. Open daily.

**Owls Head General Store,** 2 South Shore Rd., Owls Head; (207) 596-6038. With bright buoys lining the outer walls and fresh baked goods on the counter, this trim, shingled store offers a little bit of everything, from batteries to decongestant to bottles of wine and beer. It's the lunch counter, however, that brings people in: The hamburgers are legendary. Six ounces of beef, cooked how you like it, topped with lettuce and tomatoes on a toasted bun, served with a pickle spear and a mound of chips. Also on the menu are lobster rolls, chowder, home-made baked beans, a daily special, and fresh dessert—try the Grapenut custard or a slice of blueberry pie. Open year-round, closed Sun.

**Provisions Wine and Cheese,** 22 Pleasant St., Brunswick; (207) 729-9288; www.provisionsmaine.com. Providing "wines for every palate and pocketbook" and cheeses for all occasions is the mission of this specialty market, which also sells sandwiches, prepared entrees, sweet treats, and breads from Portland's **Standard Baking**

**Co.** (see p. 17). With hundreds of bottles and twice-monthly tastings, the wine section is vast but demystified by enthusiastic staff. The cheeses range from local to imported, mild to assertive. Closed Sun.

**RAYR Wine Shop,** 67 Pascal Ave., Rockport; (207) 230-7009; www.rayrwine.com. Housed in a charming Victorian storefront, this wine shop and espresso bar carries more than 500 vintages, including many rare bottles and at least 250 varieties available for less than $25. In the espresso bar, local artists display their works, drinks are made with **Rock City Coffee** (See **Rock City Coffee Roasters** on p. 178), and organic teas from **Vermont Tea Company** are brewed up. With free Wi-Fi. Open Tues through Sat.

**Rising Tide Community Market,** 323 Main St., Damariscotta; (207) 563-5556; www.risingtide.coop. Though it's recently moved to a spacious new building, this community market has retained its co-op vibe. The shelves are stocked with an abundance of natural foods—local breads, juices, wines, vitamins, bulk grains, organic produce, and more—but there's a pleasing, stripped-down quality to the place. Owned cooperatively, the store is open to the public and has a deli as well as a grocery and small gift section. Open daily.

**Treats,** 80 Main St., Wiscasset; (207) 882-6192; www.treatsofmaine .com. The pressed-tin ceiling, wide-plank country floors, and white-washed brick and wood interior are as appealing as the food in this elegant specialty foods shop. Offering wines, cheeses—including a large variety of British cheese from Neals' Dairy Yard—and a few well-chosen pantry items, as well as fresh bread, warm home-baked fruit pies, and locally roasted coffee from Bohemian Coffee Roaster in nearby Bowdoinham. Open daily.

**The Well Tempered Kitchen,** 122 Atlantic Hwy., Waldoboro; (207) 563-5762; and 78 Main St., Wiscasset; (207) 882-4142; www .welltemperedkitchen.com. The ceilings are high and the layout uncluttered at this pair of stores selling high-end cookware. Cooking essentials are beautifully displayed—arranged by color and size as well as function—and the emphasis is on the basics, from sturdy metal colanders to hand-turned wooden salad bowls. The Waldoboro location, first opened in 1994, is in a converted horse barn, while the new location shares a building with **Treats** (p. 203). Closed Sun.

**The Wine Seller,** 15 Tillson Ave., Rockland; (207) 594-2621; www.thewineseller.biz. Offering hundreds of bottles at every price point, this airy wine shop is known for its wide selection and knowledgeable staff who helps patrons choose the perfect bottle. Regular guided tastings offer tips about pairings, and location near the  harbor makes it a convenient stop if you're traveling up the coast by boat. Open daily.

**Clark's Cove Farm and Inn,** 107 Ridge Rd., Walpole; (207) 563-8704; www.clarkscovefarm.com. Stay at this beautifully manicured, 54-acre farm and inn during apple season, and you can pick your own from 27 varieties of heirloom fruit. Apples from August through late October; pears, plums, and raspberries, September through October. Open daily.

**County Fair Farm,** 434 Augusta Rd. (ME 32), Jefferson; (207) 549-3536. Apples, August through October; pumpkins, October. Open daily.

**Hardy Farms Apple Orchard,** 106 Church St., Hope; (207) 763-3262; www.hardyfarms.com. Apples, pumpkins, and winter squash, mid-September to late October. Open Wed through Sun.

**Hope Orchards,** 434 Camden Rd., Hope; (207) 763-2824; www .hopeorchards.com. Apples, late August through late October; pears, mid-September through October. Open Thurs through Sun.

**Lamb Abbey Orchards,** 2009 North Union Rd., Union; (207) 470-0447; www.lambabbey.com. Though not yet open to the public, this 15-acre orchard is growing 230 varieties of heirloom fruit trees, including 120 varieties of apples as well as pears, plums, peaches, apricots, cherries, haskaps, medlars, and pawpaws.

**Pleasant Pond Orchard,** 430 Brunswick Rd., Richmond; (207) 737-4443; www.pleasantpondorchard.com. More than 20 varieties of apples, peaches, plums, pears, raspberries, blackberries, and highbush blueberries. Open late summer through Christmas, closed Tues.

**Rocky Ridge Orchard and Bakery,** US 201, Bowdoin; (207) 666-5786; www.rockyridgeorchard.com. Farm store and bakery are open all summer; apples start in late August. Open May through Nov.

**Sewall's Orchard,** 259 Masalin Rd., Lincolnville; (207) 763-3956. The oldest certified-organic apple orchard in Maine. Open Aug through Nov, Tues to Sun.

# Downneast Maine

With its craggy granite cliffs and piney, windswept islands, Downeast Maine's distinctive image is hard to resist. In the briny water, brightly colored buoys mark the lobster traps deep below, and the cold spray of the Atlantic is alluring and wild. Acadia National Park, with its rocky outcroppings and panoramic ocean views, draws thousands each year, and midsummer brings the island communities to life, their populations tripling and their lobster shacks boiling for another season. The charming towns of Bar Harbor, Blue Hill, and Ellsworth bustle with tourists all season. Further along the coast, the pace slows and communities are centered around the water and, in Machias, the University of Maine.

Originally the home of the Wabanaki Indians—whose oyster middens, discovered by archeologists digging at sites of Native American encampments in Acadia, date back more than 6,000 years—the region was settled by French Jesuits, who arrived and founded a mission under the authority of Father Pierre Biard, in the early 1600s. Over the next 200 years, the area passed back and

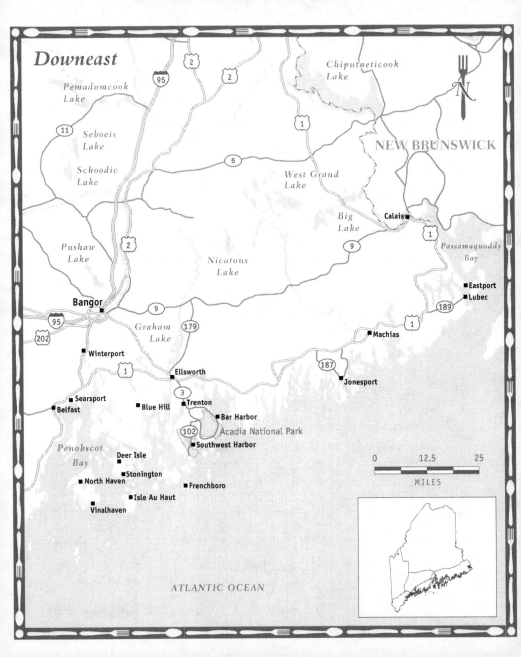

# Downeast

Pemadumcook Lake

Seboeis Lake

Schoodic Lake

Chiputneticook Lake

NEW BRUNSWICK

West Grand Lake

Calais

Big Lake

Passamaquoddy Bay

Pushaw Lake

Nicatous Lake

Eastport
Lubec

Bangor

Graham Lake

Machias

Winterport

Ellsworth

Jonesport

Searsport
Belfast

Blue Hill

Trenton

Bar Harbor

Acadia National Park

Southwest Harbor

Penobscot Bay

Deer Isle

Stonington

North Haven

Frenchboro

Isle Au Haut

Vinalhaven

ATLANTIC OCEAN

0    12.5    25
MILES

N

forth between the French and the English until the Revolutionary War, when it became a part of the United States.

By the mid-1800s, artists were drawn to the powerful beauty of Mount Desert Island, and painters of the Hudson River School put the region's iconic imagery on canvas. Later in the century, industrialists like the Rockefellers, Vanderbilts, Carnegies, and Morgans began to vacation here, building elegant wooden "cottages"—rather grand estates—to serve as rustic summer retreats.

A large seasonal community continues to vacation Downeast—including foodies from the late Julia Child to Martha Stewart, who has a home near Bar Harbor on Mount Desert Island. Sea life is a great attraction, and whales swim in the cold waters, while puffins inhabit small, rocky islands off the coast. Salmon, which run upstream from Passamaquoddy Bay, are celebrated each year in the Eastport Salmon Festival.

Year-round, the island communities are distinct, but all are dependent upon fishing and lobstering. Though it's based inland in Orono, the University of Maine's Lobster Institute, created in 1987, is devoted to the region's most recognizable export and promotes research and education on lobsters, the lobstering industry, and the lobstering way of life. Buy a bottle of Big Claw Wine, crafted from California grapes to pair perfectly with lobster and available from wine sellers throughout the state, and a portion of the proceeds benefits the institute.

Away from the coast, Downeast is blueberry country. Home to Maine's blueberry industry, more than 60,000 acres of wild blueberry barrens stretch along the region. Raked clean in summer,

the barrens turn the color of flame in fall.
Traditionally eaten by the Wabanaki, blueberries weren't cultivated commercially here until
the 1840s, but now they are the state's most
beloved berry. The University of Maine's wild
blueberry research center, Blueberry Hill Farm, is
the only facility of its kind in the country, and can be found in
Jonesboro.

In Harborside, the homestead of pioneering back-to-the-landers
Helen and Scott Nearing is now an educational retreat, and pilgrims
visit the Good Life Center and the nearby Four Season Farm, home
of gardening gurus Eliot Coleman and Barbara Damrosch.

Like the mid-coast, Downeast is home to an array of farm-to-
table restaurants, and inventive chefs like Rich Hanson, of Cleonice
in Ellsworth and Table in Blue Hill, are found as often in their fields
as they are in the kitchen. Combine freshly picked produce with
sweet berries, succulent lobster, and the myriad fruits of the sea,
and the region's culinary delights are as exciting as its coast.

## Bakeries

**Blue Hill Hearth Bakery and Pizzeria,** 58 Main St., Blue Hill;
(207) 610-9696. With artfully peeling clapboards and profusely
blooming gardens, this artisanal bakery is inviting, even before you
smell the baking bread. Offerings change daily, with rustic peasant

loaves, sweet cinnamon swirl, and weekly challah on regular rotation. Lunchtime sandwiches come on thick slices of fresh bread, and hand-tossed pizzas are made to order each weeknight. Sweet treats include cakes, pies, muffins, and enormous cookies. Open year-round, though hours vary. Closed Sun. Cash only.

**Bohemian Mama's Bakery,** Ridge Road, Addison; (207) 483-6132. This adorable bakery is a family affair, owned and run by baker Linda Clouser and her children Desiree and Adrian. The cases are filled with breads, pies, cakes, fruit and cheese buns, and assorted, generously sized European pastries—don't miss the perfect croissants. A newly installed wood-fired oven bakes savory treats, including pizza and stromboli. With free Wi-Fi. Open Fri and Sat.

**Little Urchin Bakery at North Haven Grocery,** North Haven; www.littleurchinbakery.com. Sold through the island's grocery and at the Saturday farmers' market, the crusty breads, heavenly cinnamon buns, and fruit-packed pies of this tiny bakery are some of North Haven's tastiest treats. Baker Courtney Naliboff began the business in her kitchen, and while it's outgrown that space, the bakery's treats still taste delectably homemade.

**Morning Glory Bakery,** 39 Rodick St., Bar Harbor; (207) 288-3041; www.morningglorybakery.com. Starting with fresh Maine ingredients—including local organic raw milk—and making every-thing by hand, this lovely bakery starts the day right with flaky, buttery croissants, flour-dusted bialys, and assorted muffins, scones, and Danishes (try the rhubarb cheese). Homemade soups, quiches, and sandwiches piled on the bakery's own bread are avail-able until closing. But the desserts are the real treat: glorious layer cakes, tortes, cupcakes, and pies (ginger parsnip!) fill the cases, and beautiful tiered wedding cakes can be ordered. Open daily until 7 p.m.

**Sugar and Spice Bakeshop,** 173 Main St., Ellsworth; (207) 667-0277; www.sugarspicebakeshop.com. Mother-daughter team Amanda Sprague and Lynda Kane share the helm of this sweet downtown bakeshop, offering sweets, savories, and specialty cakes. Get there early for a breakfast sandwich, served on a warm biscuit, bagel, or croissant, or stop by in the afternoon for a pick-me-up: Cookies and brownies are sold on their own or decadently sand-wiched with Shain's of Maine ice cream. Whole cakes and pies are available for order, including their signature "rapple," a double-crust fruit pie filled with raspberries and apples. Closed Sun.

# Brewpubs & Microbreweries

**Atlantic Brewing Company's Estate Brewery,** 15 Knox Rd., Bar Harbor; (207) 288-2337; www.atlanticbrewing.com. Brewing four ales year-round—Bar Harbor Real Ale, Coal Porter, Blueberry Ale, and refreshingly spicy Mount Desert Island Ginger wheat beer—five special and seasonal ales, and nonalcoholic Old Soaker Blueberry Soda and Root Beer. Free tours of the brew house run daily in the summer season, as does the all-you-can-eat outdoor Mainely Meat Barbecue, open 11:30 a.m. to 7 p.m. daily, Memorial Day to Columbus Day.

**Bar Harbor Brewing Company,** 8 Mount Desert St., Bar Harbor; (207) 288-4592; www.barharborbrewing.com. Downeast's oldest microbrewery, they've been making award-winning small-batch ales for almost 20 years. Offerings include rich, chocolaty Cadillac Mountain Stout, full-bodied Thunder Hole Ale, smoky Lighthouse Ale, and crisp True Blue blueberry wheat ale. Tastings daily at the on-site gift shop.

**Finn's Irish Pub,** 156 Main St., Ellsworth; (207) 667-2808. With dozens of mounted stools along the lengthy burnished wood bar, this Irish gastro-pub is classic and convivial. Inventive twists liven the menu: Scotch eggs are served with lemon mustard-seed aioli, shrimp cocktail is accompanied by lemon pesto, steak and mushroom pie is dotted with roast garlic and comes in a puff pastry shell. Along with the bangers and baked beans, there are a large number of vegetarian offerings, including wonderful fried long-stem baby artichokes. With a full bar, Guinness and local ales on tap, and regular live music.

**Jack Russell's Steak House & Brewery,** 102 Eden St., Bar Harbor; (207) 288-5214; www.bhmaine.com. This family-friendly pub is home to Maine Coast Brewing Company, whose craft ales are on tap and available bottled from the brewery. The steak house features massive cuts of meat—20-ounce prime rib, 12-ounce filet mignon—as well as seafood, pork tenderloin, and a kid's menu (be warned: The kid's menu includes a 3-ounce filet mignon and an 8-ounce New York strip steak). Open daily for dinner and drinks year-round.

**The Thirsty Whale,** 40 Cottage St., Bar Harbor; (207) 288-9335; www.thirstywhaletavern.com. This family-friendly tavern offers generous plates of pub food—including lobster rolls, chowders, various fried seafood, and the tasty fish club sandwich (a BLT with fried haddock)—as well as 14 beers on tap and a full bar. With live local music on Friday and Saturday evenings. Open daily for lunch, dinner, and drinks.

## Farm Stands

**Four Season Farm,** 609 Weir Cove Rd., Harborside; www.fourseasonfarm.com. The home and experimental market garden of renowned horticultural writers Barbara Damrosch and Eliot Coleman, the fields and greenhouses of this lovely farm produce vegetables year-round, making it a sustainable model for many in the region.

The gardens are beautifully arranged and carefully tended, and the farm stand features vegetables, fruits, and cut flowers that range from the standard (radishes, tomatoes, zucchini) to the sublime (artichokes, "candy carrots"). Open afternoons, June through Sept. Closed Sun.

**Hatch Knoll Farm/Garden Side Dairy,** 29 Hatch Knoll Rd., Jonesboro; (207) 434-2674; www.hatchknollfarm.com. Owned by the Roos family—Kim, Don, and their five children—this diversified farm includes blueberry barrens, vegetable fields, a flock of laying hens, and dairy goats. Stop by the farm store to pick up organic fruit spreads, fresh and aged goat cheeses, eggs, goat-milk soaps, and more. Open year-round though hours vary—call ahead or plan to use their honor system.

## Farmers' Markets

**Bar Harbor–Eden Farmers' Market,** YMCA parking lot, Bar Harbor; (207) 223-2293. May through Oct, Sun, 10 a.m. to 1 p.m.

**Bucksport Riverfront Market,** Main Street, Bucksport; (207) 469-7368. May through Sept, Sat, 9 a.m. to 3 p.m.

**Ellsworth Farmers' Market,** parking lot of Maine Community Foundation, Ellsworth; (207) 667-9212; www.ellsworthfarmers

market.com. June through Oct, Mon and Thurs, 2 to 5:30 p.m., and Sat, 9:30 a.m. to 12:30 p.m.

**Machias Valley Farmers' Market,** US R 1, Machias; (207) 483-2260. May through Oct, Sat, 8 a.m. to noon.

**Milbridge Farmers' Market,** center of town, Milbridge; (207) 546-2395. June through Oct, Sat, 9 a.m. to noon.

**North Haven Farmers' Market,** at the ball field, North Haven. June through Sept, Sat, 9 to 11 a.m.

**Northeast Harbor Farmers' Market,** behind Kimball Terrace Inn, Northeast Harbor; (207) 546-2395. June and July, Thurs, 9 a.m. to noon.

**Southwest Harbor Farmers' Market,** parking lot of St. John the Divine, Southwest Harbor; (207) 546-2395. June through Oct, Fri, 9 a.m. to 1 p.m.

**Winter Harbor Farmers' Market,** Newman Street and Main Street, Winter Harbor; (207) 537-5673. End of June through Labor Day, Tues, 9 a.m. to noon.

**Bagaduce Lunch,** 19 Bridge Rd., Brooksville; (207) 326-4729. Situated on the bank of the rushing Bagaduce River, this small family-owned and family-run take-out fish stand is as renowned for its lovely view as it is for its generous portions. From the picnic tables, take in the scene as eagles roost over the nearby cove and locals fish from a bridge over the reversing falls—the rapids change direction with the tides. On the menu, fish sandwiches hold a half pound of fried haddock, breaded to order; lobster rolls brim with sweet meat from lobster hauled by owner Judy Astbury's brother; and fried baskets overflow with seafood, made from the same recipe for four generations. Open seasonally.

**Lunt & Lunt and Lunt's Dockside Deli,** Lunt Harbor, Frenchboro; (207) 334-2902 (July and August) and (207) 334-2922 (September through June); www.luntlobsters.com. The Lunt family has been operated fishing businesses in Lunt Harbor since the 1820s, and this year-round lobster pound and seasonal restaurant continue the family tradition. A wholesale and retail business, Lunt & Lunt sells live lobsters year-round from its dock (as well as fuel and marine products in the summer). The seasonal deli serves homey sandwiches, steamed lobsters and clams, seafood rolls, ice cream, and freshly made desserts—try the homemade peanut-butter cups, as well as a limited breakfast menu and Wicked Joe Coffee (brewed in Brunswick). With free Wi-Fi on the dock. Deli open from early July through Labor Day; closed Sun.

# THE CHALLENGE OF THE
# PERFECT BOILED LOBSTER

Maine native Colin Woodard is the author of *The Lobster Coast,* a cultural and environmental history of coastal Maine and its lobstering communities. He's spent a great deal of time on the coast and can now be found in Portland or at www.colinwoodard.com. His thoughts on the perfect lobster:

There's nothing technically challenging about cooking the perfect boiled lobster. It's not that much different from cooking pasta: You have to boil water, put your prey in it, keep an eye on the time, and know how to test it for readiness to avoid having it overcooked or underdone. The challenge for some is that the lobster, unlike pasta, is tossed into the pot alive. Cooking lobster at home is fundamentally a test of one's commitment and mettle, not their culinary skills.

Some reassure themselves that lobsters, as lowly decapodous crustaceans, don't really mind being boiled alive. I'm certain this isn't the case. Their brains may be a simple bundle of nerves, but they're still nerves. Death comes quickly in the pot, but I doubt it's

**Lunt's Gateway Lobster Pound,** 1133 Bar Harbor Rd., Trenton; (207) 667-2620; www.luntsgatewaylobster.com. The walls are lined with kitschy collectibles and the tables are covered with simple oilcloth at this lobster pound and casual seafood restaurant, family owned for more than 40 years. Located across the road from the Bar Harbor Airport, it's often the first place hungry visitors see, and

painless. A better way to look at it is that (a) it's a lot better way to die than the lobster would likely experience on the seafloor, where they're often swallowed whole by codfish, to be slowly digested, or simply dismantled by a larger lobster or other prey, and (b) it's a better fate than the chicken, cow, and pig in your refrigerator probably experienced. Here's one of the few times many people actually kill their food and eat it, and I think it honors the animal more than outsourcing the task. Revel in the ritual, and be proud your meal lived its life in its natural environment and, particularly if sourced from Maine, was harvested by one of the world's few truly sustainable fisheries.

Apart from that, boiling a lobster is really easy. Make sure you have a pot big enough to completely submerge all the lobsters you plan to cook. Add a tablespoon or so of salt per quart of water and bring to a full-on boil. Put the lobster in, claws first, immediately cover, and set the timer. A pound-and-a-quarter lobster takes 8 or 9 minutes, a one-and-a-half- to two-pounder, 8 to 11. Test it at the early end of the time frame by trying to lift one by its antenna. If it pulls out, the lobster is ready. Serve with melted butter and enjoy!

the restaurant's quality matches its convenience: Seafood is fresh, desserts are homemade, and service is friendly and attentive. A challenge for the daring: Successfully conquer a 3-pound (or larger) steamed lobster and your photo will grace the Wall of Fame. Open May through Oct.

**Pectic Seafood,** 367 Bar Harbor Rd., Trenton; (207) 667-7566 or (877) 667-7566; www.pecticseafood .com. "If life gets hectic, go to Pectic!" is the motto of this family-owned fishmonger and market. Fresh seafood, live lobsters, and crabmeat fill the cases, and owners Paul and Teresa Cecere smoke their own salmon and mussels—as well as ribs and pulled pork. Homemade soups and chowders are available for takeout, as are prepared entrees, wines, and specialty foods. An in-house bakery, making breakfast treats and desserts, also offers gluten-free goodies. Open daily year-round.

**Thurston's Lobster Pound,** 1 Thurston Rd., Bernard; (207) 244-7600; www.thurstonslobster.com. Perched above the working waterfront, the views from this lobster pound offer a tableau of coastal life: Watch lobster boats tie up and unload their traps as you dine. The menu is simple: Start with mussels or clams by the pound, or a cup of chowder or lobster stew, enjoy a boiled lobster with drawn butter, corn, slaw, and a roll, and finish with a slice of homemade pie, fruit crisp, or blueberry cake. With wine by the glass or bottle and a large selection of beers. Open for lunch and dinner daily, Memorial Day to Columbus Day.

**Trenton Bridge Lobster Pound,** 1237 Bar Harbor Rd., Trenton; (207) 667-2977; www.trentonbridgelobster.com. With a long row of open pots boiling seawater over smoking wood fires, you can't miss this iconic lobster pound, just before the bridge to Mount Desert Island. Owned by the same family for four generations, the pound has been boiling lobster the old fashioned way since 1956, evolving with the times to offer mail-order seafood, from live lobsters to local scallops and steamer clams. One thing they don't offer, however, is fried food: Trenton Bridge Lobster Pound is proudly grease-free. All seafood dishes begin with lobsters, crabs, and clams that have been steamed or boiled. Restaurant open Mon through Sat in summer; lobster pound open year-round.

**Union River Lobster Pot,** 8 South St., Ellsworth; (207) 667-5077; www.lobsterpot.com. On the banks of the Union River, the tanks of this seasonal restaurant hold nearly 1,000 pounds of live lobsters, and classic shore dinners of boiled lobster, steamed clam, and local mussels from Blue Hill Bay Mussel Company are piled high. The menu ranges from traditional saltwater-boiled lobsters to spicy mussels with coconut, cilantro, and *sriracha* sauce. Entrees are served with warm homemade bread, and desserts—from summer berry crisp to decadent Toll House pie—are made in-house. Open nightly, June through Oct.

## Food Happenings

**August**

**Frenchboro Lobster Festival,** Frenchboro; www.frenchboro online.com. Now in its fiftieth year, this annual crustacean celebration offers scenic boat rides through the picturesque harbor, live old-time music on the porch of the Frenchboro Parsonage, and a dinner featuring boiled lobster, coleslaw, potato chips, soda, and homemade pie.

**Machias Wild Blueberry Festival,** 7 Center St., Machias; (207) 255-6665; www.machiasblueberry.com. Sponsored by the Centre Street Congregational Church, this weekend festival features an all-ages Blackfly Ball, a hands-free pie-eating competition, cooking contests, a blueberry quilt raffle (hand stitched by community women), live music, road race, and parade. The much anticipated Blueberry Musical, performed in the church sanctuary, features different blueberry-themed numbers each year—from "Rakealot" (a spoof of the Broadway hit *Camelot*) to the local "village people" adapting the tune of "YMCA" to the words "Wild Blueberry." Area blueberry farms open up for tours during the festival; pick up a map at the information booth.

**Maine Lobster Festival in Winter Harbor,** Winter Harbor; www.acadia-schoodic.org/lobsterfestival. Held for more than four decades at various points on the western side of the Gouldsboro Peninsula, this one-day festival features a road race, craft fair, famed Maine Lobster Boat Races, a lobster dinner, a bagpipe concert, and a parade down Winter Harbor's Main Street. Always the second Sat in August.

## September

**Eastport Salmon Festival,** downtown Eastport; www.eastport salmonfestival.com. For more than 20 years, this three-day festival has celebrated the salmon of Passamaquoddy Bay. Popular events include a 5K run, a guided walking tour, boat tours of the salmon pens, and the highlight: a grilled salmon lunch.

**Mount Desert Island Garlic Festival,** Smuggler's Den Campground, Southwest Harbor; www.nostrano.com. A celebration of the "stinking rose," this one-day festival began in 1998 as a harvest party for Frank Pendola's garlic crop. In the years since, it's blossomed into a community event featuring local brewers, restaurants, and musicians, as well as garlic producers, and has served as a fund-raiser for local nonprofits.

## October

**Acadia's Oktoberfest,** Smuggler's Den Campground, Southwest Harbor; (207) 244-9264 or (800) 423-9264; www.acadiaoktoberfest .com. A two-day family festival with live music, dozens of local food vendors, and a craft tent, the main event is the brew tent, where 20 of Maine's top breweries sample craft beers. Twenty-one and older only admitted to the brew tent.

**Foliage, Food, and Wine Festival,** Blue Hill; (207) 374-3242; www.bluehillpeninsula.org. A weekend of leaf peeping, tastings, tours, and more, this four-day festival features panel discussions of local farming, guided walks, tastings of local products—from regional apples to smoked seafood—themed dinners, cooking workshops, and a treasure hunt.

## The Maine Ice Cream Trail

**Ben & Bill's Chocolate Emporium,** 66 Main St., Bar Harbor; (207) 288-3281 or (800) 806-3281; www.benandbills.com. Though originally an import—the company was started in Vineyard Haven, Massachusetts, in 1956—this family-owned candy store and ice-cream shop has been a local fixture for more than 30 years. Sixty-four flavors of hard-serve flavors are made on-site and served daily, in addition to a dozen gelatos. The main event is the famed Lobster Ice Cream: butter-flavored ice cream packed with hand-picked cooked lobster meat. In the summer season, hundreds of patrons line up daily to sample this curiosity, which is available by the scoop, and by the pint, quart, and half gallon for shipping. Open seasonally, from Mar through Dec.

**John's Ice Cream Factory,** 510 Belfast Augusta Rd., Liberty; (207) 589-3700. Considered by many to be the best ice cream in the state, this off-beat shop features creamy scoops of hard pack in fresh, intense flavors. Blackberries in Cream balances tart, concentrated fruit with buttery sweetness; chocolate is rich and smooth;

and toasted coconut has a lingering, nutty taste. Flavors change regularly, so call ahead if you're craving something special.

**Mount Desert Island Ice Cream,** 325 Main St., Bar Harbor; (207) 460-5515; and 7 Firefly Lane, Bar Harbor; (207) 801-4007; www.mdiic.com. Not your father's hard scoop, this maverick gourmet ice cream shop features "fearless flavors"—inventive, addictive combinations. Ice creams include Chocolate Wasabi, Blackstrap Banana, Sherry Catalana, and Zabaglione Raisin, as well as summer classics like peach, salt caramel, and rich Callebaut chocolate. Sorbets take it up a notch, with offerings that range from orange-tarragon to beet-ginger to blueberry-basil (just try it!). With a line of drink mixes that includes a sampling of sorbet flavors, and Sweet Cream Canine Ice Cream, sold by the pint. With a **new location in Portland's Old Port** (51 Exchange St., 207-210-3432).

## *Landmark Eateries*

**Helen's Restaurant,** 28 East Main St., Machias; (207) 255-8423; $$. The sign on this converted house sports an *H* designed from a knife, fork, and spoon, and locals have been dining under the flatware since 1950. Though it's changed ownership in recent years, the kitchen still turns out heaped mounds of whole belly clams and perfectly fried haddock, sweet and juicy beneath a crunchy golden crust, and deconstructed lobster rolls: a bowl of freshly picked lobster, bathed in melted butter, with soft buttered bread tucked beneath. The famed berry pies combine fresh and cooked fruit in a tart filling, mellowed somewhat by the cloud of whipped cream floating on top.

**The Jordan Pond House,** Acadia National Park; (207) 276-3316; www.jordanpondhouse.com; $$$. This venerable teahouse and restaurant has been serving summer visitors to Acadia National Park since 1870. Situated on an overlook with views of Jordan Pond, Penobscot Mountain, and "the Bubbles" (North and South Bubble Mountains), visitors can enjoy light tea or a refreshing glass of just-squeezed lemonade on the lawn or a full meal in the garden-side dining room. The menu includes famed popovers, served warm from the oven, rich lobster stews and rolls, seafood entrees, and house-made ice cream. Open daily from late May to late October.

**Jordan's Snack Bar,** 200 Downeast Hwy., Ellsworth; (207) 667-2174; $$. This local landmark has been a seasonal favorite for three decades. Known for fresh crab rolls—never made from frozen meat, they're only offered when a hand-lettered sign in the window reads FRESH CRABMEAT TODAY—and perfectly battered onion rings, the menu also includes hot dogs, burgers, and addictive fried clams. Soft-serve ice cream is available in dipped cones, sundaes, and blended with fresh fruit. Open Apr through Oct.

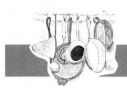

**Blueberry Point Chefs,** Perry; (207) 853-4629; www.blueberry pointchefs.com. In the sunny kitchen of a 150-acre blueberry farm overlooking breathtaking Passamaquoddy Bay, chef Audrey Patterson teaches small classes to cook cuisines that span the globe from Caribbean to classic French. In addition to cooking, the Ice House Wine Club holds weekly wine tasting through the summer season and culminates in a fall wine dinner. Private classes and corporate retreats can be arranged. With a seasonal shop carrying artisanal cheeses and fine wines. Open May through Oct. Visit their website for class details.

**Pairings,** 279 South Main St., Winterport; (207) 223-4500; www .winterportwinery.com. Next door to the **Winterport Winery** (p. 232) and started by its owners, Michael and Joan Anderson, and their associate Jody Connor, this cooking school began with a common question at their tasting room, "What's a good food to go with this wine?" Now resident chef Laurie Turner helps participants answer the question, leading classes that range from kitchen essentials to gourmet demonstrations. For those who prefer to simply taste, monthly Wine Dinners are held, in which diners watch and learn as foods are paired with carefully chosen wines (by reservation only). Check the website for upcoming classes.

**Bar Harbor Cellars at Sweet Pea Farm,** 854 ME 3, Salisbury Cove, Bar Harbor; (207) 288-3907; www.barharborcellars.com. Offering wines made from the nearly 1,000 grapevines planted in their own vineyards, and grapes imported from small co-ops throughout Europe and North America, this boutique winery is making several reds and whites, two fruit wines, and one ice wine. In late June, attend the cellar's annual Mussel and Wine Festival, a fund-raiser for the Angel Flight charity. With tastings and tours daily, Memorial Day to Columbus Day.

**Bartlett's Maine Estate Winery/Spirits of Maine Distillery,** 175 Chicken Mill Pond Rd., Gouldsboro; (207) 546-2408; www .bartlettwinery.com. Since 1975 Bob and Kathe Bartlett have been making award-winning wines from Maine's native fruits, and their offerings range from crisp apple and pear whites to robust blueberry reds. Their repertoire also includes dessert wines, sophisticated aperitifs—try the Apple Blush—and meads. Sample all in the tasting room, and take a bottle (or a case) home for a taste of the coast. The winery is off the beaten path—23 miles east of Ellsworth—look for the triangular granite sculpture and you'll know you're there. Open June through Oct, and by appointment.

**Black Dinah Chocolatiers,** 1 Moore's Harbor Rd., Isle Au Haut; (207) 335-5010; www.blackdinahchocolatiers.com. Sleek, elegant chocolates grace the tempered orange cases at this chocolate shop and cafe, just out of the woods at the base of Black Dinah Mountain. Made from local cream and butter and sustainably grown cacao from Belgium, Venezuela, and Peru, these luscious, whimsically named confections are infused with herbs and spices, nuts, and spirits. Whenever possible, ingredients come from local sources: the Maine Mint features a chocolate mint leaf from **Four Season Farm** (see p. 214), the Chèvre & Nib incorporates goat cheese from nearby **Sunset Acres** (see p. 231), and the rhubarb features stalks from the inn down the road. Don't miss the Flagship Caramel—buttery caramel scented with vanilla bean, enrobed in chocolate and sprinkled with sea salt—or its cousin, the Sea Turtle, with cashews and Brazil nuts. The cafe also includes freshly baked goods made by owner-chocolatier Kate Shaffer, organic coffees and teas, and free Wi-Fi (rare in these parts). Cafe open June through Sept; chocolates made and shipped to order year-round (also available at specialty shops throughout the state).

**Harmony Mill Farm,** 133 Fitchburg Rd., Waltham; (207) 584-2035. Milking a small herd of organically raised Jersey cows, farmers Deb Dik and Jon Pierce craft aged raw-milk cheddars, heat-treated ricotta, and ricotta salata cheeses at this idyllic farm on the shores of Graham Lake. Raw whole and skim milk are sold off the farm in returnable glass bottles. Call ahead to schedule a visit.

**Monica's Chocolates,** 100 County Rd. (ME 189), Lubec; (866) 952-4500; www.monicaschocolates.com. Chocolatier Monica Elliott began making chocolate at her father's elbow in her native Peru. It's his recipes for traditional Peruvian sweets that fill her signature bonbons: creamy confections, packed with nuts or dried fruit and dipped in rich bittersweet chocolate. Other treats include the Pistachio Crème, filled with organic Sicilian pistachio paste; the Pisco, filled with Peruvian Pisco liqueur and raisins; and that Maine classic, the needham (see p. 88), topped here with almonds, pecans, or blueberries. Open Mon through Fri, year-round.

**Raye's Mustard,** 83 Washington St., Eastport; (800) 853-1903; www.rayesmustard.com. "Taste the flavor that modern technology left behind" at this century-old mustard mill in the country's easternmost town. In operation since 1900, when J. Wesley Raye began producing mustard for Maine's sardine industry, the mill is still run by the Raye family and makes mustard the old fashioned way: soaking the mustard seed in cold spring water and white vinegar and grinding it between stones, as it's been done since the Middle Ages. Tours allow you to watch the process as thick yellow mustard flows like lava from between the grindstones. Now with 25 flavors, ranging from classic yellow Down East Schooner to subtly herbed Winter Garden. Open year-round, Mon through Fri and sometimes Sat.

**Seal Cove Farm,** 202 Partridge Cove Rd., Lamoine; (207) 667-7127; www.mainegoatcheese.com. Since their beginnings in 1976 with one Saanen doe, goatherds and cheesemakers Barbara Brooks and Lynn Ahblad have expanded their operation to produce more than two tons of cheese per month. Trained in France, they make a variety of cheeses, from mild, creamy, fresh chèvres to pungent aged chèvres and semifirm Tommes. More than 100 goats roam the farm, and spring visits may include the chance to bottle-feed a kid. With a summer farm stand. Call ahead to arrange a visit.

**Shalom Orchard Organic Farm and Winery,** 158 Eastbrook Rd., Franklin; (207) 565-2312; www.shalomorchard.com. The first certified-organic winery on the East Coast, this diversified farm specializes in wines pressed from their own organic fruits. Offerings currently include blueberry, pear, and apple wines, cranberry cyser (cranberries fermented with apple cider), and sweet honey mead. New fruit wines for the coming seasons include kiwi, raspberry, and blackberry, and specialty maple and wintergreen. In addition to the winery, owner-farmer-vintners Charlotte Young and Jim Baranski operate a CSA (community supported agriculture), raise chickens and Rambouillet sheep, and invite pick-your-own apples in the orchard, now with more than 1,000 trees. Call to arrange a visit.

**Sunset Acres Farm & Dairy,** 769 Bagaduce Rd., Brooksville; (207) 326-4741; www.sunsetacresfarm.com. On this small saltwater farm, dairy goats bound through the fields to the water edging their pasture, and farmers Anne Bossi and Bob Bowen make fresh chèvres, award-winning bloomy rind cheeses, aged Camembert, ash-dusted "Stonington Granite" pyramids, and the rare and much-coveted demi-Brie. Spreadable cheeses contain chopped herbs from their own gardens, as does their crumbled feta. Call ahead to arrange a visit.

**Winterport Winery,** 279 South Main St., Winterport; (207) 223-4500; www.winterportwinery.com. Winemaker Michael Anderson began fermenting as a hobby decades ago, but since 2001 he's been making wine full-time, bringing his family into the business along the way. Fruit wines are his specialty, including blueberry (both sweet and dry), apple, pear, and raspberry, among others. Several years ago, the family began brewing craft ales, and the facility is also home to Penobscot Bay Brewery, known for its signature Old Factory Whistle Scottish Ale; they've teamed with Stone Fox Creamery in Monroe to create Bay Brew Ice Cream, which offers their Half Moon Stout by the scoop. Try it all at their tasting room, open Mar through Dec.

## *Restaurants*

**2 Cats Cafe,** 130 Cottage St., Bar Harbor; (207) 288-2808 or (800) 355-2808; www.2catsbarharbor.com; $$. The cafe at this charming inn serves breakfast, lunch, and snacks throughout the day at sunny indoor tables and a shaded outdoor patio. Warm bread and buttery biscuits and muffins are turned out by the on-site bakery each morning, and menu offerings range from smoked trout omelets to lobster eggs Benedict to homemade granola, sold by the bowl and the pound. Portions are generous and ingredients are local—fresh herbs are gathered from the inn's garden—and organic, whenever possible. The two friendly felines of the name wander freely around; if you're a cat fancier, check out the collectibles in the gift shop.

**The Artist's Cafe,** 3 Dublin St., Machias; (207) 255-8900; $$$. The walls of this small hilltop restaurant are lined with owner Susan Ferro's own paintings—her artistry ranges from pigment to produce—and her menu is arranged with a careful eye. One of the area's early proponents of farm-to-table dining, Ferro has crafted her dishes to showcase what's available locally, and preparations change regularly. Serving sandwiches named for artistic movements—try the Surrealist—and sweet treats for weekday lunch, and hearty entrees and an assortment of generously portioned rich desserts for dinner. Reservations recommended. Open early spring through late October.

**Barncastle Hotel and Restaurant,** 125 South St., Blue Hill; (207) 374-2330; www.barn-castle.com; $$. The cozy dining room at this historic inn offers an eclectic mix of rustic Italian and New England comfort food. Inventive pizzas from the wood-fired oven are available on white or spelt dough, and can be topped with everything from broccoli, feta, and walnuts to smoked shrimp, mussels, and scallops. Sub sandwiches are served on oven-toasted baguettes, and entrees range from Naskeag crab cakes to baked stuffed potato. With a full bar, wines by the glass and bottle, and a range of local and imported beers. Open nightly for dinner, year-round.

**The Brooklin Inn,** ME 175, Brooklin; (207) 359-2777; www .brooklininn.com; $$$. The tiny coastal village of Brooklin, on Eggemoggin Reach, is famed for its wooden boat-building school and its resident celebrity, the late writer E. B. White. The inn has been a fixture for generations, and its dining room and Irish pub are popular with locals and visitors alike. Chef Marcus Ted Williams's dining room menu changes daily to reflect what's seasonally available, but it always includes elegant preparations of local seafoods—if it's on the menu, don't miss the Maine seafood bouillabaisse. The pub features burgers of local beef on home-baked buns, marinated steak, and fresh-caught fish from the Gulf of Maine. With an extensive wine list and craft beers on tap. Open year-round, nightly in summer, Wed through Sun in winter.

**Brown's Coal Wharf,** 5 Boatyard Rd., North Haven; (207) 867-4739; $$. This casual, relaxed restaurant sits in the marina, perched over the water, with spectacular ocean views. The menu includes dishes from the island and "from away." The former includes seafood risotto, fried battered fish and Maine shrimp, and locally caught lobster; the latter includes barbecued ribs smothered in blueberry bourbon sauce, pan-seared chicken, and a variety of sandwiches and burgers. Open for lunch and dinner in summer.

**Burning Tree,** ME 3, Otter Creek; (207) 288-9331; $$$. Since 1987, chef-owners Allison Beal and Elmer Beal Jr. have served fresh, healthy meals created from regionally sourced ingredients in this bucolic island restaurant. The daily catch from local fishermen is paired with vegetables from the restaurant's gardens, mushrooms foraged in nearby woods, and cheese from local producers to create dishes that emphasize the flavors of the region. The changing menu features at least 10 seafood and 3 vegetarian entrees daily, and offerings can range from pan-fried sage-and-almond flounder to crispy kale and oven-roasted littleneck clams to minted edamame wontons in miso. Serving dinner nightly, closed Tues. Reservations strongly recommended.

**Cafe This Way,** 14½ Mount Desert St., Bar Harbor; (207) 288-4483; www.cafethisway.com; $$$. Behind the white shingles and rustic gardens of this seasonal restaurant, the space opens into a surprisingly cavernous, ruby-red lounge. Hearty homemade breakfast is served on Formica-topped tables, and offerings range from the kitchen's own corned beef hash to the McThis Way Big Breakfast Sandwich: fried eggs, tomatoes, cheddar cheese, and a choice of meat or veggie bacon on a big English muffin. Closed in the afternoon, the restaurant reopens for supper, serving inventive dishes like smoked duck–wrapped scallops, grilled quail, Korean tuna tartare (with kimchee and lotus chips), and lobster cocktail parfait with fresh pineapple, poblano peppers, and avocado cream (and those are just the appetizers!). With a full bar, homemade desserts, and nightly specials. Open for breakfast and dinner, mid-April through October.

**Cleonice Mediterranean Bistro,** 112 Main St., Ellsworth; (207) 664-7554; www.cleonice.com; $$$. Chef-owner Rich Hanson's elegant bistro brings the flavors of the Mediterranean Downeast, serving tapas, paella, and Italian *timpano*, as well as entrees of fresh-caught seafood and locally raised meats and poultry. Much of the restaurant's produce comes from Hanson's farm in Bucksport, and the menu changes regularly to reflect the harvest. The raw bar and seafood tapas are particularly fine, with *opah crudo* (sometimes referred to as Sicilian sushi), fluke seviche, spice-rubbed tuna carpaccio, and grilled baby octopus joining the classic oysters and clams. With a full bar and specialty cocktails.

**Eat A Pita/Cafe2,** 326 Main St., Southwest Harbor; (207) 244-4344; $$. With potted herbs out front, a breezy screen door, and daily specials chalked on a board, this comfortable restaurant is a cheerful treat. Sandwiches—pitas and panini—are stuffed with fresh veggies, and lunch and dinner entrees are healthy and flavorful, from carrot ginger soup to burgers with turkey bacon. All of this encourages a guilt-free splurge on rich, homemade dessert (if it's on the board, try the bread pudding).

**El El Frijoles,** 41 Caterpillar Hill Rd., Sargentville; (207) 359-2486; www.elelfrijoles.com; $$. "Sargentville's best choice for delicious Mexican food" is also its only, but this cheerful spot in the barn behind owners Michael Rossney and Michele Levesque's home delivers the goods. Using local, organic ingredients, the couple makes fresh tacos, empanadas, burritos, and quesadillas filled with spiced lobster and crab meat, shredded pork, *pollo asado* (chicken stewed in red mole sauce), and simple black beans and cheese. Start the meal with crisp cabbage salad dressed with lime and cilantro and finish with homemade *dulce de leche.* To drink, try a class of *horchata,* a sweet cinnamon rice milk. Open late May to late September, and occasionally through the winter.

**Galyn's,** 17 Main St., Bar Harbor; (207) 288-9706; www.galynsbar harbor.com; $$$. Since 1986, this casually upscale restaurant near the waterfront has served local seafood, steak, and pastas. Lobster comes several ways—boiled in the shell, sautéed with butter and sherry, baked in enchiladas—and local crabs, scallops, and fish are offered grilled, baked, and sautéed. Desserts are homemade and include a spiced blueberry-apple crisp and rich, warm Indian pudding. With slow-roasted prime rib every Friday and Saturday. Open daily, mid-March to November.

**The Harbor Gawker,** 26 Main St., Vinalhaven; (207) 863-9365; $$. Owned by the Morton family since it opened in 1975, the Gawker—as it's known—is a local landmark, named for the historical island term for people living on the inlet to Carver's Harbor. With an improbably extensive menu—close to 100 options—its most popular offerings are still the classics: tasty chowder, lobster and crab rolls, and assorted seafood specialties. Soft-serve ice cream is a cornerstone of the business, and the first Saturday in May marks the annual Free Ice Cream Day, begun decades ago on the first day of the summer season, when the island's school bus would swing by the shop so that each student could get a free cone. Open seasonally.

**Havana,** 318 Main St., Bar Harbor; (207) 288-2822; www.havana maine.com; $$$. With vivid colors, rattan furniture, and more than a hint of spice, this upscale restaurant has brought Latin flair to coastal Maine for more than a decade. The menu isn't strictly Cuban, revealing influences that span the globe—appetizers range from sea scallops with pickled local pumpkin to wild mushroom spring rolls with Japanese buckwheat noodles, and entrees include mixed seafood stew with coconut broth, seared tuna with crispy chipotle polenta cakes, and jerk chicken or tofu. Desserts are divine; don't miss the sweet polenta cake with mascarpone whipped cream, candied jalapeño sauce, and pink peppercorn pineapple salsa. At 25 pages, the wine list is a hefty tome, but staff is happy to help you navigate. With a new outpost in Portland's Old Port, **Havana South** (44–50 Wharf St., Portland; 207-772-9988). Open year-round.

**The Haven Restaurant,** Vinalhaven; (207) 863-4969; $$$. This local favorite has a creative, eclectic menu and a commitment to using local ingredients. Reservations are recommended, as seating fills early. Closed February to mid-May.

**H.J. Blakes,** 9 Main St., North Haven; (207) 867-2060; $$. In the island's tiny downtown, this whimsical seasonal cafe serves seafood rolls, sandwiches, and prepared entrees to eat on the outdoor deck or to take away. With a surprisingly varied menu that ranges from BLTs to peanut noodles. Open for lunch during July and Aug.

**Lily's Cafe,** 450 Airport Rd. at ME 15, Stonington; (207) 367-5936; $$. Chef-owner Kyra Alex has been serving up weekday breakfast and lunch and Friday dinner for more than a decade at this cozy island cafe. The menu is simple and tasty, featuring such comfort foods as fried chicken and macaroni and cheese, in addition to more sophisticated fare. Famed for her quiche, soups, and scones—in late summer, try the wild blackberry—Alex has recently revised her cookbook, which is available for sale at the restaurant. Also for sale are gourmet pantry staples, including imported pastas and olive oils. Closed Sat and Sun.

**Lompoc Cafe,** 30 Rodick St., Bar Harbor; (207) 288-9392; www .lompoccafe.com; $$. With a bocce court in the garden under the watchful eyes of the totem owl, and a laid-back attitude that nicely matches the creative but casual menu, this cafe is a hidden gem. The menu changes seasonally but often includes house-pickled juniper cucumbers and spicy dilly beans, falafel burgers, various thin-crust pizzas, and the famed Bang-Bang sandwich: a deceptively simple combination of fried chicken breast, spicy slaw, and aioli on crusty bread. Combinations can be quirky—mint-buttermilk dressing, honey-harissa carrots—but here, they work. With more than a dozen craft beers on tap and regular live music. Open year-round, though hours vary.

**Maggie's Restaurant,** 6 Summer St., Bar Harbor; (207) 288-9007; www.maggiesbarharbor.com; $$$. With an elegant atmosphere—white table linens, muted terra-cotta walls, French doors opening onto the outdoor patio—this seasonal restaurant is known for its inventive seafood and attentive service. The lobster crepes, filled with succulent meat in a creamy sherry sauce, are a signature dish, and other favorites include garlicky mussels and mixed seafood stew. Reservations essential. Open for dinner, June through Oct. Closed Sun.

**McKay's Public House,** 231 Main St., Bar Harbor; (207) 288-2002; www.mckayspublichouse.com; $$. In a beautifully restored historic Victorian building on Main Street, this casual restaurant serves "elevated pub fare," elegant entrees, an extensive list of craft beers and carefully selected wines by the glass and bottle. Menu highlights include homemade pretzels rolled in smoked salt;

lamb burgers; and lobster mac and cheese, here made with truffled cream sauce, cavatappi noodles, and spring peas. Serving dinner nightly, year-round; closed the month of Jan.

**Mother's Kitchen,** 1502 SR 102, Town Hill; (207) 288-4403; www .motherskitchenfoods.com; $. For more than a decade, this gourmet sandwich shop has served lunch from its homey counter. Sandwich names may be obscure to outsiders, but their flavors are satisfying and perfect for a picnic. Try the Humble Farmer, with Havarti dill, cukes, tomato, lettuce, and sprouts, and the Charlie Noble, with homemade chicken salad with walnuts and tarragon, cranberry sauce, and lettuce. Call ahead and your sandwich will be waiting. Also with fresh baked goods. Open Mon through Fri, 9 a.m. to 2 p.m.

**Nebo Lodge,** 11 Mullins Lane, North Haven; (207) 867-2007; www .nebolodge.com; $$$. Owned by the Pingree family—Congresswoman Chellie Pingree, and her daughters Hannah, a state representative and former Maine Speaker of the House, and Cecily, a filmmaker—this beautifully appointed inn holds the island's only year-round restaurant. Chef Amanda Hallowell's menu emphasizes local ingredients, from a breakfast sausage of famed North Haven lamb to a dinner entree of seared Vinalhaven halibut with oregano stuffing, pancetta, locally foraged fiddleheads, and spring parsnip *frites*. The bar, with weathered counters and copper accents, features delicious cocktails—try the Aerial View with Lillet, soda, bitters, and fresh mint, or the sparkling Italian Lesson with Prosecco, cognac, bitters, and a sugar cube. Small bites, from nuggets of fried cod to local vegetable bagna cauda, can be ordered at the bar. Open year-round.

**Nostrano,** Bar Harbor; (207) 288-0269; www.nostrano.com; $$$. Chef-owner Frank Pendola came to Maine in 1992 as a molecular biologist working with the Jackson Laboratories; he gardened and cooked as a passionate weekend hobby. Today Pendola cooks full-time, making delectable country Italian meals, smoking Atlantic salmon and barbecue in-house, and running the annual **Mount Desert Island Garlic Festival** (see p. 223). Housed in the lower level of his home, the restaurant is family-style, with an open kitchen and multiple courses. By reservation only.

**Redbird Provisions Restaurant,** 11 Sea St., Northeast Harbor; (207) 276-3006; www.redbirdprovisions.com; $$$. Every glorious detail is in place at this carefully curated restaurant: Tables are scattered along terraces and in the abundant gardens, votives flicker on elegantly set tables, fresh and potted flowers bloom from corners and windowsills. The menu changes seasonally but regularly includes house-made pastas studded with seafood and garden-fresh vegetables, meats paired with foraged mushrooms, and salads featuring house-made ricotta. Open Memorial Day through Labor Day. Reservations recommended.

**Red Sky,** 14 Clark Point Rd., Southwest Harbor; (207) 244-0476; www.redskyrestaurant.com; $$$. Something in this unpretentiously elegant restaurant—the wood-paneled ceilings, the row of small porthole-like windows—gives an impression of the snug belly of a ship. The menu of chef-owners James and Elizabeth Geffen Lindquist changes to reflect what's seasonally available, but includes a variety of seafood dishes, from peekytoe crab salad with citrus to lobster paired with risotto, as well as sustainably raised meats and house-made pastas. Fresh bread is baked on-site, as are rich desserts, often paired with **Mount Desert Island Ice Cream** (see p. 225). With a full bar featuring delicious cocktails (try the blackberry) and a lengthy wine list. Closed Jan.

**Rupununi,** 119 Main St., Bar Harbor; (207) 288-2886; www .rupununi.com; $$. This casual bar and grill, named for a South American river, has an aquatic feel to it, with stylized fish adorning one wall, an immense freshwater aquarium stocked with the fish of the Rupununi River, and a menu that features Maine's best seafood. In addition, offerings include Niman Ranch and locally sourced natural meats, handmade pastas, and burgers that include ostrich, lamb, and American-raised Kobe beef. Live music, from youth trios to New Orland jazz ensembles, perform regularly. With 60 beers on tap and bottled, a large wine list, and a full bar. Open daily for lunch, dinner, and drinks.

**The Seasons of Stonington Restaurant and Bakery,** 27 Main St., Stonington; (207) 367-2600; www.seasonsofstonington.com;

$$$. With vast windows and an outdoor deck overlooking Stonington Harbor, this year-round restaurant serves beautiful food in an elegant setting. Chef Kristian Burrin's creative menu is eclectic: pan-fried halibut is paired with tabbouleh and green pea–white truffle puree; crab dip is seasoned with chili and Parmesan and served with candied cherry tomatoes and black-olive jelly. The attached bakery provides European-style artisanal breads and pastries for the restaurant and for takeout. Open year-round, though hours vary.

**Table,** 66 Main St., Blue Hill; (207) 374-5677; www.farmkitchen table.com; $$$. The Bucksport farm of James Beard Award–nominated chef-owner Rich Hanson (also of **Cleonice,** see p. 236) is the source of much of the produce—and some of the meat—on the menu at this rustic restaurant and bistro. Offerings are casual but exquisitely executed: a turkey BLT is made with house-smoked turkey breast, Curtis Smokehouse bacon from nearby Warren, and local tomatoes and greens, served with house-made mayonnaise on **Borealis** bread (see p. 14), while Aroostook County lamb chops are paired with sorrel-mint gremolata and roasted potatoes. Don't miss the artisanal cheese plate, featuring selections from the area's best cheesemakers. Closed Jan through Mar.

**Town Hill Bistro,** 1317 SR 102, Bar Harbor; (207) 288-1011; www .townhillbistro.com; $$$. The menu at this local favorite ranges from classics to curiosities; staid house-made charcuterie and pâté may be on the same menu as grilled yellowfin tuna with mixed olives, gin-spiked lemonade, and mashed artichoke, or sirloin with a stout-chocolate demi-glace. The atmosphere is cozy—seating is limited to about 30 patrons—and the service is engaged and attentive. Open year-round, with limited hours in the off-season. Reservations recommended.

**The Whale's Rib Tavern at Pilgrim's Inn,** 20 Main St., Deer Isle; (207) 348-6615 or 888-778-7505; www.pilgrimsinn.com; $$$. In the restored barn of the historic Pilgrim's Inn (built in 1793 and listed on the National Register of Historic Places), this casual seasonal restaurant offers a changing menu that ranges from small bites like Blue Hill mussels in garlic, wine, and butter to hearty meals like blue cheese–crusted beef tenderloin. Desserts are simple and satisfying: seasonal fruit crisps and chocolate caramel tart sprinkled with sea salt. With changing hours, call ahead.

**XYZ,** 80 Seawall Rd., Southwest Harbor; (207) 244-5221; www .xyzrestaurant.com; $$$. Xalapa, Yucatan, Zacatecas—XYZ—are three regions of Mexico known for their culinary traditions, and this casual wood-side restaurant aims to recreate the flavors of their rustic fare. Incorporating locally sourced ingredients and making all but bread and tortillas from scratch, the menu includes flavors unfamiliar to the coast: chicken in a simple mole sauce of chiles, fruit, and chocolate; pork rubbed with achiote paste and citrus, baked, and coarsely chopped; mushrooms stewed in chipotle. Drinks include Mexican beers, a carefully chosen wine list (including many

South American bottles), and four types of tequila. For dessert, don't miss the perfect flan, paired with coffee from a cooperative in Chiapas, Mexico. Reservations are recommended. Open Memorial Day through Columbus Day, though hours vary.

## Specialty Stores & Markets

**Blue Hill Co-op Community Market & Cafe,** 4 Ellsworth Rd., Blue Hill; (207) 374-2165; www.bluehillcoop.com. Founded in 1974, this natural foods market and cafe began as a co-op (and remains a cooperative enterprise) but is now open to the public, selling the peninsula's widest variety of fresh produce, artisanal cheeses, organic and pasture-raised meats, fair-traded coffees and teas, and kitchen staples (packaged and in bulk). The cafe serves soups, salads, and sandwiches—both vegetarian and non—as well as freshly baked pastries, for eating in or taking out. Roast chicken, seasoned with the cook's choice of rub or marinade, is available daily. With occasional cooking demonstrations by the co-op's "Health Angels." Open daily, year-round.

**Carvers Harbor Market,** 36 Main St., Vinalhaven; (207) 863-4319; www.carversharbormarket.com. The island's only full-service grocery store, this family-owned market may look a bit utilitarian from the outside, but inside it's warm and well-stocked. The shop includes a deli and butcher's counter, an on-site bakery, fresh produce and dairy, dry goods, and a large freezer case, and owners Barb and Cy Davidson are happy to make special orders. The only liquor store on the island, they've recently expanded their already extensive selection of wines and beers to include more organic varieties. Open daily year-round.

**The Cave,** 123 Reach Rd., Brooklin; (207) 359-8008; www .thecavebrooklin.com. The atmosphere is warm and inviting at this specialty foods shop, where lush cheeses age in "Betty," the store's temperature- and humidity-controlled cooler, and wines and chocolates are artfully arranged in wooden crates and rustic cabinets. The store's focus is the good stuff: artisanal cheeses, rich (mostly Maine-made) chocolates, and a carefully curated list of wines. Imported oils, pastas, jams, and fresh breads are sold as well, and sandwiches and soups are made daily. Open Tues through Sat, year-round.

**The Good Kettle,** 247 US 1, Stockton Springs; (207) 567-2035; www.thegoodkettle.com. This new cafe and specialty market offers local and imported wines, craft beers, and cheeses, as well as soups, sandwiches, prepared entrees, and packed picnics. Sandwiches are named for Downeast landmarks, and many are dabbed with Good Kettle's own marmalades and chutneys, also sold by the jar. Complete entrees and savory soups are available frozen, and sweet treats like bread pudding and chocolate mousse are made in-house. In the heat of summer, this is one of the few markets where you can pick up a pint of luscious ice cream from Monroe's Stone Fox Creamery. Open year-round, closed Tues.

**Rooster Brother,** 29 Main St., Ellsworth; (207) 667-3825 or (800) 866-0054; www.roosterbrother.com. A cooking shop, coffee roastery, tea merchant, bakery, specialty foods purveyor, and licorice mecca, this charming store is housed in a towering Victorian building that looks over the Union River. Baked goods are scrumptious—don't miss the Ultimate Chocolate Dessert, a rich flourless chocolate cake—and specialty foods include a variety of Maine-made treats, from **Raye's** mustards (p. 230) to Maine maple candies. But coffee is the true star: Green beans are carefully selected and roasted on-site, their perfume curling through the store. Grinders and other coffee accoutrements are for sale, and staff is eager to help you make the perfect cup at home. If you're a fan of licorice, the shop offers 17 varieties from across the globe. Open year-round, closed Sun.

**Sawyer's Market,** 353 Main St., Southwest Harbor; (207) 244-3317; www.mdiwine.com. In a lovely recessed store front, this family-owned market has been a local landmark since 1946, selling organically grown produce; custom-butchered meats; fresh seafood; warm baked goods; an extensive list of wines, beers, and spirits; and a variety of prepared foods, deli meats, and cheeses. The market specializes in boat provisioning—pick up a form or fill it out online and they'll deliver to the town dock or Great Harbor Marina. At the checkout, take note of the mounted photo: loyal customer Julia Child with the market's previous owner—an endorsement if ever there was one. Open daily, year-round.

**Wild Blueberry Land,** 1067 US 1, Columbia Falls; (207) 483-2583 (BLUE). This strange blue dome looks like something out of *Willie Wonka*—vivid, round, and enormous—and is devoted to promoting the state berry. Owned by the retired manager of Maine's blueberry research farm in nearby Jonesboro, the shop is a celebration of the blueberry: Here you can find blueberry jams, blueberry pancake mixes, and dried blueberries, among other treats. Harvest equipment, including blueberry rakes, is on display, as well as a video about the berry. Open June to Dec; call for hours.

## Pick Your Own

**Beddington Ridge Farm,** ME 193, Beddington; (207) 638-2664. Wild blueberries. Open during dry weather in Aug and Sept; please call ahead.

**Blue Barren Farm,** 88 Pea Ridge Rd., Columbia; (207) 483-4196. Various fruits and vegetables, as well as famed preserves. Open late June through Sept, Wed through Sun, noon to 5 p.m.

**Hillcrest Orchards,** 560 Maine Rd. South, Winterport; (207) 223-4416. Apples; open daily in season.

**Hog Bay Blueberries,** 207 Hog Bay Rd., Franklin; (207) 565-3584. Blueberries; open late July through mid-September, daily 9 a.m. to 5 p.m.

**Hooper's,** 856 Back Brooks Rd., Monroe; (207) 525-3236. Apples, winter squash; open September through mid-October, Sat and Sun, 8 a.m. to 6 p.m.

**Merrill Apple Farms,** US 1A, Bangor Road, Ellsworth; (207) 667-5121. Apples; open daily in season.

**Molly's Orchard,** Point Street, Columbia Falls; (207) 483-4178. Strawberries and apples; in season open daily until dark.

**Silver Ridge Farm,** 699 McDonald St., Bucksport; (207) 469-2405. Strawberries and pumpkins; open 8 a.m. to 8 p.m. daily during the season. Call ahead for crop conditions.

# Central Maine

Away from the tourist destinations of Maine's coastal waters and wooded mountains, the central part of the state is a quiet region with a rich history of agriculture and industry. The landscape is a tapestry of sparkling lakes and rolling emerald pasturage, dotted by family farms and orchards continuing the work of previous generations. This is historically the heart of Maine's farmland, and commercial dairies, egg farms, and apple orchards are scattered through the area, though on a relatively small scale. These are human-size farms, not industrialized, and many are diversified, filling their old post-and-beam barns with cattle, sheep, goats, and pigs, and growing hay and enough produce to sell at farmers' markets and stands along the roadside. An emerging community of artisanal cheesemakers has sprung up, and custom butchers specialize in humanely processing organic and pasture-raised animals.

Unity is the home of MOFGA—the Maine Organic Farmers and Gardeners Association—and the site of the annual Common Ground Country Fair, a celebration of sustainability that brings 60,000 visitors to the fairgrounds each year. Nearby Unity College is an

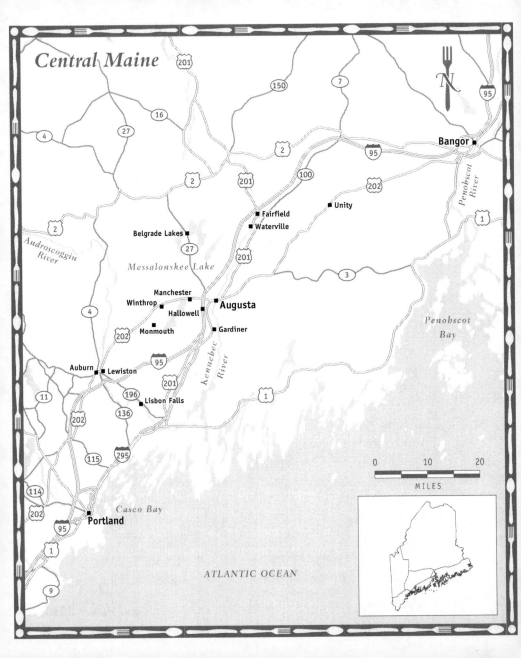

"environmental college" focusing on outdoor learning, community involvement, and issues of environmental responsibility. Another plus for budding farmers, central Maine is also home to two of New England's largest seed companies, Johnny's Selected Seeds in Winslow and Fedco Seeds in Waterville.

At the center of the state is its capital, Augusta, one of the smallest state capitals in the country. It's the site of Old Fort Western, America's oldest wooden fort (circa 1754), a National Historic Landmark on the banks of the Kennebec River, which is now a museum, store, and interpretive center. Just decades after the riverbanks were settled by Europeans, by the 19th century the Kennebec was lined with lumber and fabric mills, as well as paper mills that established a publishing industry in Augusta.

Further down the river, historic Hallowell was the center a thriving ice industry, in its heyday shipping massive cubes down the Kennebec and as far as the West Indies. Now the area has a vibrant artistic community, as well as a picturesque antique river port downtown.

A century ago, the entire region hummed with industry, and great mill complexes sat at the edges of both the Kennebec and the Androscoggin Rivers. Millwork brought an influx of immigrants to towns throughout the 19th and early 20th centuries, and their influences can still be felt on the culture and cuisines, from the French-Canadians in Lewiston to the Lebanese in Waterville. More recently, immigrants from troubled spots around the world have sought refuge in central Maine. Augusta is home to a small Cambodian population that arrived in the mid-1980s, while a large number of Somalis settled in Lewiston in the early 2000s.

After decades of disuse, the mills are now being reimagined as spaces for offices, restaurants, and small-scale manufacturing—look for microbreweries. A creative economy and the fusion of many influences have begun to sweep the region: Young chefs and producers have moved into mill complexes and downtowns, bringing energy, new flavors, and life to the buildings. College students at

## AMERICA'S FIRST ORGANIC GROWER'S ASSOCIATION

Since Helen and Scott Nearing moved to coastal Maine in search of "the good life," the state has attracted generations of homesteaders seeking a quiet plot of land on which to grow. The **Maine Organic Farmers and Gardeners Association,** known throughout the state as **MOFGA,** was founded in 1971 to help organic farmers learn from each other, increase local food production, and raise awareness of healthful, environmentally sound food practices. It is the oldest organization of its kind and has grown into the largest, expanding its offerings to include organic certification, myriad workshops, and the popular **Common Ground Country Fair** (see p. 269), which draws 60,000 people to the organization's rural fairgrounds each September. Though its headquarters are in Unity, MOFGA is a resource throughout the state, and its success is a testament to the commitment Mainers have to great local food and a sustainable environment. To learn more about MOFGA, visit their website: **www.mofga.org.**

Bates (in Lewiston) and Colby (in Waterville), are taking part in the renaissance. From cafes to breweries to cinemas, exciting things are happening. In communities like Lewiston, Somali shops are opening in abandoned downtown storefronts that once housed French-Canadian wares, and community gardens are tended by Africans and Acadians, side by side.

## Bakeries

**Black Crow Bakery,** 232 Plains Rd., Litchfield; (207) 268-9927; www.blackcrowbread.com. In a charmingly renovated antique barn, owner-bakers Mark and Tinker Mickalide make scrumptious breads, cookies, and sticky buns in their wood-burning brick oven. Artisans to the core, they use whole grains that they've milled on premises, eggs from their own chickens, and slow-rising natural starters; apple bread is likely to include fruit they've picked from their own heirloom tree. Bread varieties change daily, though the schedule is listed, and special orders can be accommodated. Don't miss sweet Apricot Almond, with toasted nuts, dried fruit, and a drop of honey, and the daily Tuscan. Come early, they often sell out. Open Tues through Sat.

**Hillman's Bakery,** 16 Western Ave., Fairfield; (207) 453-6300. A wall of wedding-cake tops greets you upon entering this unassuming bakery, and the smell of sugar floats through the air.

First opened in 1960 by owner Larry Hillman's father, things here are still done the old-fashioned way: Bread cools on racks behind the counter, and customers can watch everything being made on-site, from morning bismarcks to lunchtime meat pies. Decorated cakes are a specialty, but the more homespun menu items are equally tasty: chewy oatmeal bread, flaky-crusted French

## MAKIN' WHOOPIE

Whoopie pies are so beloved in the state of Maine that former governor John Baldacci once proclaimed a holiday in their honor. Shaped like a hamburger, these sweet treats are made of two cakey rounds filled with sugary cream. Purists consider chocolate buns with vanilla filling to be the only true combination, but bakers have been known to take liberties, using vanilla or pumpkin cake, and spiking the icing with everything maple syrup to Grand Marnier. Even the venerable **Labadie's Bakery** in Lewiston (see p. 257), which has been making whoopie pies since 1925 and is considered by some whoopie boosters to be the birthplace of the pie, makes a few nonstandard flavors. In summer, the sides of US 1 are lined with stands whose hand-lettered signs read HOMEMADE WHOOPIE PIES. They may not be professional bakers, but it might be worth a stop. To learn more about the history of the whoopie pie, check out *Making Whoopies: The Official Whoopie Pie Book* by Maine author Nancy Griffin (Down East Books, 2010).

Canadian *tourtières* (pork pies), hermit cookies, and surprisingly good cannoli.

**Labadie's Bakery,** 161 Lincoln St., Lewiston; (207) 784-7042; www.labadiesbakery.com. Selling whoopie pies from the same red-brick storefront since 1925, this local landmark is now a 24-hour operation, working round the clock to supply their mail-order business as well as the retail outlet. Whoopie pies, for the uninitiated, consist of two moist rounds of chocolate cake filled with sweet vanilla cream. Labadie's takes some liberties, offering peanut butter filling, vanilla cake, and the Pink Whoopie (vanilla cake filled with vanilla cream and raspberry jelly and sprinkled with coconut) in addition to the classic. Fresh crème horns, and warm honey-dipped doughnuts and bismarcks are also for sale.

**Roadside Bakery and Cafe,** 829 Main St., Monmouth; (207) 933-4544; www.roadsidebakerycafe.com. Gluten-free baked goods are the specialty of the house at this little bakery, and wheatless breads, muffins, cakes, and pie crust can be ordered in advance (give two to three days notice for orders). Also serving home-made breakfast and lunch and freshly baked desserts, cakes, pies, and breads (gluten-free and wheat based). Open daily.

# Brewpubs & Microbreweries

**Baxter Brewing Co.,** Bates Mill, Lewiston; (207) 333-6769 or (877) 319-4408; www.baxterbrewing.com. This eco-friendly micro-brewery is the first in the state to offer craft brews in cans. Founder Luke Livingston cites environmental concerns and quality assurance as the reason for their packaging: Aluminum is both easier to recycle and better for the brew, keeping out UV rays that spoil beer over time. Located in a sprawling Civil War–era textile mill, the brewery currently offers two beers, the hoppy Stowaway IPA, and the subtle Pamola Extra Pale Ale, named for a Native American god of thunder, whose form is a flying moose (also the brewery's logo). Open for tours and tastings Tues through Sat.

**Fat Toad's Pub,** 655 Maine Ave., Farmingdale; (207) 629-5111; www.fattoadspub.com. Cheekily billing itself as the town's largest pub (also its only), this friendly roadside tavern in a converted house is small and cozy and offers 14 brews by the pint—taps are mounted on the tailgate of an old Chevy—dozens of beers by the bottle, a full bar, and a menu of classic pub foods, from jalapeño cheddar burgers to a solidly good Reuben. Open daily for lunch, dinner, and drinks.

**The Kennebec Wharf,** 1 Wharf St., Hallowell; (207) 622-9290. This local landmark is a dive in the best sense: on the bank of the Kennebec—just feet from the water—the tavern floods regularly. With a full bar, beers on tap, and a menu of pub standards, the atmosphere is convivial, and there's live, local music several times a week. Open daily for lunch, dinner, and drinks.

**The Liberal Cup,** 115 Water St., #1, Hallowell; (207) 623-2739. With rough-hewn beams, exposed brick, and chalkboards keeping track of dart wins, the atmosphere at this cozy brewpub is inviting, as is the menu: brewer-owner Geoff Houghton's craft ales on tap (try the rich Tarbox Cream Stout), matched with hearty gourmet fare. Pub favorites like fish-and-chips, garlic mashed potatoes, cobb salad, and beer cheese soup are always on the menu, and the annual autumn Brewer's Dinner lets the chefs show their chops; past dinners have included pistachio chicken pâté with sauce vert, smoked paprika and sweet-spiced Muscovy duck breast with plum compote, and stout-and-chocolate crème brûlée. With live music. Open daily for lunch, dinner, and drinks.

**Mainely Brews Restaurant and Brewhouse,** 1 Post Office Sq., Waterville; (207) 873-2457; www.mainelybrews.com. This laid-back pub in the heart of downtown offers a large menu and six house ales—all named for Waterville landmarks—brewed by **Black Bear Microbrew** (see p. 301) in Orono, as well as more local and imported beers—bottled and draft—and a full bar. The food is classic tavern fare—chicken wings, nachos, burgers, sandwiches, and a few entrees, though the vegetarian offerings are surprisingly varied. Early in the night, the place is family friendly, but it's crowded with students from nearby Colby College and locals who come to shoot pool, hear live music, and shout out trivia answers (Thursday is Trivia Night). With seasonal outdoor seating on the patio. Open daily, serving lunch Mon through Sat.

**Old Goat,** 33 Main St., Richmond; (207) 737-4628. In a converted bank in the center of town, this local favorite has revolving beers on tap, scrumptious pressed panini sandwiches, and an old-time atmosphere (helped by the staid interior) that includes cribbage games and darts. With live music on weekends. Open daily for lunch, dinner, and drinks.

## Farm Stands

**Goranson Farm,** 250 River Rd. (ME 128), Dresden; (207) 737-8834; http://home.gwi.net/~goransonfarm/gfourfrm.htm. This certified-organic farm stand offers produce, berries and other fruits, cut flowers, herbs, and seedlings. A range of baked goods (try their homemade chicken pie), fresh eggs, dried beans, and their own pasture-raised chicken and pork are also available. Open daily from mid-May through Oct and weekends in Nov. In winter call for availability of veggies from the root cellar.

# FIDDLEHEAD FERVOR

Curled tightly like the scroll of a violin (hence the name), these tender unfurled ferns mark the height of spring in Maine. When the fiddleheads have arrived, winter is officially over, and the seasons have turned! Beginning in early May, foragers throughout the state wade along the banks of streams, harvesting young ferns, dusty with brown fuzz, from the edge of the water. Once cleaned, fiddleheads are vivid green, with the texture of asparagus and an earthy, almost mushroomy flavor. In season, they're sold in specialty shops, by the side of the road out of honor-system coolers, and from the back of station wagons— if there's a dripping canoe on top, you know they're fresh. Local chefs revel in this first flavor of the season, incorporating fiddleheads into everything from tempura to tapenade. They're surprisingly easy to cook—simply trim the ends and parboil for at least a minute to get rid of the sharp tannins (when the water is the color of tea, they're ready). Once prepared, they can be chilled and tossed in a salad, sautéed with garlic, or used as you would any green. Warning: Not all ferns are edible, so make sure you buy fiddleheads from an experienced forager.

**Jillson's Farm and Sugarhouse,** 143 Jordan Bridge Rd., Sabbatus; (207) 375-4486; www.jillsonfarm.com. Since 1966, the Jillson family has operated a farm stand and sugarhouse, selling vegetables and cut flowers in season, and maple syrup, handmade pickles (don't miss the tangy green tomatoes), relishes, jams, dried beans, and local dairy and meats year-round. In early spring, the shop hosts sugar parties as the maple syrup is boiled. Open daily, year-round.

**Kinney's Sugarhouse and Maple Supplies,** 39 Maple Lane, Knox; (207) 568-7576; www.maple confections.com. Tapping 185 acres of sugar bush, this sweet farm store sells maple syrup and a range of maple products, all certified organic by the Maine Organic Farmers and Gardeners Association. They are the largest producer of maple candy in the state, and other products include maple cream (also called maple butter), granulated maple sugar, and cinnamon maple sugar. Supplies and advice for tapping your own trees are also available at the shop. Open Mon through Fri. In maple season (late February through early April), visit their sugarhouse at 200 Abbott Rd.

**Nezinscot Farm,** 284 Turner Center Rd., Turner; (207) 225-3231; www.nezinscotfarm.com. This year-round farm store offers seasonal produce, owner Gloria Varney's exceptionally fine aged artisanal cheeses, fresh baked goods, natural meats, and more. The farm operates an organic dairy, and includes 250 acres of lush, rolling pasturage and crops. A small teahouse, overlooking the back vegetable garden, is available for reservation from mid-May through October for a full English or Asian tea—each includes seasonal fruit accompanied by either warm scones and clotted cream (English) or sticky rice (Asian). The farm hosts occasional musical jam nights; knitters love the store's second floor, filled with yarns from the farm's Cormo and Shetland sheep, llamas, alpacas, and goats. Open year-round, closed Mon.

**Town House Farm,** 35 Townhouse Rd., Whitefield; (207) 549-5670. This licensed dairy offers creamy Ewegurt (sheep's milk yogurt), Moogurt (organic cow's milk yogurt), briny feta cheese, semi-firm Greek-style halloumi, and Ballstown 1790, a mild aged cheese, at their self-serve store, open Mar to Nov. If you can't make it to the farm, look for their products at natural food stores around the state.

## Farmers' Markets

**Auburn Mall Farmers' Market,** Porteous rear lot, Turner Street side, Auburn; (207) 336-2411. May through Oct, Thurs and Sat, 9 a.m. to 3 p.m.

**Augusta River Market,** old Edward's Mill site on Water Street, Augusta; (207) 626-0514. June through Sept, Sat, 8:30 a.m. to 1 p.m.

**Fairfield Farmers' Market,** 81 Main St. (Nazarene Church parking lot), Fairfield; (207) 948-5724. May through Oct, Wed, 2 to 6 p.m., and Sat, 9:30 a.m. to 1:30 p.m.

# Blueberry Pie

Maine's blueberries are legendary, prized for their sweetness and concentrated flavor, immortalized in Mainer Robert McCloskey's classic children's book Blueberries for Sal *and enjoyed at their peak in July and August, when US 1 is lined with roadside stands selling berries by the pint. In Maine, blueberries make their way into ice cream, salsa, vodka, and more. There's something perfectly summery, though, about blueberry pie. My mother-in-law, Nancy Schatz, began making this pie in her mother's Portland kitchen and won first prize with the recipe at the 1991 Old Hallowell Days bake-off. It's so good that it was featured in the cookbook* More from Magnolia *by Allysa Torey, from which this version is adapted.*

### Crust:

2½ cups all-purpose flour

3 tablespoons sugar

1 teaspoon salt

4 tablespoons unsalted butter, chilled and cut into small pieces

3 tablespoons vegetable shortening, chilled and cut into small pieces

5 tablespoons orange juice

### Filling:

3 cups fresh Maine blueberries

1 cup sugar

3 tablespoons quick-cooking tapioca

3 tablespoons brandy

2 tablespoons lemon juice

¼ teaspoon cinnamon

2 tablespoons unsalted butter, chilled and cut into small pieces.

**To make the crust:** *Combine flour, sugar, and salt in a large bowl. Using a pastry cutter, work in the butter and shortening until the mixture is the consistency of coarse cornmeal. Sprinkle orange juice over the mixture and toss with a fork until the dough is moistened. Gather the dough into two balls, wrap with plastic, and refrigerate until chilled (about 20 minutes). While dough is chilling, make the filling.*

**To make the filling:** *Combine blueberries, sugar, tapioca, brandy, lemon juice, and cinnamon in a large bowl and toss until fruit is evenly coated.*

*Preheat oven to 425 degrees. On a lightly floured surface, roll each ball of dough into a circle, approximately 10 inches in diameter. Press one circle into a 9-inch pie tin, leaving about ½ inch around the edge. Pour in the fruit filling, dot with remaining chilled butter, and place top crust over the fruit. Pinch edges of the dough to seal, and slash a few vents in the top crust.*

*Place pie on a baking sheet and bake for 15 minutes, then lower the oven temperature to 350 degrees and continue baking until crust is lightly browned, 30 to 40 minutes. Allow to cool at least 2 hours before serving. Garnish with a big dollop of whipped cream.*

*Serves 6–8.*

Recipe courtesy of Nancy Schatz.

**Lewiston Farmers' Market,** Kennedy Park, Lewiston; (207) 777-5131. July through Oct, Tues, 2 to 6 p.m.

**Manchester-Mayflower Farmers' Market,** next to Manchester post office on ME 17, Manchester; (207) 621-1981. May to Thanksgving (weather permitting), Wed, 3 to 6 p.m., and Sat, 10 a.m. to 2 p.m.

**Waterville Farmers' Market,** Appleton and Main Streets, Waterville; www.watervillefarmersmarket.org. Summer market: May through Nov, Thurs, 2 to 6 p.m. Winter market: Dec through Apr, every third Thurs, 2 to 4 p.m.

 *Food Happenings*

## June

**Festival FrancoFun,** 46 Cedar St., Lewiston; (207) 689-2000. Sponsored by the Franco-American Heritage Center (Le Centre d'Héritage Franco-Américain), this annual festival celebrates the contributions and living legacy of the city's French-speaking Canadian community, who immigrated to the area in droves in the mid-1860s to work in the textile mills. The three-day festival includes a daily breakfast of traditional foods, performances by local entertainers, and delicacies that range from *poutine* to *creton* to salmon pie.

## July

**Central Maine Egg Festival,** Crosby Street, Pittsfield; (207) 257-4208; http://eggfest.craftah.com. "Brown eggs are local . . . and local eggs are fresh" is the motto of this annual celebration of the brown egg industry, held every fourth Saturday in July since 1973. With a parade; an Early Bird Breakfast featuring an enormous frying pan that measures 5 feet across; a quiche, cheesecake, and pie cook-off (entries must use at least three eggs); a chicken barbecue; and a fireworks display.

**Moxie Festival,** Downtown Lisbon Falls; www.moxiefestival.com. Thousands descend upon the little town of Lisbon Falls each July for its annual celebration of Maine's official soft drink. The three-day festival includes parades, live music, a firefighters' muster, craft tents, and a book sale to benefit the local library—and gallon upon gallon of Moxie by the bright orange can, over vanilla ice cream, and even as a braise in "Moxie pulled pork."

## August

**Taste of Greater Waterville,** Downtown and Castonguay Square, Waterville; (207) 873-3315. Sample the flavors of local eateries, from pulled pork to panna cotta, at this one-day festival. Featuring street-side dining, a beer garden (21 plus), live music, and children's activities.

# Maine's Got Moxie!

Love it or hate it, Maine's official soft drink brings out strong feelings. Originally created as a patent medicine and "nerve food" by Dr. Augustin Thompson of Union, Moxie has been sold as a beverage since 1884. Its trademarked bittersweet flavor is generally attributed to gentian root, though the formula is a carefully guarded secret—the label offers precious few tantalizing clues. In the 1910s and '20s, Moxie's advertising campaign was so effective that the term *moxie*, meaning "courage, daring, and verve," made its way into American slang. Over the years, the drink's popularity has waned, and it's now sold exclusively in New England. In Maine, you can grab an orange can in almost every convenience store, visit the **Moxie Museum** in Lisbon Falls (Kennebec Fruit Company building, 2 Main Street; 207-353-8173), or, at the select few diners that have it on tap, simply tell your waitress to "Make Mine Moxie!"

**Winslow Blueberry Festival,** Winslow Congregational Church, 12 Lithgow St., Winslow; (207) 872-2544. For more than four decades, this annual celebration and fund-raiser has served up blueberries provided by the Houston family, who donate more than 500 pounds of berries each year. The festivities begin with an all-you-can-eat blueberry pancake breakfast and continue with live music, a rummage sale, silent auction, face painting, and the sale of hundreds of blueberry pies and muffins.

## September

**Common Ground Country Fair,** 294 Crosby Brook Rd., Unity; (207) 568-4142; www.mofga.org. Billed as a "celebration of rural living," this three-day festival draws more than 60,000 people to the tiny town of Unity, where the **Maine Organic Farmers and Gardeners Association** (p. 254) is headquartered. Amidst organic gardens and open barns, speakers in tents educate visitors on everything from goat care to political action, and demonstrations range from sheering and spinning fleece to using garden tools and safe bicycling. All food vendors must use certified-organic ingredients grown in Maine, which in past years has inspired a contraband coffee cart just outside the fairgrounds. Volunteers at the children's area help little ones make banners and flags for the popular parade of vegetables, and horse-drawn wagons carry families around the extensive grounds. Campsites available.

**Monmouth Apple Fest,** 748 Main St., Monmouth; (207) 933-2287. In the heart of apple country, this one-day community festival is a tribute to the iconic fruit. Featuring apple-barrel car rides, apple exhibits, the Apple Pie Cafe, wagon rides, and fresh pressed cider.

## October

**Manchester Apple Festival,** Manchester; (207) 215-7487. This annual one-day festival, sponsored by **Lakeside Orchards** (see p.

290), kicks off with a pancake breakfast and road race, and includes home-cooking demonstrations, the Maine State Apple Pie Eating Championship, an apple-pie baking contest, and the Great Apple Race across Muck Pond. Live music accompanies the festivities, and visitors can pick apples, sample fresh cider, and take horse-drawn wagon rides at the orchard. The day ends with a bean supper and community concert.

**Swine and Stein Octoberfest,** Water Street, Gardiner; (207) 582-3100. Craft beers and local pork are showcased in this one-day family festival, celebrating the diverse flavors of Maine. Adults can taste brews from throughout the state, kids can hit the dunk tank and compete in stick-pony races, and the whole family can oink out on the swine, prepared in dozens of ways by local chefs.

## The Maine Ice Cream Trail

**Deb's Ice Cream and Mini Golf,** 32 Water St., Randolph; (207) 582-1835. With homemade ice cream and a well-worn minigolf course, this local landmark is popular with local teens, many of whom wield the scoops. Ice creams are made on-site, as are treats like ice-cream cakes, and, of course, gooey sundaes (try the maple syrup). With outdoor seating and a drive-through window. Open daily in season.

**Gifford's Famous Ice Cream,** 170 Silver St., Waterville; (207) 872-6631. This seasonal stand is on the site of the now defunct but much beloved Rummels, and though it's been a Gifford's for almost 20 years, locals still can't resist reminiscence and comparison. Ice cream, by Skowhegan-based **Gifford's** (see p. 309) is creamy and rich, and includes Maine favorites like Grapenut and Moose Tracks. With batting cages and minigolf from the old days. Open seasonally.

**Old Colony Ice Cream,** 28 Bowdoin St., Winthrop; (207) 377-7788. Tucked on a back street, this seasonal stand is a hidden gem and has been a favorite among locals for decades, serving homemade ice cream, sundaes, and treats. Flavors are creamy classics—don't miss peppermint stick, packed with crunchy bits of candy. Open seasonally.

**Tubby's Ice Cream,** 76 Main St., Wayne; (207) 686-8181; www.tubbysicecream.com. Made from scratch on-site, the ice-cream offerings at this seasonal stand change daily and are available by the scoop, the hand-packed pint, and in treats that range from sundaes (topped with home-made fudge or butterscotch sauce) to the popular Frozen Frenzies: ice cream blended with your choice of mix-ins. Lobster rolls and homemade lobster stew are also available, as well as a range of sandwiches. Open seasonally.

**A-1 Diner,** 3 Bridge St., Gardiner; (207) 582-4804; www.a1diner .com; $$. In a classic silver dining car on a downtown street that straddles the river, this landmark diner has been serving up traditional diner fare since 1948. The decor is pure period—a checkered floor, powder-blue stools, and an illuminated clock above the counter—but the menu is more inventive, offering surprising, far-ranging specials in addition to well-executed standards. Steaks, fries, BLTs, and buttery biscuits (famed in the region) share the bill with Thai crab cakes, Moroccan stew, and a range of specials. For dessert, there are classics like apple crisp, carrot cake, and tapioca pudding, as well as zesty lemon coconut pie, seasonally changing puddings, and the decadent, justly renowned warm brownie cup. Get there early; since the diner was featured in Guy Fieri's *Diners, Drive-Ins and Dives*, tourist traffic has gotten heavy. Open daily.

**Fast Eddie's Drive-In,** 1308 US 202, Winthrop; (207) 377-5550; $$. Though it's only been around for a little more than a decade, this '50s-style drive-in—complete with poodle-skirted waitresses and outdoor speakers tuned to doo-wop music—has become a fixture. With diner food and an indoor ice-cream parlor serving up scoops of homemade hard-pack ice cream, the drive-in is a flashback to another time. Weekly Cruise Nights attract classic-car aficionados, converging in everything from Model Ts to Thunderbirds, for onion rings, a Coke, and a trip down memory lane. Open daily; closed briefly in winter.

**Graziano's Casa Mia,** ME 196, Lisbon; (207) 353-4335; www .grazianoscasamia.com; $$. With boxing memorabilia on the walls and garlicky goodness in the air, "every meal is a knockout" at this expansive Italian restaurant. Former boxer and former athletic commissioner for the state of Maine Joe Graziano founded the restaurant in 1969, transforming a rowdy saloon that was popular with mill workers into the family-friendly eatery his children run today. Legend has it that Joe's skills in the kitchen and the ring were called on in the early days, though now the only fights patrons encounter are in the photographs lining the walls. The menu is classic Italian: fettucine Alfredo, eggplant parmigiana, spaghetti puttanesca, and the like, with hearty portions, savory tomato sauces, and mounds of mozzarella. In the heart of Maine's farmland, the Graziano family has made a commitment to serving exclusively local, grass-fed beef. Open Thurs through Sun for lunch and dinner.

**Hi Hat Pancake House,** 380 Maine Ave., Farmingdale; (207) 582-9842; $$. Though its tall, faded sign still reads HI HAT DRIVE IN, the days of car service are long past at this local landmark. Instead, go inside, seat yourself, and enjoy diner breakfasts and pancakes of all description. Flapjack offerings include simple buttermilk, fruit-dotted blueberry, chocolate or butterscotch chip, but the house special is bacon: crispy strips of bacon are crumbled onto the batter as it cooks on the griddle. Lavished with butter and syrup, these are a surprising treat. The restaurant makes its own jams, fruit syrups and breads, which are available at the table and for sale. Open daily for breakfast, lunch, and dinner.

**The Red Barn Drive In Restaurant,** 455 Riverside Dr., Augusta; (207) 623-9485; www.redbarndrivein.com; $$. Since 1977, this family-owned eatery has served fried seafood and chicken, lobster rolls and stew, and crisp onion rings from its big red barn. It's a fast, casual restaurant—place your order at the outside window or indoor counter and pick it up a few minutes later, mounded in cardboard boats and disposable cups on a red plastic tray. The food itself is tasty and fresh, with succulent scallops and tiny, sweet Maine shrimp fried to a golden brown, juicy chicken in a crusty coat, speckled chunks of lobster, and piping hot fries. With outdoor seating in warm weather. Open Tues through Sun for lunch and dinner, Mon for lunch.

**Roy's All Steak Hamburgers,** 5 Washington St., Auburn; (207) 783-4304; www.roysgolf.com; $. A Maine classic, this year-round hamburger stand delivers on its name: Order a hamburger and fries, and from the other side of the counter you can watch the Grade A sirloin being ground and shaped into patties and the potatoes being crinkle cut by hand. Burgers come dressed with mustard, ketchup, grilled onions, and pickle relish, and tables have bottles of vinegar for dousing the fries (ask at the counter for more ketchup). Cap your meal with a scoop of Gifford's ice cream, or with a round of golf on their adjacent course. Open daily.

**Sam's Italian Foods,** 268 Main St., Lewiston; (207) 782-9145; www.samsitalian.com; $. In 1939, Sam Bennett opened a small sandwich shop in Auburn to serve quick meals to the mill workers. Over the years, the company has grown, adding pizzas, pastas, and Italian entrees to its long list of Italian sandwiches, as well as famed whoopie pies. Now with locations throughout central Maine.

**Simone's Hot Dog Stand,** 99 Chestnut St., Lewiston; (207) 782-8431; $. Steamed "red snappers," Maine's signature scarlet-hued hot dogs, are on the menu at this family-owned corner restaurant, which has served the "twin cities" of Lewiston and Auburn for nearly a century. Though the menu also features diner breakfast and lunch, it's all about the weenies. Franks come on a warm, fluffy split bun and are topped with onions, relish, and ketchup ("the usual"), or with cheese, chili, or sauerkraut; a shaker of celery salt sits next to the salt and pepper counter. Open daily for breakfast and lunch, closed Sun.

## Made or Grown Here

**Kennebec Cheesery at Koons Farm,** 795 Pond Rd., Sidney; (207) 547-4171; www.kennebeccheesery.com. On 92 acres of pasture overlooking picturesque Messalonskee Lake, cheesemakers Jean and Peter Koons raise Alpine goats and Katahdin sheep and make small batch cheeses that reflect their blended heritage—she's from

# WINERIES IN SOUTH-CENTRAL MAINE

Maybe it's the rolling hills, or the long winters that inspire dreams of Napa. Whatever the origins, south-central Maine is home to a small but growing community of winemakers. Though their operations aren't yet open to the public, look for these labels at local specialty shops and local restaurants or order a taste of Maine online.

**Maine Coast Vineyards,** Falmouth; www .mainecoastvineyards.com

**Tanguay & Son Winery,** Lewiston; (207) 740-6873; www.tanguaywinery.com

**Younity Winery & Vineyards,** Unity; (207) 948-7777; www.unitywinery.com

New Zealand, he grew up here on the family farm—and techniques Jean has learned making cheese on three continents. Cheeses are made from both goat's milk and organic Jersey cow milk from nearby Woodside Farm, and include goat and cow chèvre "cobbles," fresh goat's milk feta, snowballs (mushroomy French Chaource), yogurt (cow's and goat's milk), and occasionally ricotta. Fresh lamb is available in season. Products sold at local farmers' markets and on the farm. Call ahead.

**Maurice Bonneau's Sausage Kitchen,** 36 Main St., Lisbon Falls; (207) 353-5503; www.sausagekitchen.com. Beneath a swinging sign that reads MY WURST IS BEST, this tidy store sells just one thing: sausage. From fiery smoked chorizo to mild, fresh Swedish potato sausage, the offerings span the globe and include something for every carnivorous palate. All sausage is made on premises from natural pork, lamb, turkey, and beef, and smoked sausages are cured in the on-site smokehouse. It's a pork lover's paradise, with more than 50 types of sausage, and assorted jerkies and trail sticks. Open Tues through Sat.

## Restaurants

**Big G's Deli,** Benton Avenue, Winslow; (207) 873-7808; www .big-g-s-deli.com; $$. This deli, bakery, and restaurant is known for its extensive list of cleverly named mile-high sandwiches served on home-baked breads. Local politicians, celebrities, and employees are immortalized at the deli in combinations that range from straightforward (the Jacques Cousteau sandwich, with seafood salad, sprouts, tomato, and Jack cheese) to experimental (the Willy Nelson, with turkey, sauerkraut, onions, pepperoncini, and cheddar) to mind boggling (the Jimmy Buffet omelet, filled with pineapple, bananas, coconut, dates, and walnuts). Owner Gerald Michaud Jr. still mans the kitchen, presiding over the ovens that turn out hundreds of loaves, pastries, and baked treats daily. Save room for dessert: It's considered by some to have the best whoopie pies in the state. Open daily for breakfast, lunch, and supper.

**Cloud 9 at the Senator Inn and Spa,** 284 Western Ave., Augusta; (207) 622-0320; www.senatorinn.com; $$$. The dining room at this elegant hotel and spa is whimsical, with a decor that combines bright accents, contemporary artwork, and comfortable, overstuffed seating. The menu is creative, with an emphasis on locally sourced ingredients, fresh seafood, and light options for the health conscious, which include a variety of entree salads—the lobster cobb salad is a treat. Desserts range from virtuous to decadent, and all baked goods, including the warm bread basket delivered to each table, are made in-house. Open daily for breakfast, lunch, and dinner.

**Country Cafe,** Hallowell Road, Litchfield; (207) 268-4003; $. At a tiny country crossroads, next to the local post office, this casual restaurant serves down-home cooking made from scratch. Sit at one of a handful of tables or the few seats at the counter and start your day with fresh home-made muffins (banana and blueberry are winners), an omelet, or a stack of pancakes. At lunch, try a hot open-faced turkey sandwich or fried seafood—and save room for a wedge of coconut cream pie.

**FishBones American Grill,** 70 Lincoln St., Lewiston; (207) 333-3663; www.fishbonesag.com; $$$. Amid weathered masonry and solid wooden beams in the newly renovated Bates Mill complex, this upscale seafood restaurant specializes in grilled and roasted entrees, arranged beautifully on the plate. The menu influences are varied, and offerings range from seared tuna sashimi on ramen noodles to Cajun sea scallops with lentil ragout to "deconstructed" shepherd's pie with grilled lamb, roasted vegetables, and garlic mashed potatoes. An extensive wine list is featured in monthly reservation-only wine dinners. Serving lunch and dinner, Tues through Fri, dinner Sat, and brunch on Sun.

**Fuel,** 49 Lisbon St., Lewiston; (207) 333-3835; www.fuelmaine .com; $$$. Possibly the only restaurant in town with *sous vide* preparations on the menu, this hip eatery in downtown's historic Lyceum Hall takes its inspiration from French bistro cooking, with a smattering of American comfort foods for good measure. Housed in a restored Victorian theater, the dining room has a welcoming feel that's both elegant and a little gritty: Butcher paper covers the white table linen, votive candles illuminate the exposed brick walls. The changing menu offers classic French dishes with a few fun twists—a lamb sirloin in red wine sauce comes dotted with grapes, while flounder filets are paired with chunks of Maine lobster. If you're feeling adventurous, try the Feed Me Justin, a four-course tasting for the entire table created by chef Justin Oliver. Open for dinner, Tues through Sat.

**George's Restaurant,** 4 Union St., Waterville; (207) 872-2629; $$. With oilcloth on the tables and a salad bar in the corner, this casual restaurant may not look extraordinary, but among locals, it's a landmark. Originally opened more than 30 years ago as Sitto's, a Lebanese grocery, bakery, and restaurant catering to the city's tight-knit Syrian and Lebanese immigrant community (drawn to the area at the turn of the 20th century by the promise of mill work), the restaurant is now owned by brother-and-sister team Patricia and Ed McMahon. Though their heritage is different, the menu is substantially the same, with hand-rolled grape and cabbage leaves, kibbe and kofta (spiced meatballs), as well as pasta specials, seafood, and the King Steak, a massive slab of beef, cooked to order. Open for lunch and dinner, Wed through Sat.

**The Last Unicorn Restaurant,** 8 Silver St., Waterville; (207) 873-6378; www.lastunicornrestaurant.com; $$. For more than 30 years, this casual restaurant has been a fixture, drawing patrons downtown for hearty comfort foods, globally inspired specials, and brunch under the umbrellas on the street-side outdoor patio. The menu is eclectic and blends influences that range from local favorites to owner Joe Plumstead's heritage and travels. You'll find Chesapeake crab cakes (Plumstead hails from Maryland) next to Thai sizzling catfish, next to macadamia-crusted chicken with lemon, ginger, and Brie next to Italian rib eye steak, and somehow it all comes together deliciously. With a full bar—if you're not driving, try the island rum punch. Open daily for lunch and dinner.

**Marché,** 40 Lisbon St., Lewiston; (207) 333-3836; www.marche maine.com; $$. This "sassy little sister" of nearby **Fuel** (see p. 279) specializes in lunch, serving fresh crepes, sandwiches, and salads in a quietly elegant space separated into two dining rooms: the formal Salon Bleu, and the funkier Bar Rouge. The menu includes savory and sweet crepes, ranging from delicate lobster with wilted spinach and lemon beurre blanc to hearty mushrooms with tomato compote, spinach, basil, and béchamel to the French dessert classic, Nutella. Sandwiches are thick and made to order, and braised short ribs and rotisserie chicken are seasoned and cooked to tender perfection. On Monday evenings, the kitchen reopens for an intimate four-course prix-fixe meal (reservations necessary). Open Mon through Fri for lunch (11 a.m. to 2 p.m.).

**Pepper and Spice,** 875 Lisbon St., Lewiston; (207) 782-7562; www.pepperandspice.com; $$. With more than 300 items on the menu, this unassuming restaurant—set back from the road beneath a blue vinyl awning—is as surprising as it is tasty. Noodles and curries are light (especially the popular pad thai) and can be spiced to taste, and the menu offers an abundance of vegetarian and seafood dishes. Staff is friendly, unobtrusive, and incredibly attentive. Open daily for lunch and dinner.

**Purple Cow House of Pancakes,** 6 US 201, Fairfield; (207) 453-1371; www.purple cowmaine.com; $. This wacky pancake house includes a drive-through window that features home-cooked breakfast and a kitschy decor teeming with cartoon characters and retro memorabilia. Owner Yann Milcendeau, originally from Morocco, has perfected the diner menu, serving breakfast all day, more than a dozen pancakes—ranging from raspberry to onion—and homey sandwiches like cream cheese and olive. Dinners run the gamut, from baskets of sweet fried smelts to fettucine in homemade Alfredo sauce. Open daily.

**Riverfront Barbeque and Grille,** 300 Water St., Augusta; (207) 622-8899; www.riverfrontbbq.com; $$. The smells of Southern barbeque may seem surprising on the banks of the Kennebec River, but this casual restaurant brings smoke and spice to Augusta's historic downtown. Housed in an old paper warehouse, the atmosphere is comfortable, and the food is made from scratch: slow smoked ribs, pulled pork, shredded beef brisket, and smoked chicken are menu favorites. Pair them with coleslaw and jalepeño corn bread, and you'll swear you're in a warmer climate. The upstairs Gin Mill, a lounge built in tribute to the Prohibition-era secret storehouse workmen found in the base-ment, offers a light menu, full bar, and extensive list of single-malt scotches and single-batch bourbon. Open daily for lunch and dinner; Gin Mill open nights Thurs through Sat.

**Rolly's Diner,** 87 Mill St., Auburn; (207) 753-0171; www.rollys diner.com; $. In an unassuming white clapboard building just across the river from Lewiston, this homey diner serves some of the best comfort food in the region. From Mémère Blais Crepes, served plain or filled with lemon curd, berries, brown sugar, and whipped cream, to baked beans, sausage or *creton* from nearby Mailhots, the French-Canadian offerings are superb. Classic diner breakfasts and lunches include steak and eggs, omelets, and a variety of sandwiches and burgers. Also available for catering; for festive occasions, order one of the surprisingly intricate fruit sculptures. Open daily for breakfast and lunch.

**The Sedgley Place,** 54 Sedgley Rd., Greene; (207) 946-5990 or (800) 924-7778; www.sedgleyplace.com; $$$. With dining by reservation only, this country inn offers several dinner seatings each night, serving five-course meals created from ingredients grown on the restaurant's own certified-organic farm in nearby Leeds. Owners Paul and Suzanne Levesque operate the restaurant and farm with two of their grown children, giving the restaurant, in a Federal home circa 1786, a comfortable, homelike quality. Menus change weekly, reflecting what's in season. Dinner by reservation only. Closed Mon.

**Slate's Restaurant and Bakery,** 163 Water St., Hallowell; (207) 622-4104; www.slatesrestaurant.com; $$. A local landmark, this off-beat restaurant has been a hangout for local artists and intelligentsia for decades. Over the years, the menu has grown from its veggie burrito and sprouty sandwich origins, and it now includes grilled pizzas on whole wheat crust, country chicken pie, hand-rolled pastas, and a variety of grilled meats. The "afternoon" menu, offered between lunch and dinner service, includes a range of appetizers and light entrees—don't miss the warmed Brie with smoked shrimp. The bakery provides all the restaurant's breads and pastries and also offers takeout and coffee. With weekend brunch and Monday live music. Open daily, though hours vary.

**Village Inn Restaurant,** 157 Main St., Belgrade Lakes; (207) 495-3553; www.villageinnducks.com; $$$. This beloved inn and local landmark is famed for its many preparations of roast duckling. Perched at the lake's edge, with unsuspecting waterfowl drifting by, the atmosphere is elegant, as is the menu, starting with grilled duck sausage, lobster crepes, and escargot. The roast duckling is napped with your choice of many sauces, from tangy orange-cranberry to spicy Madagascar with green peppercorns. The seasonal inn has views of Great Pond. In the off-season (in fact, year-round), roast ducks can be ordered by mail, prepared by chef Susan Grover and shipped overnight. Open seasonally, Apr to Dec.

**Weathervane Restaurant,** ME 17, Readfield; (207) 685-9410; $$$. With an outdoor deck overlooking Maranacook Lake, this year-round local favorite serves down-home cooking: steaks, baked and fried seafood, house-made soups, and gooey desserts. At night, the downstairs hosts live music in the lounge; occasionally, the Weathervane House Band—including the owners—gets up to jam.

## Specialty Stores & Markets

**Ballard Meats & Seafood,** 55 Myrtle St., Manchester; (207) 622-9764. For more than 30 years, this family-owned shop near Lake Cobbosseecontee has sold live lobsters, fresh shellfish and seafood, and specialty cuts of beef. Serving both retail and wholesale customers, the shop's not fancy, just solidly good: thick steaks, creamy fresh scallops, and tanks full of large lobsters. Call in advance and they'll cook your lobsters and steamers perfectly to order.

**Barrels Community Market,** 74 Main St., Waterville; (207) 660-4844; www.barrelsmarket.com. Conceived as a "year-round Common Ground Fair," (p. 269) this nonprofit market in the historic Barell Block building brings local, sustainably produced natural and organic produce, meats, dairy, and crafts to the community. Most products are grown or raised within 20 miles of Waterville, and others are sourced whenever possible from within Maine's borders. Vegetables and fruits are sold during the seasons when they're plentiful—don't come here for bananas or zucchinis in winter. With a special emphasis on regional treats like pickled fiddleheads, beet relish, and smoked mussels and shrimp. Closed Sun.

## Somali Stores of Lewiston

Somali refugees began arriving in Lewiston in 2001, fleeing their country's brutal, ongoing civil war, which began in the early 1990s. Over the past decade, their community has grown to more than 2,500 immigrants. A fascinating culture has emerged, with mosques coexisting with French-Canadian Catholic churches, and empty storefronts downtown are being revitalized as markets catering to the predominately Muslim Somali population.

**A&R Halal Meat,** 199 Bartlett St., Lewiston; (207) 786-0018

**African Store,** 258 Lisbon St., Lewiston; (207) 577-4677

**Al-Hudda Halaal Grocery Store,** 253 Lisbon St., Lewiston; (207) 784-0300

**Aliyows Store,** 191 Lisbon St., Lewiston; (207) 795-1111

**Baraka Store,** 234 Lisbon St., Lewiston; (207) 782-7838

**Barwaqo Halal Store,** 274 Lisbon St., Lewiston; (207) 577-2988

**DurDur,** 268 Lisbon St., Lewiston; (207) 786-3275

**Mogadishu Store,** 240 Lisbon St., Lewiston; (207) 777-7757

**E. W. Mailhot Sausage Co.,** 258 Bartlett St., Lewiston; (207) 786-2454. Specializing in French-Canadian meat products, this family-owned meat shop has been serving the Franco-American community of Lewiston for more than a century, turning out *cretons* (pork spread, like pâté), *tourtière* (pork pie), salmon pies, and pound after pound of homemade pork sausage, made according to a secret family recipe. Mailhot's products are now distributed throughout the region, but they're all made in the shop, by hand, under the guidance of this generation's sausage maker, Marc Mailhot.

**Farmers' Gate Market,** 170 Leeds Junction Rd., Wales; (207) 933-3300; www.farmersgatemarket.com. This custom butcher shop is committed to supporting local farmers who raise grass-fed beef and pastured pork, and it works exclusively with farmers who meet the shop's rigorous criteria for environmentally sound farming practices and humane animal treatment. Meats come from pastured animals that were raised in Maine and are cut to order by butcher Leon Emery, who has 40 years of experience. Open Tues through Sat. See Farmers' Gate Market's recipe for **Yankee Pot Roast** on p. 288.

**Jorgensons' Cafe,** 103 Main St., Waterville; (207) 872-8711. This independent coffee shop and cafe features locally roasted Carrabassett coffees by the cup or the pound, a variety of teas, and a changing, chalked menu of sandwiches, fresh cakes, and Kennebec Chocolates. Popular with students at nearby Colby College, the cafe offers gift baskets put together by owners Steve and Ginny Bolduc available for local delivery to your favorite homesick kid. With free Wi-Fi. Open daily.

**Joseph's Market,** 74 Front St., Waterville; (207) 873-3364; www .josephmkt.com. A small family-owned butcher shop with its roots

# Yankee Pot Roast

*This bone-in neck roast is beloved by frugal New Englanders, who traditionally cook it all day in a slow oven, warming the house as it perfumes it. Butcher Leon Emery of the **Farmers' Gate** in Wales (see p. 287), has been cutting meat for more than 40 years and is seeing a resurgence of interest in these simple, traditional cuts of beef. When patrons are searching for a good recipe, this is what he and shop owner Ben Slayton recommend.*

*Fry up some Farmers' Gate bacon and pour off some of the fat, then take a 2- to 4-pound neck roast, cover it with salt and pepper, and brown it in the bacon grease. Remove roast and sauté some onions and carrots. Put roast in a Dutch oven, fill with a mixture of stock and red wine, chunk up the bacon and throw it in, add the onions and carrots, rough cut some garlic cloves, throw a few sprigs of rosemary in, cover, and place in a 250 degree oven for the better part of the day. Enjoy warmth and savory aroma. Devour the roast with side of baked potato.*

*Serves 4–6.*

Recipe courtesy of Farmers' Gate Market (p. 287).

in another time: The Josephs have served the community for more than 80 years, starting as a corner store that sold cigarettes, beer, and sundry items to workers at the local Wyandotte Mill, where Lebanese immigrant John R. Joseph Sr. worked before opening this shop. In the 1930s, the store began selling groceries and meats, and over the years it's become known for its fresh meats and produce, custom cuts of beef, pork, and lamb, and personalized customer service. In recent years, current owner Kevin Joseph has begun offering cooking courses at the shop, teaching patrons such essential and often forgotten skills as boning a chicken, properly frying pork chops, and working with inexpensive cuts of beef. Closed Sun.

**Kennebec Home Brew,** 235 Farmington Falls Rd., Farmington; (207) 778-5276; and 662 Maine Ave., Farmingdale; (207) 623-3368; www.kennebechomebrew.com. The shelves at these two small shops are stocked with fermentation vessels, stoppers, and labeling equipment, as well as dozens of types of grains, hops, yeasts, and malt extracts—in short, everything a home brewer or winemaker could possibly need. In addition to gear, the shops' mission extends to education, and helpful staff offers recipes and advice. Both locations open daily.

**Ricker Hill Orchards,** 295 Buckfield Rd. (ME 117), Turner; (207) 225-5552; www.rickerhill .com. There are apples to pick in the rolling acres of orchard outside, but the seasonal bakery and market are worth a trip in themselves. Fresh, homemade doughnuts are available all day (try the apple), and seasonal pies with crisp, flaky crusts are filled with raspberries, blueberries,

and, of course, apples. Snacks and locally made jams, jellies, and salsa are sold in the market, as well as wooden toys, scented candles, and assorted gifts. Open daily, Apr through Dec.

**Riverside Farm Market and Cafe,** 291 Fairfield St., Oakland; (207) 465-4439; www.riversidefarmmarket.com. What began as a small, seasonal farm stand has grown over the past two decades into this lovely specialty foods market and cafe, with views of Messalonskee Lake and the farm's own vineyard (wines will be sold soon under the label Laissez Faire). The market features fresh baked goods, cheeses, olives, artisanal vinegars, and an extensive collection of small-batch boutique wines, both imported and local. The cafe serves lunch, dinner, and Sunday brunch—don't miss sweet and savory *ployes*. Hours change seasonally for both cafe and market.

## Pick Your Own

**The Apple Farm,** 104 Back Rd., Fairfield; (207) 453-7656; and **Lakeside Orchards,** 318 Readfield Rd., Manchester; (207) 622-2479; www.lakesideorchards.com. Two orchards owned by the same family, offering 16 varieties of apples and 3 varieties of pears. September through mid-October. Open daily.

**Bailey Orchard,** North Hunts Meadow Road, South Windsor; (207) 549-7680. More than 50 varieties of apples, as well as plums, pears, crabapples, and pumpkins. Mid-August through early November, open daily.

**Benoit Orchard,** Ferry & Cotton Roads, Lewiston; (207) 783-0875. Apples, native plums, and pumpkins; mid-August through October. Open daily.

**Boothby's Orchard,** 366 Boothby Rd., Livermore; (207) 754-3500; www.mainehoneycrisp.com. More than 3,000 trees on 7 acres. Offering hay rides on the weekends. Apples, early August through October.

**Chick Orchards, Inc.,** 155 Norris Hill Rd., Monmouth; (207) 933-4452. With more than 800 acres in production, this is the largest family-owned farm in New England. Apples; open daily, Sept through Oct and on weekdays through Nov.

**Elm Crest Farms,** 127 Norris Hill Road, Monmouth; (207) 933-3778. Apples, pumpkins, and winter squash; open weekends, mid-September through late October.

**Gagnon Family Orchard,** 75 Saunders Rd., Greene; (207) 576-0541. Highbush blueberries in September and apples from September through October.

**Goss Farm,** 158 Megquier Hill Rd., Poland; (207) 998-2565. Apples and peaches, if weather permits. Open June through Sept. Closed Sun.

**Greenwood Orchards,** 174 Auburn Rd., Turner; (207) 225-3764. Apples, August through December.

**Harndon's Family Farm,** 1152 Main St., East Wilton; (207) 645-2568. Apples, mid-September through mid-October; closed Sun.

**Kents Hill Orchard,** 1625 Main St., Kents Hill; (207) 685-3522. Apples, Labor Day through late October. Open daily.

**Lemieux's Orchard,** Priest Hill Road, North Vassalboro; (207) 923-3518. Apples, late August through late October. Open daily.

**Maine-ly Apples,** ME 7, Dixmont; (207) 234-2043. Twenty-three varieties of apples, with prepicked pumpkins and squash; mid-August through October. Open weekends.

**Mount Nebo Orchard,** 339 Wings Mills Rd., Mount Vernon; (207) 685-3627. Strawberries from June through early July and apples from mid-August through October. Closed Tues.

**Schartner Farms,** ME 220, Thorndike; (207) 568-3668. Apples, pumpkins, and winter squash; Labor Day through October. Open daily.

**Shackley Hill Orchard,** Shackley Hill Road, Livermore; (207) 897-4283. Apples, open mid-August through October.

**Stukas Farm,** 144 Ferry Rd., Lewiston; (207) 786-2639. Apples, mid-August through October. Open daily.

**Wallingford's Fruit House,** 1240 Perkins Ridge, Auburn; (207) 784-7958. Apples, mid-August through Halloween. Open daily.

**Whit's Apples,** 42 Case Rd., East Winthrop; (207) 395-4436. Apples, mid-August through October. Open daily.

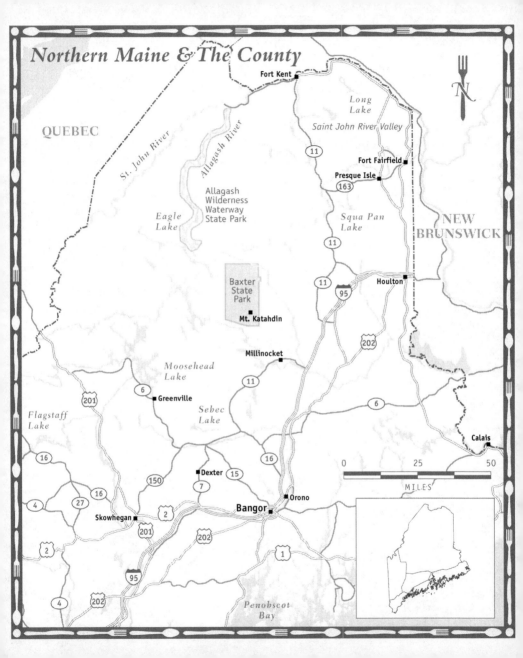

# Northern Maine & The County

QUEBEC

St. John River

Fort Kent

Long
Lake

Saint John River Valley

Allagash River

11

Fort Fairfield

Presque Isle

163

Allagash
Wilderness
Waterway
State Park

Eagle
Lake

Squa Pan
Lake

NEW
BRUNSWICK

11

Baxter
State
Park

11

95

Houlton

Mt. Katahdin

202

Millinocket

11

Moosehead
Lake

6

6

201

Greenville

Flagstaff
Lake

Sebec
Lake

Calais

16

16

150

Dexter

15

0          25          50

MILES

16

7

4

27

16

Orono

Skowhegan

2

Bangor

201

202

2

1

95

4

202

Penobscot
Bay

# Northern Maine & The County

The untamed north woods of Maine, with their crystalline lakes, wandering moose, and towering pines, are enchantingly beautiful, intensely rugged, and sparsely populated. Here, at the culmination of the Appalachian Trail in Baxter State Park, Mount Katahdin rises from the woods, while further north, the Allagash Wilderness Waterway challenges intrepid rafters and canoeists. For more than a century, this was the heart of the state's lumber industry, and throughout the 1800s French-Canadian lumberjacks came south to log the region, sending timber to the shipyards on the coast. They brought with them their own culinary traditions, and in the logging camps they adopted new ones, especially the practice of cooking dried beans—yellow eyes, Jacob's cattle, and soldier beans—in heated holes in the ground ("bean holes"), a technique learned from the local Penobscot Indians. (For a taste of traditionally cooked beans, visit the Patten Lumbermen's Museum in Patten for

## PLOYES TO POUTINE:
## A GLOSSARY OF FRANCO-AMERICAN FOODS

The Upper Saint John River Valley of Aroostook County is a melting pot of Acadian and Quebecois culinary influences. Many of Maine's favorite Franco-American dishes bear names incomprehensible to those "from away." Here's a brief glossary:

*Beignets:* here, chunks of apple dipped in batter and cooked in boiling maple syrup

*Boudin:* blood sausage

*Crepes:* thin wheat-flour pancakes

*Cretons:* pork pâté

*Croccignoles:* twisted pastry deep-fried in fat

*Fricot:* chicken stew, traditionally served with pâté roulés

its annual August Bean Hole Supper. The museum is located at 61 Shin Pond Rd.; 207-528-2650; www.lumbermensmuseum.org.)

East of the woods, the fertile Saint John River Valley in Aroostook County is the state's largest agricultural region. Commonly referred to simply as The County, this was once considered the breadbasket of New England, and it is still a patchwork of rippling golden grain and vast stretches of potato fields. The region is sparsely populated and relatively remote, dominated by the British and French-

*Gortons:* pork cracklings

*Le pâté chinois:* casserole of mashed potatoes, ground meat, and corn (shepherd's pie)

*Pâté roulés* (confusingly, sometimes simply called *poutines*): rolled flour dumplings boiled in stock

*Ployes:* buckwheat flatbreads (pancakes) cooked on a griddle

*Pot-en-pot:* meat pie for a party cooked in a roasting pan, layering sliced potatoes and strips of dough with at least four meats—usually including venison, wild birds, rabbit, pork, and beef—and covered with piecrust before baking

*Poutine:* fried potatoes and cheese curd covered in hot gravy

*Tourtières:* meat pies filled with pork, beef, veal, chicken, or a combination of meats

Canadian influences of the earliest European settlers. There's also a taste of Scandinavia in the area that dates from the formation of the Swedish colony (now the town of New Sweden) in 1870. For the last century, The County has been known particularly for its potatoes, and tubers are available by the seed, the sack, and in exquisite locally made chips.

Bangor, the cultural and economic seat of the region, has been called the "Queen City of the East" for its beautiful old churches, leafy shade trees, and Greek Revival and Victorian houses, remnants of the lumber barons of the city's heyday. Now the town is noted for its cultural life: The Bangor Symphony Orchestra is the oldest continually operating symphony orchestra in the country, and the city has a variety of public music, theater, and artistic events. The proximity of Orono, home of the University of Maine, adds to the vibrancy of the city. Bangor is also the gateway to Acadia and all points north: I-95 crosses the city before heading straight up to Houlton, and scenic US 1A connects with the interstate to take visitors Downeast. The Bangor International Airport is both a civil and a military airport, and arriving tourists may also see the airport's famed troop greeters—members of the community who meet each arriving military plane to welcome service members home.

The traditional foods of northern Maine—potatoes, beans, *ployes,* freshwater fish—are humble, hearty, and satisfying. In recent years, organic farmers have been drawn to The County because of affordable, expansive land, and growers' cooperatives have emerged to sell produce throughout the region. On a large scale, Backyard Farms of Madison has begun to grow vine-ripened tomatoes year-round in their immense, 42 acres of greenhouses, and their tomatoes are available throughout the Northeast. With nods to the culinary past and the visionary agricultural future, farm-to-table restaurants are emerging, while local landmarks continue to go strong.

## Bakeries

**Abbot Village Bakery & Cafe,** ME 15, Abbot; (207) 876-4243. Specializing in pies—sweet, savory, and whoopie—this local favorite also offers doughnuts (get there early to try the chocolate coconut), classic cookies like date bars, and heartier fare like Maine baked beans and chicken potpie packed with chunks of meat and thick gravy, to eat in or take out.

**Bagel Central,** 33 Central St., Bangor; (207) 947-1654; www .bagelcentralbangor.com. In a cavernous, cheerfully painted downtown storefront, this bagel shop and deli makes 16 types of bagels fresh daily, serving them with a schmear of cream cheese, or sandwiched around eggs and lox. Omelets, lunch sandwiches, and a few deli favorites (blintzes and knishes) are also on the menu, and fresh baked bread, including Friday challah, is sold by the loaf. Closed Sat.

**County Junction Market Bakery,** 53 Main St., Houlton; (207) 532-2218. In the heart of the historic Market Square district, this organic bakery retains the building's original pressed-tin moldings and weathered fixtures, and adds an appealing array of baked goods, from breads and bagels to pastries and sweet treats. Also with a market of Maine-made and organic goods. Open Mon through Fri 7 a.m. to 4 p.m. and Sat 7 a.m. to 2 p.m.

**Farms Bakery and Coffee Shop,** 118 Bennett Dr., Caribou; (207) 493-4508. With hot coffee and fresh baked goods—try the chocolate croissants and the walnut and cinnamon pastries. Open Tues through Sat. Cash only.

**Frank's Bakery,** 199 State St., Bangor; (207) 947-4594 or (888) 561-5611; www.franksbakery.com. Family owned since 1947, this bakery specializes in cakes, catering, and fruit tarts, made by daughter Bernadette Gaspar, known around the shop as "the Queen of Tarts." Beloved in the community, over the years the shop has turned out generations of wedding cakes, and loyal patrons return for intricately decorated cakes to celebrate baby showers, birthdays, anniversaries, and graduations. Prepared entrees are also available. Closed Sun.

**Gosselin's Bakery,** 34 Harlow St., Bangor; (207) 947-5600. The smell of hot oil billows out as you open the door to this local landmark, known for its old-fashioned doughnuts. Pastries stick to your ribs—they're a meal in themselves—and famed doughnuts range from cakey to jelly filled.

**Sadie's Bakery,** 5 Water St., Houlton; (207) 532-6650. Since 1948, this sweet storefront bakery has turned out fresh, homemade doughnuts every day. Flavors are simple—plain, molasses, and chocolate—and a single variety is offered each morning. Also selling bread, turnovers, assorted pastries, and cookies. Closed Mon.

# *Brewpubs & Microbreweries*

**Abel Blood's Pub,** 100 E. Main St., Dover-Foxcroft; (207) 564-3177; www.abelbloodspub.com. Serving more than 70 imported and domestic beers, this friendly tavern, named for the town's first settler, offers a classic pub menu of thick sandwiches, juicy burgers, hearty comfort food, and a small kids' menu. With weekly live jazz on Wednesday. Open nightly, Wed through Sat.

**Black Bear Microbrew,** 19 Mill St., Orono; (207) 949-2880; www .blackbearmicrobrew.com. Owner and brewmaster Tim Gallon brings a sense of *terroir* to his brews; local hops are added to his Harvest Hops Ale within hours of picking, and fragrant fruit goes in his summer Bluesberry Ale. Beers are available on tap at restaurants throughout the state, and in growlers and 22-ounce bottles at the brewery. Call ahead to arrange a visit.

**Kennebec River Brewery,** US 201, The Forks; (800) 765-7238; www.northernoutdoors.com. Located in a rustic North Woods resort, this craft brewery has been making ales and lagers since 1997. Starting with pure Kennebec Valley water, two-row malted barleys, and domestic and imported hops, draught beers are cask conditioned. India Pale Ale is available bottled year-round, Summer Ale and Sledhead Red are bottled seasonally, and a dozen others—from Whitewater Wheat to Penobscot Porter—are only sold on tap at the brewery. If it's available, don't miss Arthur's Hazelnut Brown, a nutty, roasted, English-style brown ale.

**Oak Pond Brewing Company,** 101 Oak Pond Rd., Skowhegan; (207) 474-3233; www.oakpondbrewery.com. Owner-brewers Nancy and Don Chandler brew five ales and lagers year-round and two seasonal ales at this microbrewery housed in a converted barn. Tours take visitors through the entire production, starting at the grain silo (where you're encouraged to taste the malted barley) and ending at the tap, where you can sample the brews. In winter,

## ALLEN'S COFFEE FLAVORED BRANDY

For more than 20 years, **Allen's Coffee Flavored Brandy** has been the top-selling spirit in Maine. Though it's produced by M. S. Walker in Somerville, Massachusetts, the neighbors to the north are its most loyal consumers, for reasons as mysterious as they are notable. Perhaps it's the flavor: Made with an extract from Brazilian coffee beans, Allen's has the bitter bite of coffee without the heavy sweetness of many liqueurs. Perhaps it's the community presence: Allen's sponsors stock car–racing teams and music festivals throughout the state. Perhaps, in thrifty northern New England, it's the value, with bottles of this domestic spirit selling for a fraction of the cost of imports like Kahlua and Tia Maria. Whatever the reasons, Allen's is the drink of choice for generations of Mainers. Look for it by the bottle, and (often with an ironic wink) on drink menus throughout the state.

try the rich, nutty Storyteller Doppelbock; in summer, grab a few bottles of smooth Laughing Loon Lager. Open late afternoon, Mon through Fri, all afternoon Sat, and by appointment. Call ahead for tours.

**Sea Dog Microbrewery and Restaurant,** 26 Front St., Bangor; (207) 974-8009; www.seadogbrewing.com. Brewing dozens of award-winning ales and lagers in three brewpubs, this microbrewery offers beers for every taste, from fruity Apricot Wheat to malty Old Gollywobbler Brown Ale. The menu offers solid pub fare, from thick burgers to fried fish, and a surprising number of dinner salads. Look for the dog in the yellow fishing cap. **Other locations** are in South Portland (125 Western Ave., 207-871-7000) and Topsham (1 Bowdoin Mill Island, 207-725-0162).

## Farm Stands

**Avalon Acres Orchard & Farm,** 234 Dexter Rd., Saint Albans; (207) 938-2501. Farmers Wendy and Mark Sheriff tend more than 20 varieties of apples, as well as pears, plums, cherries, and high-bush blueberries on this diversified farm. In summer, an assortment of vegetables is sold from the farm stand, and in the fall you can pick your own fruit on weekends. Stand is open weekends and by chance—look for the flag; if it's flying, they're open.

**Country Junction Greenhouse & Gardens,** 1204 Main Rd., North Bradford; (207) 327-1398; www.countryjunctionmaine.com. A family business with greenhouses that foster perennials, fruit tree saplings, and vegetable and flower seedlings year-round ("It's spring in the greenhouse"); in summer months, they add a vegetable stand. Call ahead, hours vary seasonally.

**Skylandia Organic Farm,** 61 Main St., Grand Isle; (207) 895-5234 or (207) 316-5321; www.crownofmainecoop.com. The late Jim Cook, pioneering founder of Crown of Maine Organic Produce, a cooperative that markets foods from dozens of northern Maine producers, started this diversified organic farm in 1994. His daughter, Marada, continues to farm the land, selling summer vegetables, winter greenhouse greens, and root crops into the late fall. Call ahead, hours vary.

## Farmers' Markets

**Bangor-European Farmers' Market,** Buck Street across from Bangor Auditorium, Bangor; (207) 326-4741. Year-round, Sat 9:30 a.m. to 1 p.m.

**Brewer Farmers' Market,** Brewer Auditorium parking lot in Wilson Street, Brewer; (207) 948-5724. May through October, Tues to Fri 8 a.m. to 1 p.m. and Sat 8 a.m. to 3 p.m.

**Calais-Sunrise County Farmers' Market,** Union Street, Calais; (207) 853-4750. June through October, Tues 11 a.m. to 3 p.m.

**Caribou Farmers' Market,** 75 Bennett Dr., Caribou; (207) 498-6156. June through September, every day. Hours vary.

**Dexter Farmers' Market,** ME 7, between Dexter and Corinna. June through October, Fri 9 a.m. to 1 p.m.

**Eastport-Sunrise County Farmers' Market,** next to Raye's Mustard on Washington, Eastport; (207) 853-4750. June through October, Thurs 11 a.m. to 2 p.m.

**Eddington Farmers' Market,** 906 Maine Rd. (ME 9), Eddington; (207) 537-5673. June through October, Sun 10 a.m. to 1 p.m.

**Fort Kent Farmers' Market,** across from Saint Louis Parish, Fort Kent; (207) 834-6399. June through September, Tues and Thurs all day; Sat 7 a.m. until sold out.

**Houlton Farmers' Market,** US 1, Houlton; (207) 794-8306. May through October, daily until noon.

**Houlton Market Square Farmers' Market,** next to Temple Theater on US 1, Houlton; (207) 448-2037. June through September, Thurs 9 a.m. to 1 p.m.

**Orono Farmers' Market,** Steam Plant parking lot, UMO campus, Orono; (207) 257-4103. June through October, 2:30 to 5:30 p.m.; and May through November, Sat 8 a.m. to 1 p.m.

**Presque Isle Farmers' Market,** Aroostook Center Mall, US 1, Presque Isle; (207) 455-8386. May through October, Sat 9 a.m. to 2 p.m.

**Skowhegan Farmers' Market,** Aubuchon parking lot on Russell Street, Skowhegan; (207) 324-0331. July through October, Sat 9 a.m. to 1 p.m.

 *Food Happenings*

**February**

**Annual Moosehead Lake Chocolate Festival,** Masonic Hall, 281 Pritham Ave., Greenville; (207) 695-2702. This delectable afternoon event features dozens of chocolate desserts. Thirty-five of the region's best pastry chefs make their favorite cocoa concoctions; the entry fee ($10) allows tastings of twelve.

## June

**Maine Swedish Colony Midsommar Celebration,** Station Road and Capital Hill Road, New Sweden; (207) 896-3641; www.maineswedishcolony.info. This annual commemoration of the founding of Maine's Swedish colony in 1870 is a celebration of all things Swede. Displays by the historical society, wooden *dala* horse painting, Viking lawn bowling, and Majstang (the decoration of the maypole) are capped by a Swedish supper of meatballs, ham, mashed potatoes, *rotmos* (rutabaga casserole), pickled herring, and Scandinavian desserts. In mid- to late June.

**The Maine Whoopie Pie Festival,** 20 East Main St., Dover-Foxcroft; (207) 564-8943; www.makingwhoopies.net. This one-day celebration of the "official dessert of Maine" is so popular that in 2010, Governor John Baldacci officially proclaimed the day of the festival Maine Whoopie Pie Day. Dozens of bakers bring thousands of pies—cakey rounds of chocolate filled with creamy white filling—to downtown Dover-Foxcroft for tastings, whoopie pie-eating contests, and voting for the coveted People's Whoopie Pie award. But it's not all sugary treats: The day begins with an annual Earn Your Whoopie Pie 5K road race.

## July

**Maine Potato Blossom Festival,** 18 Community Dr., Fort Fairfield; (207) 472-3802; www.potatoblossom.org. For more than

## Maine Potatoes

Arriving in the early 1800s, the first white settlers to Aroostook County began planting potatoes almost as soon as they'd cleared fields from the forests. The cool climate and fertile soil created ideal conditions for the tubers, and by the middle of the last century, Maine was the country's leader in potato production. Between 1928 and 1958, Aroostook County grew more potatoes than any other state in the nation. Over the past 50 years, potato production has declined, and fewer families are farming, but in Maine, The County is still synonymous with potatoes. Schools in the north are closed for late September Harvest Break so that kids can help their parents dig potatoes; the **Maine Potato Blossom Festival** (see p. 307) is held in Fort Fairfield; and each spring, seed potatoes from Aroostook County help gardeners across the country plant their own rows. Among the most passionate potato producers is organic farmer **Jim Gerritsen,** a potato advocate who has spoken internationally on the subject. His family's diversified **Wood Prairie Farm** offers 20 varieties of seed potatoes, from Swedish peanut fingerlings to Adirondack red. Wood Prairie Farm, 49 Kinney Rd., Bridgewater; (800) 829-9765; www.woodprairie.com.

60 years, this weekend festival, timed to coincide with the blossoming of the potato flower, has celebrated the humble heart of Aroostook County's agricultural heritage. Festivities include a

potato-picking contest, potato suppers, mashed potato wrestling, and the pageant to crown the Maine Potato Blossom Queen.

## August

**Ploye Festival,** Fort Kent; www.fortkentchamber.com. On a 12-foot griddle set up under a tent in the heart of downtown, volunteers and members of the Bouchard family (see p. 315) pour and smooth 5-gallon buckets of *ploye* batter in this one-day festival, creating their annual "world's largest *ploye*." Locals discuss the variations of their family recipes and everyone digs in while they watch the Muskie Derby that follows. Fishermen haul in giant muskellunge pikes—known as "muskies"—from the Saint John River. The muskies, which can weigh as much as 20 pounds, are then cleaned and cooked for a giant community fish fry.

## The Maine Ice Cream Trail

**Gifford's,** 307 Madison Ave., Skowhegan; (207) 474-2257; www .giffordsicecream.com. This family-owned ice-cream business began at a seasonal stand in Skowhegan and has grown to include four more stands, serving more than 1 million cones each summer; a thriving wholesale business that serves 400 independent ice-cream shops throughout New England; and a retail arm that sells quarts and half gallons in supermarkets around the state. Made with hormone-free milk from Maine dairy farmers, the ice cream has won numerous industry awards—and deserves every one. Flavors range from creamy old-fashioned vanilla to peanut-butter-cup-packed Moose Tracks, and scoops are ample. With **additional locations** in Bangor, Auburn, Waterville (see p. 271), and Farmington. Open Mar through Oct.

**Houlton Farm Dairy Bar,** 131 Military St., Houlton; (207) 532-2628. The first pasteurizing dairy in The County, since 1938 Houlton Farm has been Aroostook County's source for premium local milk, butter, ice cream, and more. Their glass bottles, marked in vivid orange, can be found in attics and antique stores throughout the region. The seasonal ice-cream stand sells old-fashioned hard-pack cones and treats from a walk-up window—locals swear their Grapenut flavor sets the standard. Look for the giant orange milk carton and you'll know you're there. There is a second seasonal location on Main Street in Presque Isle. Now open year-round at the Aroostook Centre Mall, Presque Isle; (207) 764-6200.

**Libby's Mill Pond Dairy Bar,** 225 Hodgdon Mills Rd., Hodgdon; (207) 532-9891. At the edge of the pond from which it takes its name, this classic ice-cream stand has been around for generations. Order a soft-serve or sherbet at the window, and enjoy it by the water. Also serving fries, burgers on the grill, and the local favorite: deep-fried pickles. Open mid-April to mid-September.

## Landmark Eateries

**Craig's Clam Shop,** 92 Main St., Patten; (207) 528-2784; $$. This beloved seasonal clam shack and dairy bar serves fried seafood, grilled burgers, and a range of wraps and salads. But clams are the main event, and flat clams, whole belly clams, and clam tenderloins come in baskets and rolls. Ice cream comes by the scoop or the treat, and milk shakes can be ordered regular, thick, or extra thick. There is a year-round restaurant, **Craig's Maine Course** in Island Falls (142 Walker Settlement Rd.; (207-463-2425).

**Dolly's Restaurant,** 17 US 1, Frenchville; (207) 728-7050; $. This humble roadside diner has been a local institution for decades, serving up Acadian specialties like hot *ployes* fresh from the griddle, ramekins of *creton* (p. 296) made with their secret blend of spices, and hearty chicken stew packed with meat and dumplings. *Ployes* are perfectly tender and served at every meal—dressed with maple syrup in the morning and hot gravy at supper. Closed Tues.

**Dysart's Truck Stop and Restaurant,** Cold Brook Road, I-95 exit 180, Bangor; (207) 942-4878; www.dysarts.com; $$. Fuel your truck, buy your heating oil, and enjoy a bowl of creamy lobster stew and a wedge of fresh baked blueberry pie at this state treasure. For more than 40 years, the Dysart family has served home-cooked food 24 hours a day, 364 days a year (they're closed from 2 p.m. on Christmas Eve to 5 p.m. on Christmas Day) at their full-service truck stop. Servings are colossal, from towering Paul Bunyan's Platter breakfasts to thick-cut meat loaf and Yankee pot roast at supper. The restaurant is famed for its baked yellow-eye beans, available 24 hours a day as a side dish or a meal, and they slow cook more than 4 tons each year. The pies, too, are justly famous, their deep, flaky crusts filled with fresh fruits and rich cream filling (try the heavenly chocolate). Desserts, breads, and sweet treats can also be ordered from their bakery, which makes everything on-site. Bring a taste home with a copy of their recently updated cookbook, *Cooking With Dysart's*; the family donates 100 percent of the proceeds to Eastern Maine Medical Center's CancerCare, and the previous edition has already raised more than $100,000 for the cause.

**Elm Tree Diner,** 146 Bangor St., Houlton; (207) 532-3777; $$. For more than 75 years, this local institution has warmed chilly winters with open-faced sandwiches, chicken potpies, chowders, and the signature Maine shrimp platter. Open at 5:30 a.m. on weekdays, regulars gather for a fresh pastry or a loaded omelet before work. After a devastating fire in 2009, the diner relocated to a new, spacious location, but its home-cooked meals have stayed the same. Open daily for breakfast, lunch, and dinner.

# Millie Chaison's Oyster Dressing

*When Portland writer Nicole Chaison's grandmother Mildred was a bride, she moved from upstate New York to Bangor, where she raised her family and made her home. Embracing the foods of Maine, she made this oyster dressing for holidays, and now Chaison, the author of* The Passion of the Hausfrau *and co-author, with Ana Sortun, of the James Beard Award–nominated cookbook* Spice, *continues the tradition. The combination is simple, the proportions are variable, and Chaison confesses that her grandmother tweaked it a little each time.*

**4 cups shucked oysters**          **½ cup heavy cream**
**One sleeve saltines, crushed**    **Salt and pepper**
**6 tablespoons butter**

*Preheat oven to 350 degrees. Put the shucked oysters in a small casserole dish and cover them with the crushed saltines. Cut the butter into 6 pats and dot over the crackers. Pour heavy cream over the top and season with salt and pepper to taste. Bake, covered, for 45 minutes, or until bubbling. Serve piping hot.*

*Serves 6–8.*

Recipe courtesy of Nicole Chaison.

**Pat's Pizza,** 11 Mill St., Orono (and locations throughout Maine); (207) 866-2111; www.patsyarmouth.com; $$. C. D. "Pat" Farnsworth opened the Farnsworth Cafe in 1931, but it wasn't until 1953 that he and his wife, Fran, added homemade pizza to the menu. It was an instant hit, especially with students at the university, and the restaurant was transformed. Now with 13 locations throughout the state, Pat's Pizza is a Maine institution. Pizzas come in two sizes, crusts come with single or double dough, and toppings range from simple to surreal—the Reuben pizza with Canadian bacon and sauerkraut, and the Cheezburglah with ketchup, mustard, hamburger, pickles, and onion fall into the latter camp. For something more traditional, try the Caterina with fresh tomato, artichoke hearts, capers, Greek olives, oregano, and provolone, or if you're feeling especially carnivorous, the meat lovers' pizza with pepperoni, ham, hamburger, bacon, and sausage. With hot and cold sandwiches, calzones, and Italian entrees. Open daily.

## Learn to Cook

**The Tasting Spoon,** Caribou; (207) 493-4607; www.jeffschipper .com. Chef Jeff Schipper, a graduate of the Culinary Institute of America and a 25-year veteran of the food and hospitality industry, offers personal-chef services and catering for small parties throughout The County. In addition, he can be hired to teach "cooking parties," during which he comes to your kitchen and prepares a meal, introducing guests to new culinary techniques and cuisines before they sit down and savor.

## Made or Grown Here

**Bouchard Family Farm,** 3 Strip Rd., Fort Kent; (207) 834-3237; www.ployes.com. Buckwheat has been cultivated in the upper Saint John River Valley of Maine since the 18th century; by 1850 visitors to the area were making note of the tasty buckwheat flatbreads, called *ployes*, that were served by Acadians at every meal. In the 1980s, the Bouchard family began growing and milling buckwheat and packaging their mix for the perfect *ployes*. It's been a hit ever since. Nutty in flavor and gluten-free, Bouchard Family Farm's buckwheat flour has gained a following and can be used in a variety of recipes. A bag of *ployes* mix (not gluten-free) brings Acadia to your breakfast table. Available at stores throughout the state or through the website.

**Dragonfly Farm and Winery,** 1067 Mullen Rd., Stetson; (207) 296-2226; www.mainewinegrower.com. Todd and Treena Nadeau, proprietors of this small vineyard and winery, planted their first grapevines in the spring of 2005 with the goal of producing a delicious, affordable Maine Reisling. Since then, their vineyard has grown to include more than 600 vines, and they're producing seven whites, four reds, and six fruit wines. The northernmost

vineyard in the state, grapes are hardy hybrids, and wines range from fruity ruby-colored Frontenac to crisp off-dry white Serendipity. With a gift shop and tasting room that sells wines by the bottles, as well as jams and gift baskets. Call ahead to arrange a tasting.

**Fox Family Potato Chips Inc.,** Tretts, 1697 Main St., Mapleton; (207) 760-8400. Fried in the back of founder Rhett Fox's rural convenience store, these thin, perfectly browned potato chips have a cultish following. The Fox family has been growing potatoes in Aroostook County since the 1800s but only started making chips in the 1990s. Cut by hand, fried in a mixture of corn and canola oils, and lightly salted, the chips taste like the last crispy French fries in the basket—dark but not burnt, and almost translucent with oil. Incredibly, these are the only chips being produced in Maine. Look for the shiny silver bag with the hand-drawn red foxes. In plain, salt and pepper, and fiery BBQ. Sold throughout the state.

**Twenty 2 Vodka,** Houlton; www.twenty2vodka.com. Husband-and-wife distillers Scott Galbiati and Jessica Jewell make award-winning grain vodka in 50-gallon batches at their microdistillery, The Northern Maine Distilling Company. The spirit is smooth and crafted for mixing; the couple posts a weekly recipe of their favorite experimental cocktails to the company's Facebook page. Next up: They're working on a vodka distilled from Aroostook County's famed crop—potatoes. Each bottle is numbered by hand; available at stores throughout the state.

## Restaurants

**Appalachian Trail Cafe,** 210 Penobscot Ave., Millinocket; (207) 723-6720; $. The portions are massive and the comfort food homemade at this casual local favorite. Serving doughnuts hot from the fryer, toast made from freshly baked loaves, and diner standards like homemade blueberry pancakes, steak and eggs, burgers and piping hot fries, and triple-decker sandwiches with chips and a pickle. In summer, the place can get crowded, as it's very popular with hikers on the Appalachian Trail—they begin wandering in at 5 a.m. for a hot meal—and with raft guides on the Penobscot River. Open for breakfast, lunch, and dinner.

**Bahaar Restaurant,** 23 Hammond St., Bangor; (207) 945-5979; $$. A meal at this tidy, well-lit restaurant is heady from the start: delicate open bottles of spices line the half wall that edges the entrance. The cuisine is Pakistani and includes flatbreads, pakoras, vegetable and meat curries, and several fish dishes. While ordering, choose your spice threshold on a scale of 1 to 10. Finish the meal with creamy rice pudding and a cup of tea; no alcohol is served. Open daily for lunch and dinner, closed Sun.

**Blue Moose Restaurant,** 180 US 1, Monticello; (207) 538-0991; $$. This beloved eatery, housed in a log cabin, serves down-home cooking at its best: shepherd's pie, prime rib, juicy burgers, and turkey with all the fixings. Fun in summer, it's especially cozy in winter, when there's a roaring fire and locals come by snowmobile—the restaurant is feet from ITS-83—to thaw. Open for breakfast, lunch, and dinner. Closed Mon.

**Coffee Pot Cafe,** 650 Broadway, Bangor; (207) 990-2633; $. When Bangor's beloved sandwich shop, the Coffee Pot, closed in 2009 after nearly 80 years in business (it opened in 1930), locals mourned its loss but swore allegiance to its memory: They would accept no substitutes. In 2010, however, two former employees, Cheryl Whittaker and Kathie Potter, brought the concept back to life, opening this cafe in a former coffee shop. The sandwich in question is packed with salami, cheese, green peppers, tomatoes, pickles, oils, and mounds of onions, all on a freshly baked roll. Call ahead, and your sandwich will be waiting.

**The Courtyard Cafe,** 61 Main St., Houlton; www.thecourtyardcafe .biz; $$. Chef-owner Joyce Transue makes everything from scratch at this casual cafe in the Fishman Mall. The menu has something for all tastes, from comfortable favorites like baked seafood casserole with crumbled crackers on top, to more sophisticated offerings like bourbon-glazed Alaskan sockeye salmon. Lunch features salads, quiches, and sandwiches on fresh baked bread. The salad dressing is so popular that it's now available bottled. Open for lunch and dinner Tues through Fri, and for dinner on Sat.

**The Fiddlehead Restaurant,** 84 Hammond St., Bangor; (207) 942-3336; www.thefiddleheadrestaurant.com; $$$. Good food without pretension is the goal of this downtown hot spot, where owners Melissa Chaiken and Laura Albin serve a menu that ranges from fennel-dusted lamb sirloin to Pepper Jack cheeseburgers. In an elegant space with high ceilings, warm wood floors, and exposed brick walls, the atmosphere is easy; water comes to the table in mason jars, attentive servers check in regularly, and the kitchen, helmed by Chaiken, is eager to work around dietary restrictions. The menu changes several times a year, always incorporating local produce and meats. Don't miss Albin's inventive cocktails, with flavors that run from smoky (martini with smoked sea salt and smoked Gouda–stuffed olives) to sweet (the excellent mango mojito). Open nightly for dinner, closed Mon.

**Friars' Bakehouse,** 21 Central St., Bangor; (207) 947-3770; www.franciscansofbangor.com; $. Franciscan friars in coarse brown robes man the ovens, counter, and upstairs chapel at this wonderful cafe, serving breakfast and lunch. In the morning, warm baked goods emerge from the oven and are offered with self-serve coffee. Later, there are thick sandwiches and hearty soups that change daily, veering from chicken noodle to Indian lentil curry. The brothers are unfailingly kind, and the atmosphere is calm and devotional—evening prayers at the bake house are sometimes open to the public. If it's busy, be prepared to share a table. And be warned: Cell phones are strictly forbidden. Cash only. Open Wed through Sat.

**Grammy's Country Inn,** 1687 Bangor Rd., Linnaeus; (207) 532-7808; $. This cozy diner promises it's a place "where you get more than you expect," and with heaping platters of home-cooked food, it delivers. The menu offers diner standards: burgers, fries, sandwiches, seafood,, and hand-cut steaks that range from a relatively demure 12 ounces to the "Monster" that tops 18 ounces. Towering homemade whoopie pies are some of the state's best, and other desserts include a great fall pumpkin pie and Maine's traditional Grapenut custard pudding. T-shirts and hats in camouflage and hunter's orange can be found behind the counter and, during the season, on regulars roaming the woods. Open daily for breakfast, lunch, and dinner.

**Harvest Moon Deli,** 18 Mill St., Orono; (207) 866-3354; www .harvestmoondeli.com; $. Serving panini, homemade soups, and fresh salads, this casual deli caters to students at the nearby University of Maine—campus is just blocks away. Panini and specialty sandwiches are named for rock-and-roll and jazz greats (though Neil Young is conspicuously absent) and can be ordered in advance. Desserts are made in-house, and coffee is fair trade. Open daily for lunch or early dinner.

**Horn of Plenty,** 382 North St., Houlton; (207) 532-2260; $$. The decor is no-frills at this unassuming restaurant, but co-owner and chef Bill Roderick's menu is epicurean. Partner Nancy Levin manages the front of the house, reciting the many daily specials and providing attentive, accommodating service. Levin and Roderick come from Rhode Island, and many dishes reference that state's Portuguese culinary influences. Other offerings range from Creole cod cakes to seared duck. For dinner, try the coffee-rubbed steak; at lunch, have a Reuben and a pile of crisp Maine potato fries. Reservations recommended. Cash or check only. Open for lunch and dinner Tues through Fri, and for dinner on Sat.

**Market/Bistro,** 735 Main St., Bangor; (207) 941-9594 and (207) 941-9480; www.marketbistrobangor.com; $$$. Owned and operated by mother-daughters trio Kim, Colby, and Miranda Smith, this downtown farm-to-table restaurant has an eclectic menu that is both classic and creative. Starters range from escargot to coconut curry shrimp, while entrees include tender lamb osso bucco and vivid vegetarian sweet potato curry. Rustic pizza offerings include the Bistro: garlic mashed potatoes topped with lobster and shaved Parmesan. Ingredients are sourced locally whenever possible, and the menu changes seasonally. Open for dinner Wed through Sat and for Sunday brunch.

**Massimo's Cucina Italiana,** 96 Hammond St., Bangor; (207) 945-5600; www.massimoscucinaitaliana.com; $$$. With charcoal walls, hardwood floors, and a marble bar, this elegant trattoria across from the courthouse serves the kind of Italian food rarely found in these parts. Chef-owner Massimo Ranni's menu reflects the flavors of his native Rome: Homemade pastas are paired with fragrant mussels in white wine and garlic, or mush-rooms and sausage with cream; baby lamb chops, a house favorite, are redolent of garlic, anchovies, and red pepper. Desserts are made in-house—don't skip the sumptuous tiramisu. Open for dinner, closed Sun.

**Nook and Cranny,** 575 Airline Rd., Baileyville; (207) 454-3335; www.nookcrannyrestaurant.com; $$$. Though the restaurant may be hard to find—the small town of Baileyville, outside of Calais, is sometimes left off the map—the atmosphere is inviting and the menu is extensive. Owners Steven and Tami Clark serve something for every taste, from escargots bathed in garlic butter to Greek souvlaki. The majority of the dishes, however, are well-executed Italian and rustic French entrees; baked, broiled, and fried seafood; and classic beef and chicken entrees, from steak au poivre to chicken piccata. Reservations recommended. Open for lunch and dinner; closed Mon.

**Porter's Family Restaurant,** ME 159, exit 276 off I-95, Island Falls; (207) 463-2215; $. The menu's not fancy at this home-style diner, but for travelers reaching the end of the interstate, it offers a welcome breakfast and lunch. Serving simple diner fare—hot breakfasts and lunch of hot dogs, hamburgers, and assorted fried baskets.

**Thistles Restaurant,** 175 Exchange St., Bangor; (207) 945-3836; $$$. Owned and operated by the Rave family—Alejandro, Maria, and son Santiago—this stylish restaurant is infused with the flavors of their native South America. Signature dishes include Argentinean-style steak with chimichurri sauce, beef empanadas, and Spanish paella (much praised by Senator John McCain on a visit to the state). The menu covers New England ground, as well, with crab cakes and clam chowder mixed among the tapas and Cuban black bean soup. The extensive list of wines is predominantly, though not exclusively, South American, but they have been chosen for pairing rather than origin. With live music on Tango Tuesdays. Open Tues through Sat.

**The Vault,** 64 Main St., Houlton; (207) 532-2222; $$. Housed in a historic bank, from which it takes its name, this charming family-owned restaurant is considered by many to be Houlton's best. The atmosphere is warm and inviting, and the food, generously portioned and cooked to order, is made from scratch. Favorites include the spinach-artichoke starter and steak, served as you like it, with a side of simple steamed vegetables. The space is small, and even with reservations you may be seated in the bank's vault (which can be fun). Open for lunch and dinner, Tues through Sat.

**Verve Burritos and Smoothies,** 2 Mill St., Orono; (207) 866-4004; www.verveburritos.com; $. Though its menu is limited to burritos, bagels, smoothies, and locally roasted Carrabassett coffee, this casual restaurant has surprisingly varied offerings. Breakfast burritos start your day with a kick: The house favorite, El Presidente is packed with scrambled eggs, bacon, spicy chorizo, black beans, cheese, salsa, and sour cream. Lunch burritos are made with your choice of chicken, steak, or chorizo, vegetables and assorted toppings and salsas on white or wheat tortillas. Pair it with a yogurt smoothie or a cup of coffee, served hot or iced. With a variety of bagels from Bangor's **Bagel Central** (see p. 299). Open daily for breakfast and lunch.

**Woodman's Bar and Grill,** 31 Main St., Orono; (207) 866-4040; www.woodmansbarandgrill.com; $$. The menu at this bar and grill ranges from well-executed pub food to filet mignon, with inventive specials and sumptuous desserts. You can't go wrong with a Woodman's burger, or the ale-battered fish-and-chips and a pint of Old Engine Oil. Weekly trivia and open-mike nights are lively and energetic. With a full bar, 10 beers on tap, and wines by the glass and bottle. Open nightly for dinner and drinks.

**Bangor Wine and Cheese,** 86 Hammond St., Bangor; (207) 942-3338; www.bangorwine.com. Past airy windows in a downtown storefront, this elegant wine-and-cheese shop has been offering well-chosen wines, craft beers, and artisanal cheeses for more than a decade. The walls are lined with hundreds of bottles—knowledgeable staff can help you navigate—and the refrigerated case holds cheeses that range from delicate morsels to mighty wheels and slabs. Monthly wine tastings and a "beer club" help patrons expand their horizons. Open daily.

**Hampden Natural Food,** 281 Western Ave., Hampden; (207) 862-2500. Since 1994, this cozy shop in a converted house has carried local and organic produce, baked goods, dairy, eggs, and specialty items. Pastas, pulses, and grains are bought in bulk and sold by the bag. With an enormous garage often used as an event space for receptions and celebrations, like tastings of Stone Fox Farm Ice Creams from Monroe. Closed Sun.

**Log Cabin Grocery,** 809 Dover Rd. (ME 7), Dexter; (207) 924-5017. This varied market carries everything from baked beans to savory chicken pies. Baked goods are made fresh in-house and range from home-style breads to cookies and brownies. Sandwiches, built on slices from the morning's loaves, are premade, and pies, both fruit and meat, are sold whole.

**Maine Maven,** 31 Mill St., Orono; (207) 866-3557; www.maine maven.com. While not strictly a food shop, this impeccable boutique features the best Maine has to offer: tasteful gifts, exquisite housewares and yummy body products. The small but thoughtfully chosen selection of edibles includes chocolates from **Black Dinah** (see p. 228), spice rubs from **Vervacious** (see p. 68), and jams and chutneys from **Stonewall Kitchens** (see p. 96). Hours can vary, so call ahead if you're coming from a distance. Closed Sun.

---

## RED SNAPPERS

To an exiled Mainer, nothing says home like "red snappers," the bright-fuchsia hot dogs that are native to the state. Natural beef and pork hot dogs, with a few generous glugs of FD&C Red #6 and #4, they're great steamed or on the grill—either will give you that juicy snap at first bite—and have a surreal technicolor look when dressed with a little mustard and relish. Once made at butcher shops throughout the state, and famously at the now-defunct Jordan Meats processing plant in Portland, these franks now come from a single factory in Bangor; **W. A. Bean & Sons Meat Market** (see p. 327) makes their own recipe and Rice's Frankforts. The big question, why so red? There are many theories, but the least cynical notes that communities that love red hot dogs (Maine isn't the only one) often overlap with communities that love vivid red chorizo. Whatever their origins, take a bite out of summer with a red snapper!

**Spice of Life Natural Foods Market,** 333 Madison Ave., Suite 10, Skowhegan; (207) 474-8216; www.spiceoflifemaine .com. When you need some whole grains, tempeh, and organically produced olive oil, this locally owned natural foods store is a great stop. Specializing in organic and minimally processed foods, with a variety of Maine-made products and bulk items. Closed Sat.

**Spring Break Maple & Honey,** 3315 US 2, Smyrna Mills; (800) 281-0021; www.mainemapleandhoney.com. Founded in 1998, this company began as a small maple operation, gradually expanding into honey. The sweet syrups and honeys are exceptionally flavorful, a characteristic attributed to the cold weather and mineral-rich soil of northern Maine. Over the years, the company has expanded to include a gift shop, featuring their own products and assorted Maine-made gifts—don't miss the maple jelly. In 2010, Spring Break Maple purchased Smith's Maple Products, making the company the largest maple-candy producer in the state. Open Wed through Sat, and by appointment.

**State Street Wine Cellar,** 195 State St., Bangor; (207) 262-9500; www.streetwine.com. In a brick bungalow, this impressive wine-and-cheese shop boasts more than 850 different vintages, 225 beers, and 50 types of cheese. A small selection of gourmet crackers and condiments complements the offerings, and knowledgeable staff helps with pairings. With monthly tastings and regular wine dinners at local restaurants. Closed Sun.

**Uncle Willy's Candy Shoppe,** 60 Main St., Houlton; (207) 532-3640. With a red-and-white striped sign and range of old-fashioned candies, this classic confectioner's in historic downtown is a throwback to another time. Owner Karen Keber opened the shop just a few years ago, but it's already become a regional destination. Offerings include hand-dipped chocolates, rock candy, barley icicles, gummy treats, candy corn, licorice, lollipops, foil-wrapped chocolates, and more. Open Tues through Sat.

**W. A. Bean & Sons Meat Market,** 229 Bomarc Rd., Bangor; (207) 947-0364 or (800) 649-1958; www.beansmeats.com. Butchering quality meats from Maine since 1860, this historic shop still specializes in steaks, chops, and roasts, cut daily. In addition, the business is now the state's sole producer of traditional "red snapper" hot dogs (see p. 326). Guardians of two recipes, they make Bean's hot dogs from their own formula, and Rice's hot dogs from the original Rice family's. Both are stuffed in snappy natural casing, available without added color or dyed pistachio red. Closed Sun.

## Pick Your Own

**Conant Apple Orchards,** 729 Stage Rd., Etna Center; (207) 269-2241. Apples; call ahead.

**Goughan Farms,** Fort Fairfield Road, Caribou; (207) 496-1731. Apples and petting farm; open weekends, late March to Christmas Eve.

**Harris Orchard,** Wiswell Road, Brewer; (207) 989-3435. Apples, mid-September to mid-October.

**Langley's Strawberries,** 123 Crogan Rd., Hermon; (207) 848-3936. Strawberries, late June to mid-July.

**North Chester Orchard,** North River Road, Chester; (207) 794-3547. Apples, pumpkins, winter squash; call for hours.

**North Star Orchards,** 97 Orchard Rd., Madison; (207) 696-5109; www.northstarorchards.me. Apples, pears, crabapples; open daily early September to Christmas Eve.

**Rollins Orchard,** 262 Dexter Rd., ME 94, Garland; (207) 924-3504. Apples, pears, plums, pumpkins, squash; open daily, early August through end of the season.

**Rowe Orchards,** ME 7, Newport; (207) 368-4777, www.rowe orchards.com. Apples and pears; open daily late August through end of the season.

**Sandy River Apples,** 240 West Sandy River Rd., Mercer; (207) 587-2563; www.sandyriverapples.com. Apples; open daily, mid-September to early November.

**Treworgy Family Orchards,** 3876 Union St., Levant; (207) 884-8354; www.treworgyorchards.com. Apples and pumpkins, with a farm stand all summer and a corn maze in fall. Closed Mon.

# Appendix A: Index of Maine Eateries

# Appendix B: Specialty Foods & Markets

## Butchers & Meat Markets

## Candy & Chocolates

# OTHER SPECIALTY SHOPS

Bessie's Farm Goods (Freeport), 112

Bouchard Family Farm (Fort Kent), 315

Camden Bagel Cafe (Camden), 198

Fox Family Potato Chips Inc. (Mapleton), 316

Hop Shop (Gray), The, 115

Kate's Homemade Butter (Old Orchard Beach), 72

Kennebec Home Brew (Farmington and Farmingdale), 289

Maine Maven (Orono), 326

Medeo European Food and Deli (Westbrook), 117

Mitchell & Savage Maple Farm (Bowdoin), 176

Morse's Sauerkraut and European Deli (North Waldoboro), 177

Oyster Creek Mushroom Co. (Damariscotta), 177

Pastor Chuck Orchards (Portland), 40

Perry's Nut House (Belfast), 178

Pineland Farms Market (New Gloucester), 118

Rabelais Books (Portland), 63

Raye's Mustard (Eastport), 230

Rock City Books and Coffee (Rockland), 178

Simply Scandinavian (Portland), 64

Smiling Hill Farm Dairy and Market (Westbrook), 118

Smokin' Good BBQ (Bethel), 143

Sun Oriental Market (Portland), 65

Urban Farm Fermentory (Portland), 65

Vic and Whit's Sandwich Shop (Saco), 119

Vervacious (Portland), 68

Wild Blueberry Land (Columbia Falls), 249

Monica's Chocolates (Lubec), 230
Uncle Willy's Candy Shoppe
    (Houlton), 328
Wilbur's of Maine Chocolates
    (Freeport), 99

## Cheese
Appleton Creamery (Appleton), 174
Cheese Iron (Scarborough),
    The, 113
Freeport Cheese and Wine
    (Freeport), 113
Harmony Mill Farm (Waltham), 229
Kennebec Cheesery at Koons Farm
    (Sidney), 275
Nezinscot Farm (Turner), 262
Seal Cove Farm (Lamoine), 230
State of Maine Cheese Company
    (Rockport), 179
Sunset Acres Farm & Dairy
    (Brooksville), 231
Town House Farm (Whitefield), 263

## Coffee
Arabica Coffee House (Portland), 36
Bard Coffee (Portland), 36
Bohemian Coffee House and
    Gelateria (Brunswick), 175
Cafe Crème (Bath), 197

Carrabassett Coffee Company
    (Kingfield), 137
Coffee By Design (Portland), 36
Jorgensons' Cafe (Waterville), 287
Little Dog Coffee Shop
    (Brunswick), 197
Maine Coast Book Shop and Cafe
    (Damariscotta), 197
North Cottage Coffee
    (Damariscotta), 197
Rock City Coffee Roasters
    (Rockland), 178
Rooster Brother (Ellsworth), 248

## Doughnuts
Congdon's Doughnut Shop (Wells), 89
Frosty's Donut and Coffee Shop
    (Brunswick), 173
Tony's Donut Shop (Portland), 34
Willow Bake Shoppe (Rockport),
    The, 154

## Gelato
Bohemian Coffee House and
    Gelateria (Brunswick), 175
Gelato Fiasco (Brunswick), 176
Gorgeous Gelato (Portland), 37
Maple's Organics (South Portland), 62

## Maple Syrup

Jillson's Farm and Sugarhouse
(Sabbatus), 261

Kinney's Sugarhouse and Maple
Supplies (Knox), 262

Mitchell & Savage Maple Farm
(Bowdoin), 176

Spring Break Maple & Honey
(Smyrna Mills), 327

## Natural Foods

Barrels Community Market
(Waterville), 285

Bath Natural Market (Bath), 196

Belfast Coop (Belfast), 196

Blue Hill Co-op Community Market &
Cafe (Blue Hill), 246

Hampden Natural Food
(Hampden), 325

Lois' Natural Marketplace
(Scarborough), 116

Morning Glory Natural Foods
(Brunswick), 201

Rising Tide Community Market
(Damariscotta), 203

Royal River Natural Foods
(Freeport), 118

Spice of Life Natural Foods Market
(Skowhegan), 327

## Seafood Markets

Bayley's Lobster Pound
(Scarborough), 78

Bob's Seafood (Windham), 79

Browne Trading Company
(Portland), 24

Fishermen's Net (Gray), 80

Free Range Fish & Lobster
(Portland), 25

Gilmore's Seafood (Bath), 162

Glidden Point Oyster Co.
(Edgecomb), 162

Harbor Seafood (Portland), 25

Hawkes' Lobster (Harpswell), 163

Lunt & Lunt (Frenchboro), 217

Pectic Seafood (Trenton), 220

Simpson's Oceanfresh Seafood
(Wiscasset), 164

## Tea

Clipper Merchant Tea House
(Limerick), The, 138

Soak Foot Sanctuary & Teahouse
(Portland), 65

## Wines & Spirits

Bangor Wine and Cheese (Bangor),
325

# Appendix C:
# Food Happenings

## Statewide

**Open Creamery Day.** Organized by the Maine Cheese Guild, this one day fall event invites visitors into creameries and dairy farms around the state. More information at www.mainecheeseguild.org.

**Maple Sunday.** Organized by the Maine Maple Producers Association, this one day event takes place in early spring at the height of the state's maple sugaring season, when sugar shacks are steamy with boiling syrup. More information at www.mainemaple producers.com.

**Open Farm Day.** A celebration of Maine's agriculture, this one day event takes place in late July, when the season is in full swing. Dozens of farms throughout the state participate, inviting visitors to wander the fields and sample produce. More information at www .getrealmaine.com.

**Maine Restaurant Week.** Restaurants throughout the state participate in this weeklong taste of Maine's finest dining. More information at www.mainerestaurantweek.com.

## Index by Month

## July

## August

## September

## October

Acadia's Oktoberfest (Southwest Harbor), 223

Brunswick Blues and BBQ Bash (Brunswick), 167

Cultivating Community's 20 Mile Meal at Turkey Hill Farm (Cape Elizabeth), 28

Damariscotta Pumpkinfest and Regatta (Damariscotta), 167

Foliage, Food, and Wine Festival (Blue Hill), 223

Fryeburg Fair (Fryeburg), 133

Great Western Maine Chili Cook Off (Waterford), 134

Harvest on the Harbor (Portland), 28

Manchester Apple Festival (Manchester), 269

Swine and Stein Octoberfest (Gardiner), 270

Vinfest (Lincolnville), 168

## November

Maine Brewers Festival (Portland), 30

# Appendix D: Further Reading

Maine is home to an abundance of food writers, and many have turned their gaze—and pens—on the Pine Tree State. Check out some of the following books for a deeper reading, or a quick taste, of Maine's food life. (Note: Food writer Nancy Harmon Jenkins writes beautifully and astutely about Maine's food culture. She has yet to collect these essays into a book, but look for them in the *New York Times* and archived online.)

*The Arrows Cookbook: Cooking and Gardening from Maine's Most Beautiful Farmhouse,* Clark Frasier and Mark Gaier, Scribner, 2003.

*Dishing Up Maine: 165 Recipes That Capture Authentic Down East Flavors,* Brooke Dojny, Storey Publishing, 2006.

*Fresh from Maine: Recipes and Stories from the State's Best Chefs,* Michael Sanders, Table Arts Media, 2010.

*Fresh Maine Salads and Superb Maine Soups and Delicious Maine Desserts,* Cynthia Finemore Simonds, Down East Books, 2006, 2007, 2009.

*The Good Life: Helen and Scott Nearing's Sixty Years of Self-Sufficient Living,* Helen and Scott Nearing, Schocken Books, 1990.

*Good Maine Food: Ancient and Modern New England Food and Drink,* Marjorie Mosser, with a foreword by Sandra L. Oliver, Down East Books, 2010.

*The Lobster Coast: Rebels, Rusticators, and the Struggle for a Forgotten Frontier,* Colin Woodard, Penguin, 2005.

*Lobster Rolls and Blueberry Pie: Three Generations of Recipes and Stories from Summers on the Coast of Maine,* Rebecca Charles and Deborah Di Clementi, Harper, 2006.

*Recipes from a Very Small Island,* Linda Greenlaw and Martha Greenlaw, Hyperion, 2005.

*Saltwater Foodways: New Englanders and Their Food at Sea and Shore, in the Nineteenth Century,* by Sandra L. Oliver, Mystic Seaport Museum, 1970.

*The Secret Life of Lobsters: How Fishermen and Scientists Are Unraveling the Mysteries of Our Favorite Crustacean,* Trevor Corson, Harper Perennial, 2005.

*What's Cooking at Moody's Diner,* Nancy Genthner, Down East Books, 2003.

# Recipes Index

# Index

red snapper hot dogs, 326
Restaurant at Center Lovell Inn, The, 141
Ribollita, 58
Richard's Restaurant, 193
Ricker Hill Orchards, 289
Rippling Waters Organic Farm, 76
Rising Tide Community Market, 203
Riverfront Barbeque and Grille, 282
Riverhouse Ice Cream, 169
Riverside Farm Market and Cafe, 290
Roadside Bakery and Cafe, 257
Robinhood Free Meetinghouse, 193
Rock City Books and Coffee, 178
Rock City Coffee Roasters, 178
Rockland Farmers' Market, 160
Rocky Ridge Orchard and Bakery, 206
Rollins Orchard, 329
Rolly's Diner, 283
Romac Orchard, 121
Rooster Brother, 248
Rosemont Market & Bakery, 64
Rosie's Lovell Village Store & Restaurant, 142
Round Top Ice Cream Stand and Factory, 169
Route 2 Diner, 142

Rowe Orchards, 329
Royal River Natural Foods, 118
Roy's All Steak Hamburgers, 274
Run of the Mill Public House, 74
Rupununi, 243

S
Saco Farmers' Market, 78
Sadie's Bakery, 300
Sam's Italian Foods, 275
Sandy River Apples, 330
Savage Oakes Vineyard and Winery, 179
Sawyer's Market, 248
Schartner Farms, 292
Scratch Baking Company, 17
Sea Basket, 164
Sea Dog Microbrewery and Restaurant, 303
SeaGrass Bistro, 109
Seal Cove Farm, 230
Seasons of Stonington Restaurant and Bakery, The, 243
Sebago Brewing Co., 75
Sedgley Place, The, 283
Sewall's Orchard, 206
Shackley Hill Orchard, 292
Shag Rock Brewing Company, 180
Shaker Pond Ice Cream, 87